MW00776114

THE ENDS OF METER IN MODERN JAPANESE POETRY

THE ENDS OF METER IN MODERN JAPANESE POETRY

TRANSLATION AND FORM

SCOTT MEHL

CORNELL EAST ASIA SERIES
AN IMPRINT OF
CORNELL UNIVERSITY PRESS
Ithaca and London

This book has been published with generous support from
Colgate University and the Tanikawa Shuntarō Fund for
publication of modern Japanese poetry.

Number 210 in the Cornell East Asia Series

Copyright © 2021 by Cornell University

All rights reserved. Except for brief quotations in a review,
this book, or parts thereof, must not be reproduced in any
form without permission in writing from the publisher. For
information, address Cornell University Press, Sage House,
512 East State Street, Ithaca, New York 14850. Visit our
website at cornellpress.cornell.edu.

First published 2021 by Cornell University Press

ISBN 978-1-5017-6117-1 (hardcover)
ISBN 978-1-5017-6119-5 (pdf)
ISBN 978-1-5017-6118-8 (epub)

Library of Congress Control Number: 2021944850

For my parents

CONTENTS

ILLUSTRATIONS

Acknowledgments

Two chapters of this book appeared in earlier versions. Chapter 2 is an amplification of "Kitamura Tōkoku and the Versification Debate in Japan, 1890–1891," *Southeast Review of Asian Studies* 38 (2016): 38–56; and chapter 5 is based on "The Beginnings of Japanese Free-Verse Poetry and the Dynamics of Cultural Change," *Japan Review* 28 (2015): 103–32. I thank Joshua Howard, president of the Southeast Conference of the Association for Asian Studies, and John Breen, editor of *Japan Review*, for permission to reuse these materials.

Octavio Paz and Eikichi Hayashiya's two Spanish translations of a haiku by Matsuo Bashō, discussed in chapter 3, originally appeared in Paz and Hayashiya, *Sendas de Oku*, copyright Fondo de Cultura Económica, 2005.

Some of the early research for this project was completed with the help of a Fulbright-DDRA Hays Fellowship, during which Kōno Kensuke of Nihon Daigaku was a model and an inspiration. At the University of Chicago, Michael Bourdaghs, Boris Maslov, Hoyt Long, and Reginald Jackson were generous with their time, insights, and guidance.

My editors at Cornell University Press, Mai Shaikhanuar-Cota and Alexis Siemon, did expert work as they steered this manuscript toward the finish line; Alexis Siemon oversaw the culminating stages. It was a joy working with them both. The three anonymous readers shared a wealth of erudition: in the draft of my manuscript, they descried something better, and they conveyed their vision in helpful and extensive comments. To their comments were added the constructive suggestions of the Cornell East Asia Series' editorial board. I only hope my revisions brought the book nearer to becoming the better thing those first readers imagined it could be. Any errors or infelicities of commission or omission, it hardly needs to be said, are my responsibility. This book also received generous support from the Tanikawa Shuntarō Fund at Cornell University.

The staff of the library at Colgate University, and especially Lisa King of the library's interlibrary loan section, provided exceptional assistance during the trying conditions of late 2020. They made resources available to users at what must be seen as considerable personal risk, and expressing my gratitude to them is truly the least I can do.

The debts I incurred to write this book go all the way back. I have happy memories of teachers from every year of my school life, and the road I have walked—from a childhood in the extreme northeast corner of Montana to an assistant professorship in Japanese at a small liberal arts university in central New York—would not even have been visible to me if I hadn't had teachers to tell me which way was forward. At the University of Chicago: René de Costa, Norma Field, Noto Hiroyoshi, and the professors I have named above; at the University of Wisconsin–Madison: Mary Layoun, Luis Madureira, Naomi Hanaoka McGloin, Akira Miura, James O'Brien, and Jane Tylus; at the University of Wyoming: Susan Aronstein, Susan Frye, Susanna Goodin, Duncan Harris, Janice Harris, Farhad Jafari, Caroline McCracken-Flesher, Carlos Mellizo, and Marlene Tromp; and the instructors at a remarkable high school in southwest Wyoming, as well as those at a remarkable school in northeast Montana—there is simply nothing I can write to convey all that they taught me. Some of them might not even remember me. But I remember them.

Many scholars shared with me their reactions to earlier versions of materials that appear in the present book. I thank the audiences at the 2016 Southeast Conference of the Association for Asian Studies at James Madison University and at the 2016 AAS in Asia conference at Dōshisha University—especially Nick Albertson, Joshua Solomon, Kathryn Tanaka, Christophe Thouny, and J. Keith Vincent—for sharing their thoughts about my analysis of Kitamura Tōkoku. I also thank the audiences at the 2018 NordMetrik conference at Stockholm University, the 2018 New York Chapter of the AAS at the University of Rochester, and the 2019 "Counter-Readings: Modern Asian Literary Histories" conference at the University of Chicago—especially Kyeong-Hee Choi, Nathen Clerici, Kristin Hanson, Amanda Kennell, Paul Kiparsky, David Krolikoski, Nick Lambrecht, Jae-Yon Lee, David C. Stahl, and Myfany Turpin—for their comments and questions on my analysis of Kanbara Ariake.

My colleagues in the Department of East Asian Languages and Literatures at Colgate University have been ideal interlocutors and companions: Nick Albertson, John Crespi, Yukari Hirata, Jing Wang, and Dongfeng Xu have answered questions, given advice, and shared all the tasks and joys that come with being a community of Asianists. Beyond my department, I am grateful to colleagues at Colgate for their camaraderie and for their many kindnesses small and great: Seth Coluzzi, Carolyn Hsu, Padma Kaimal, Spencer Kelly, Michelle Landstrom, Jacob Mundy, Marta Pérez Carbonell,

Yang Song, Meg Worley, Daisaku Yamamoto, and Yumiko Yamamoto. I also thank the Colgate University Faculty Research Council for a generous publication subvention grant.

I would like here to remember a weekend spent at the home of Mika Endō in Annandale-on-Hudson in 2014. Mika, Nick Albertson, Mamiko Suzuki, and I spent several enjoyable days writing, dining, walking, and conversing. It was at Endō Writing Camp that I wrote what would become my first accepted scholarly article, on free verse in Japanese and Arabic, and in an important sense it was there that my work found its direction.

Friends have helped to remind me of all that happens away from the writing desk. My life would be a shabbier production altogether if it weren't for the conversations I have (and will henceforth be having more regularly, now that this book is finished) with Laura, Mireille, Craig and Maggie, Charles, Amy and Ilya, Trevor, Wah Guan, Kaye, Arthur and Sophie, Casandra, Katy and Kōtarō, Jessica, and Ottilie.

Then there are my families. It has been endlessly good to live near Margot, Beth, Debra, Holly, Amber, and Morgan. Matt, Vani, Sonali, and Anjali live farther away now, but Zoom has helped shrink the distance.

My sister, Jennifer, and her family—Daryl, Ian, Megan, Ryan, and Emily—have been bringing more and more happiness, which is saying something.

My mother and father are the dedicatees of this book, and my message to them is hidden in plain sight on every page.

My husband, Nick, continues to teach me that which is best to learn.

NOTE ON TRANSLITERATION
AND PERSONAL NAMES

For Japanese, I follow a modified Hepburn transliteration system, with occasional exceptions made for the particularities of classical Japanese orthography. As for the use of Japanese characters, I have usually followed the custom of silently modernizing older forms of kanji and kana. In many of the poems, however, I hew closely to the older orthography, for which I have an affection.

When giving the title of a text originally written in Japanese, I generally provide an English translation of the title, then in parentheses a transliteration of the Japanese title followed by the original title in Japanese characters. For works of high historical import, however, I reverse this order, presenting the Japanese titles first with an English translation following in parentheses.

For Chinese, I use Pinyin transliteration.

All translations are my own unless otherwise indicated.

When quoting from Japanese critical writings, if an aspect of the diction or orthography strikes me as being potentially noteworthy, I represent the original text by including a transliteration followed by Japanese characters. At times, however, I omit the Japanese characters if the original would be clear from the transliteration alone.

The first mention of a Japanese personal name is presented in Japanese order: family name followed by given name, which is the reverse of the Western order.

The handling of subsequent mentions of personal names is complicated by the fact that many Japanese writers of the period I treat in this book are commonly known not by their given name (*honmyō* or *honmei*) but rather by their pen name or *nom de plume* (*gō* or *gagō*). For example, the novelist who was born Natsume Kinnosuke (family name Natsume) took the pen name Natsume Sōseki, which is conventionally shortened to Sōseki in critical writings about his work. In the main, I have tried to follow Japanese critical convention on personal names: hence, I refer to the poet Takamura Kōtarō as Takamura, but the poet Kanbara Ariake as Ariake.

Where I have found Japanese critical convention to be inconsistent—for example, some Japanese literary critics refer to Hattori Yoshika as Hattori, some as Yoshika—I generally default to the family name. The details are labyrinthine, but for now let this note suffice.

THE ENDS OF METER IN MODERN
JAPANESE POETRY

Introduction
Making Forms New, Making New Forms

> The kind of classicizing fixed-form poetry that took the 7-5 rhythm as its basis has now virtually disappeared. Within not even a hundred years of Japanese poetry history, it has altogether vanished.
>
> —Kuroda Saburō, *Shi no tsukurikata* (1969, 12)

> Who today would dare to write a rhymed poem, in alexandrines—if not to commit a new transgression of a new norm?
>
> —Tzvetan Todorov, *Les genres du discours* (1978, 46)

The years 1882–1907 saw several waves of innovation in Japanese poetry, due to changes in how Japanese writers— and Japanese readers more generally—interacted with literary institutions in other countries and other languages. In 1882 there appeared in Japanese the first anthology of translated European-language poems; in 1907 the first free-verse Japanese poetry in a modern stylistic register was written, establishing the form in which the preponderance of long Japanese lyric (that is, longer than seventeen-syllable haiku or thirty-one-syllable tanka) is written today. The quarter-century under examination in this book—a period during which Japanese poets engaged in formal experimentation to a degree unmatched in any other period of comparable length in Japanese history, a time of creativity fed and sustained by precedent-setting translations of European-language verse—is therefore critical for understanding modern Japanese literature.

The experimenters themselves evidently saw the merits of creating new kinds of poetry in Japanese, but some critics and readers regarded the new poetry with revulsion. Revulsion is not too strong a word, in some cases. There were many shades of vituperation, from mild to extreme, directed toward the new poetries. On the milder side, one writer claimed that laughter came from all four directions in response to the first Japanese translations of European verse (Kunikida [1897] 1972, 120). More severely, a Japanese

1

poet's symbolist poetry led one reviewer to proclaim, "I hate his poems" (Matsubara et al. [1908] 1972, 266). Still another critic, on first reading Japanese free-verse poetry, declared that it made him "want to vomit" (quoted in Hitomi 1954, 49). The new forms of Japanese poetry created during these years, whether in Japanese originals or appearing in Japanese translations, encountered resistance from many quarters, and that manifold resistance is the thread that holds together the chapters of the present study.

I will say more below about that resistance, but first I want very briefly to give readers a glimpse of the poetry that elicited such resistance. The poem that is frequently declared to have been the earliest free-verse Japanese poem in a modern stylistic register is "Rubbish Heap" (Hakidame 塵溜), first published in a poetry magazine in 1907 by Kawaji Ryūkō 川路柳虹 (1888–1959), a poet only eighteen years old at the time. Ryūkō revised the poem for his epochal 1910 poetry collection, *Flowers by the Wayside* (*Robō no hana* 路傍の花), from which I quote the poem's second stanza. The unnamed and unmentioned speaker directs the reader's attention to the titular rubbish heap:[1]

Within the heap of rubbish there are rice bugs moving, larvae;
the worms, soil-eaters, lift their heads;
the sake bottles are in pieces, and scraps of paper are rotting and dank;
small mosquitoes wail as they fly away.[2]

hakidame no uchi ni wa ugoku ine no mushi, unga no tamago,
mata tsuchi o hamu mimizura ga kashira o motage,
tokkuribin no kakera ya kami no kirehashi ga kusare musarete
chisai ka wa wamekinagara ni tonde yuku.

塵溜の中には動く稲の蟲、浮蛾の卵、
また土を食む蚯蚓らが頭を擡げ、
徳利壜の醶片や紙の切れはしが腐れ蒸されて
小さい蚊は喚きながらに飛んでゆく。

(*rubi* as in the 1910 version, Kawaji 1910, 158–59)

Trash was not then (and still is not) conventionally seen as a subject for poetry composition. This poem's insistent contemplation of insects and their environment may have stood outside the horizon of most poetry readers' expectations in Japan in 1907, but there were also Japanese readers—less numerous, but no less important—who had already encountered ugliness as a subject in European-language poetries. In the first line of the following stanza, the speaker calls attention to the insects' status as subjects in their own right, making an implicit claim upon a reader's sympathy: "Even here there is a world of suffering without end" (159; *soko ni mo taenu kurushimi no sekai ga a[ru]* そこにも絶えぬ苦しみの世界があ〔る〕). By minutely observing the life in a pile of waste matter and imagining that life from the inside, Ryūkō advertised his support for a poetry of new possibilities. Perhaps some readers thought his poetry was trash, but Ryūkō himself thought it more interesting to turn trash into poetry.

Japanese critics soon also realized that Ryūkō's poetry had another distinction: it eschewed metrical predictability. It was, in short, free verse. Different languages have different ways of raising metrical expectations in poetry: in English, for example, patterns in poetry usually involve a recurring arrangement of stressed and unstressed syllables in a line ("Shall Í compáre thee tó a súmmer's dáy?"), and hence English is typically said to have an accentual prosody. In Japanese, patterned verse involves an iteration of phrases of a certain number of syllables: for this reason Japanese prosody is said to be syllabic.[3] The haiku, for instance, is a short poem in seventeen syllables composed of phrases of five, seven, and five syllables. Five- and seven-syllable phrases are the fundamental building blocks of traditional Japanese poetic meter, a point to which I will return below. The distinguishing metrical trait of Ryūkō's poem is that the number of syllables varies from one line to the next according to no predictable pattern: in the stanza quoted above, for example, the first line has twenty-four syllables, the second nineteen, the third twenty-six, and the fourth seventeen. How many syllables the next line will have is not something that can be foreseen in a poem like Ryūkō's: his "Rubbish Heap" must be seen as an instance of what in English we would call free verse.

Free verse is poetry by virtue primarily of the fact that it has lines; it declares itself free because of all the other formal traits it does not have. Predictability is anathema in free verse, so the characteristics of recursive poetry—such as any regular pattern involving rhyme, meter, stresses, or number of letters or syllables—are perforce absent from free-verse poetry; or, if they are present, they may not predominate. For our purposes, I should note that the patterns being avoided by free verse depend in part upon the language in which the poetry is written. For example, English-language free-verse poetry generally eschews both meter and rhyme. In Japanese free verse, however, the avoidance of rhyme is a nonconsideration, because rhyme was never a traditionally assumed feature of formal poetry in Japanese. Hence *free verse* does not designate the same thing in every language: the patterns being avoided by any given free-verse poem are determined very much by the time, place, and language in which that poem is written.[4]

As the above definition of free verse implies, part of the story of Japanese free verse is the story of the rejection of other forms of Japanese poetry. The most famous form of Japanese poetry outside of Japan is probably the haiku, a poem in a 5-7-5 syllable pattern. Poets who wrote haiku—or, as poems of that form were known in earlier centuries, *haikai* or *hokku*—embraced other restrictions upon their verses, too, such as the requirements to include seasonal words (*kigo*) and so-called cutting words (*kireji*). Within Japan, it was not the haiku but the slightly longer *waka*, later called tanka[5]—poems in 5-7-5-7-7—that enjoyed, for many centuries, the greatest prestige. In the long history of Japanese poetry there have been many other forms, as well, such as the comic, haiku-like *senryū* (5-7-5), the *sedōka* (5-7-7-5-7-7), the *dodoitsu* (7-7-7-5), and the linked verse forms such as the *renga* (sequences of linked *waka*). Many Japanese poets even wrote *shi*, which were later called *kanshi*— poetry in literary Chinese—in the centuries when Chinese was regarded as the language of scholarship. All such forms were prosodically regular and typically involved the counting of syllables. Importantly, all were quite short (relative, at least, to European-language poetries): even the longest Japanese verse form, the *chōka* (alternating lines of seven and five syllables, no fixed length), seldom ran to more than a few dozen lines.[6]

By contrast, free-verse poems can have any number of lines, and the counting of syllables plays no part in their composition, except negatively. Free verse differed radically, therefore, from what Japanese readers used to associate with poetic language.

So, however, did poetry in European languages, even when that poetry was formally regular. But it is no exaggeration to say that up until the mid- to late nineteenth century, Japanese readers in general had no exposure to European-language poetries. The background to this generalization requires a long examination of historical conditions, which I describe in chapter 1, but for the present it will suffice to say that when Japanese readers in large numbers began encountering the poetries of Europe, their experience was, in an important sense, altogether new. Like Chinese verse, with which many Japanese readers at the time had at least a passing acquaintance, nineteenth-century poetry in European languages tended to rhyme. But unlike Chinese verse, many forms of which arranged the syllables according to tonal patterns, European poetries arranged their words to fit patterns of stressed and unstressed syllables, in some languages, or patterns of long and short syllables, in others. In the late nineteenth century when Japan was entering into closer relations with the more globally active nations of Europe and their cultures, Japanese modernizers felt compelled to learn about European culture, and quickly. For poetry, that meant translation.

The Japanese writers who introduced translations of European-language poetries to the Japanese reading public in the late nineteenth century had to make decisions about poetic form. Take a poem like the English poet Thomas Gray's (1716–71) "Elegy Written in a Country Church-yard" (1751), a 128-line poem in quatrains of iambic pentameter, rhyming throughout on alternating lines (*abab*, *cdcd*, etc.). Should the Japanese translation of Gray's poem also attempt rhyming, ten-syllable lines arranged in quatrains, thereby hewing closely to the form of the original? Should each quatrain be trans-lated as, say, a single *waka*, condensing forty syllables of English (four lines of iambic pentameter) into thirty-one of Japanese while at the same time localizing the poem by relying on the verse form most familiar to Japanese audiences? Should each line be translated rather as a haiku—seventeen syl-lables in Japanese to approximate the ten syllables of each English pentam-eter line? Should the poem be rendered instead as a *chōka*, a verse form that had acquired, among many Japanese readers, a reputation for staleness? As it happens, the translator of the most notable early Japanese version of Gray's poem, Yatabe Ryōkichi 矢田部良吉 (1851–99), ultimately opted for a course close to the latter, except that he refused to call the translation a *chōka*, lest the negative associations of that term cling to the translation—and thus to the original. Yatabe, who collaborated with two other scholars on an influ-ential translation anthology, *Shintaishi shō* 新体詩抄 (New-style poetry col-lection, 1882), instead called the form into which he translated Gray's poem a *shintaishi* (new-style *shi*)—repurposing a word (*shi*) that had hitherto been used to name poetry in literary Chinese. This new term became the name of a new kind of Japanese poetry. *Shintaishi* tended at first to adhere rigidly to twelve-syllable lines in 5-7 or 7-5, although eventually other prosodic outlines were invented.

At every turn, the Japanese critical conversation in 1882–1907 about new-ness in poetry was intertwined with parallel conversations about Japan's putative standing on an international stage. Ideological concerns were at the forefront of critics' minds: as Japanese writers and thinkers weighed the meaning of Japan's new entanglements with the governments and cultures of Europe and North America, they found it necessary to rethink what it meant to write poetry in Japanese. How should one defend the corpus of Japanese verse from the scrutiny of observers abroad who counted Milton and Homer among their classics? By what criteria should one assert the par-ity (to say nothing of the superiority or inferiority) of Japanese literature? How should one justify the composition of poetry at all when the energies of every Japanese citizen were needed for learning the sciences, the technical skills, and the organizational expertise required of an industrializing, militarizing country? Above, I claimed that the translator of Gray's "Elegy" had to make a decision about the form the translation would take, but that choice followed upon a prior choice regarding which poem to translate. A translation of an acknowledged classic in the literature of an imperial power or of any other admired culture needs to be seen as an engagement with, and not simply a concession to, that other literature's standards and perceived prestige.

The close connection between form and translation in the history of modern Japanese poetry is important, because it provides a window onto a problem that has occupied literary scholars in recent years: the broader significance of intercultural borrowing and adaptation. By attending to how literary forms change when writers borrow them from one language and recreate them in another, we learn something fundamental about how the implied and explicit values of different literary cultures interact.

Forms on the Move

In the last decade many scholars have taken up the subject of cross-cultural formal comparison with a new urgency, motivated by the intensification of textual transmission and circulation across linguistic, national, and media boundaries. One recent study that contextualizes the problems that arise in cross-cultural morphology is Ilya Kliger and Boris Maslov's *Persistent Forms: Explorations in Historical Poetics* (2016), which presents translations of seminal works by the Russian thinker Alexander Veselovsky (1838–1906), along with critical essays about the field that Veselovsky founded: historical poetics. The phrase *historical poetics* cuts both ways: it is both a poetics of history and a diachronic account of literary phenomena.

Kliger and Maslov's *Persistent Forms* describes Veselovsky's work as having a "historical vision of genre as a persistent form," a vision shared in outline, as Kliger and Maslov claim, by such later critics as Mikhail Bakhtin and Fredric Jameson (2016, 6–7). In this vision, the study of literature benefits from taking literary genre as the unit of analysis, because attention to genre requires a constant examination and reexamination of the relative proportions of invention and (possibly inadvert) homage in any literary text. The emphasis of Veselovsky's account, however, falls on forms' persistence, so that, as Victoria Somoff notes, "Veselovsky's vision of literary history rules out the emergence of a genuinely new artistic form" (2016, 66).

Somoff argues that "the question of how something 'new' comes about—a new communicative format, genre, narrative strategy, and so forth—can be restated as the problem of how 'old' (or pre-given) patterns, be they artistic or ideological, can be *forgotten*," a problem that Veselovsky left unresolved, as Somoff maintains (70).

The challenge of accounting for formal novelty requires, I think, a supple grasp of the many things newness can mean. To speak of "genuinely" new forms is to set a high standard, one that would seem to discount any literary form that has been adopted from one literature to another—since an adopted form is anything but new. (By that standard, sonnets—or free-verse poems—written in Japanese would not be new, because such poems had been written in other languages first. Try telling that to the first readers of such poems in Japanese.) Part of the challenge lies in the framing of the question about new forms. Maslov observes that there are many critical methodologies that overlook, or cannot accommodate, "the effects of the borrowing of formal elements across cultural boundaries that render their ideological associations moot, and their allusiveness irrelevant" (2016, 140). Even in monocultural accounts of literary language, however, "genuine" novelty still poses a challenge to the explicator: seemingly new forms could be explained away, according to this view, as being merely rearrangements of the elements of old forms.

A recent work that attempts to account for newness by examining localization as a poetic strategy is Ignacio Infante's *After Translation: The Transfer and Circulation of Modern Poetics across the Atlantic* (2013). Infante's work destabilizes received ideas about poetic modernism by denationalizing that movement, zeroing in on a multidirectional process of "poetic transfer" between poets writing in English, Spanish, Portuguese, and French—not always as their native languages (14–15). For Infante, the various poets in his study are united by a fascination with the unknown—or, as Infante puts it, by "the productive experience of being engaged by an unknown 'stranger'" (17). In this case a "stranger" is a text that (I paraphrase) provokes a desire to overcome the distance that putatively separates self from other: for a poet confronted with such an alluring textual stranger, the question is whether the foreign text can be productively brought into the poet's home language. The viability of that poetic transfer is open to significant doubt, however, when what is formally possible in the source language is perceived as being unimaginable in the host language.

Infante introduces the notion of the "stranger" in the course of his examination of another important essay working at the intersection of translation

and form: Dilip Parameshwar Gaonkar and Elizabeth A. Povinelli's "Tech-
nologies of Public Forms," which privileges ethnographic and political over
aesthetic and literary considerations of textual phenomena (2003, 391–92).
For Gaonkar and Povinelli, an "ethnography of forms" must attend to "cul-
tures of circulation," examining closely the movements of texts and thereby
laying bare the divergent social conditions at every node in any text's itiner-
ary through the world (391). If a text undergoes a transformation when it
enters a new spatiotemporal context, that fact registers a sociopolitical dif-
ference: inequalities are inscribed in the reception history of a text, and part
of that reception history is the text's "transfiguration" (another key term
for Gaonkar and Povinelli) through circulation (394). The authors express
dissatisfaction with much translation theory, with its too-frequent attention
to "the question of how to translate well" (393)—a concern that reduces
the analysis of translation to a mere weighing of equivalences, when one's
real concern should be to account for how "flows and forms [are] integrally
related" (387).

The present study, by attending closely to the interplay between transla-
tion and invention in the creation of new forms of Japanese verse, offers
a provisional methodology for analyzing the translation of literary form.
While I agree with Gaonkar and Povinelli's insistence that "flows and forms"
are inextricable, I try to keep at bay the false (as I see it) dichotomy they pre-
sume between the social and the aesthetic. Gaonkar and Povinelli caution
against "succumb[ing] to the temptation of reading for meaning" (386)—but
I take it to be the case that a text's meaning does have a connection with how
the text is circulated. Readers for whom a text is repellent—for reasons of
either form or content, possibly both—will sometimes express their displea-
sure by refusing to participate in a text's circulation; they might go so far as
to attempt to prevent its circulation. The same could be said for publishing
houses, for translators, and so forth. A text's circulation—including but not
limited to its adaptation, localization, or translation—can encounter impedi-
ments at any time or place, and those impediments can bring its circulation to
a halt, both locally and in limit cases even globally. The reasons for such resis-
tance are seldom purely and only aesthetic *or* purely and only sociopolitical—
although subsequent explanations of those reasons might favor one fac-
tor over the other. While Gaonkar and Povinelli recommend "orient[ing]
analysis toward the calibration of vectors of power rather than vectors of
meaning-value" (396), the present study will, I hope, reward the attentions
of readers who are invested in both kinds of analysis.

Because the long period during which nearly all Japanese readers knew
next to nothing about European-language literatures was followed by a rush

to acquire knowledge of those literatures, the course of modern Japanese poetry offers a particularly intriguing set of test cases for any theory of formal circulation. When the floodgates opened, there was a rearrangement of literary ecologies on both sides of the invisible barrier that had hitherto kept Japanese literature in and European literature out: longer lyric forms came to Japan and were adapted in a spirit of radical experimentation, while shorter Japanese forms such as the haiku and the tanka caught the interested eye of European-language poets on the lookout for ways to unsettle assumptions about poetic form. In other words, the history of modern Japanese poetry provides another way to understand questions of world literature.

World Literature, Japanese Poetry, and Comparative Morphology

On the subject of the novel, the literary theorist Franco Moretti has written that the invention of a new literary form is a comparatively rare occurrence: it is invented once and then disperses (2000, 61).[7] Poetic forms are another example of the phenomenon Moretti describes, and not only in Japan.[8] The sonnet, for instance, was invented once and then taken up and repurposed, first by other poets in its home language, then by poets in other languages. Therefore, to dwell overmuch on the moment of invention—to dwell overmuch on the writer who originated a form—is, as Moretti argues, to overlook the position in which the near-totality of writers find themselves, which is that of borrower. Most writers do not invent the forms in which they write; they adapt them. In the world-systems view of intercultural relations that Moretti derives from the sociologist and historian Immanuel Wallerstein, there is a division between core cultures and cultures on the periphery: core cultures are perceived as being dominant in multiple ways, not only culturally but also economically, militarily, politically, and so on. As Moretti reminds us, most cultures are peripheral most of the time. Literatures everywhere, regardless of their degree of relative centrality, are productive of new materials and new forms, but it is only the literature at the center that wins in the cultural marketplace—by having its forms and themes taken up by so-called peripheral cultures. What we would expect to see in the case of longer lyric poetry in Japan would therefore be an instance of borrowing pure and simple: Japanese poets and critics, on learning of the prestige of long-form poetry in urban France and the publishing centers of the Anglosphere, would create local analogues, replicating in Japanese the forms found in the European hubs of culture.

In a sense, that simplification is what we find with the new forms of verse in Japanese, but a more granular view reveals differences that are stark enough to suggest that a diffusionist model needs to be refined for each particular literature, and even each literary form.[9] We could pose the following brief but I think fundamental questions about diffusionism: Under what circumstances, if any, can a so-called peripheral culture resist adopting the forms created by a core culture? Is it possible to specify when such resistance would be effective, and when ineffectual? The history of Japanese verse forms in 1882–1907 presents data that can be interpreted in opposing ways— either as validating Moretti's model of diffusionism, or as circumscribing it with so many qualifications that it becomes at best a caricature. The case for validating the model is easy to make: long lyric poetry based on European forms came to Japan, took root there, and stayed.

There are two reasons to take a closer look. The first is the phenomenon of modern free-verse poetry in Japanese. Free verse in Japan began with what we might call a trial invention by a young poet named Kitamura Tōkoku 北村透谷 (1868–94) as early as 1889—a trial that was attempted, apparently, without Tōkoku's having any knowledge of European-language free verse (as shown in chapter 2). The prosodic features that made Tōkoku's poetry distinctive, however, were not recognized by critics. That was in spite of the fact that there had been several writers of significance (treated at the end of chapter 1) who had called for a metrically looser poetry to counterpoise the alleged monotony of *shintaishi*—the metrically regular kind of longer poetry, as mentioned above, that had been invented in 1882 for translating European poetries. What these points taken together suggest is the obvious but essential conclusion that a literary form, once invented, might not be propagated even in its home literature: the conditions can be unfavorable for a number of reasons—the absence of a market of readers or critics, the robustness of competition from already-existing forms, and so on. A model such as Moretti's—as he himself would recognize—has little to say about a form that goes dormant or fails altogether. The contrast between the earlier but unrecognized free-verse poetry of 1889 and the recognized invention of Japanese free verse in 1907 (considered in chapter 5) is instructive: those later poems were seen as succeeding at something new rather than failing at something old, and that reception made all the difference. The nearly twenty-year interval between these two inventions of Japanese free verse can be explained (as in chapters 3 and 4 below) by examining the strategies—largely successful ones—adopted by haiku, tanka, and *shintaishi* poets in the 1890s and early 1900s to buttress their forms against critical attacks.[10]

The second reason is that although traditional poets and *shintaishi* poets both attempted to defend their forms against criticisms, only the former succeeded. The *shintaishi* went into a decline so sharp as to seem an extinction, so that the postwar poet Kuroda Saburō 黒田三郎 (1919–80), looking back from the second half of the twentieth century, could write the words that serve as one of the epigraphs to this introduction, marveling at the death of the *shintaishi*. As a poetic form, the *shintaishi* had had staunch defenders as well as voluble opponents, but there was no question that it was a viable and—at least in its time—even a vibrant new type of Japanese verse, the medium in which every poet wrote who had aspirations to appear up to date. The fact that this poetic form, created as an analogue to European-language verse forms, had so brief a period of viability is, as I present it in this study, another aspect of modern Japanese literary history that a diffusionist model could account for only with difficulty.

These differing descriptions of the period under examination arise, I would argue, in part from their different foci: the story of the free-verse poem ends on a vector toward increasing diffusion, while that of the new-style poem ends on a vector toward contraction and obsolescence. In their details, both stories call a diffusionist model into doubt. If all long European-style poems are treated as members of a single class, however, then the period 1882–1907 can be described as the time when European verse came to Japan and established a place for itself—so far a permanent one—among the other still-extant Japanese poetic forms. What I want to call attention to is not the greater persuasiveness of one account or the other, but rather a feature of the relation between premises and conclusions: questions of form need to be answered differently depending on one's unit of analysis. Moretti's essay originally centered on the novel—a capacious, one might even say a catch-all, designation for literary prose narratives of a certain length. The various subsets of the category *novel*—such as historical novels, science fiction novels, *Bildungsromane*, and so forth—are distinguishable not by form but by story content. With poetry—another capacious category—the distinction between subsets is just the converse: content is relatively immaterial,[11] since formal features such as number of lines, number of beats per line, and rhyme scheme are what most clearly distinguish one poetic form from another. Following the life cycle of any single poetic form will bring to light phenomena different from those revealed by a study of poetry in its broadest sense, to say nothing of the novel.

Theoretical questions aside, the first and best reason to attend to the Japanese poetry and criticism that provide the archive for this study is their interest. The poems themselves reward careful reading and rereading, especially the Japanese translations of European-language poems. The latter assertion may surprise some readers. I certainly esteem highly the original poems that I have included, but the translations, too, merit close attention. The translated poems function as snapshots, representing the translators' best (at the time) solutions to the problem of creating, for their Japanese contemporaries, analogues in Japanese of poems originally written by unfamiliar poets working in unfamiliar literary traditions. The poetry translators quoted in the present study straddled two eras, in a sense: they were young at a time when what we might call a classical Japanese education, which typically would have entailed deep training in ancient Chinese and Japanese texts, was still a living memory; at the same time, they were among the earliest Japanese to learn the classics of European literatures. The translators' cultural polyopia is one of the reasons why so many of their works remain valued exemplars even today.

As for the Japanese poetry criticism cited and paraphrased in this book, it is little known outside Japan and deserves wider recognition, especially in light of the continuing prevalence of "European practices of knowledge production," as Revathi Krishnaswamy has put it, in Anglophone academic literary theory and beyond (2010, 401).[12] This latter point relates to what I take to be the other principal justification for a study such as this one: it brings recent critical discussions about literary globalization into contact with new corpora of evidence, thereby reformulating the terms of those discussions. Throughout this study, I establish connections between my primary sources and more recent theories, but I intentionally give pride of place to criticism written by contemporary late nineteenth- and early twentieth-century observers, for two reasons. First, I believe that my primary critical sources in themselves already provide a theoretical framework that is crucial for understanding the poetry I introduce in this book. Second, I would wager that Anglophone readers who come to this book are likely to be familiar with recent theorists—such as Emily Apter, David Bellos, Michael Emmerich, Naoki Sakai, Lawrence Venuti, Judy Wakabayashi—but are probably less familiar with writings by Hattori Yoshika, Ikebukuro Kiyokaze, Ueda Kazutoshi, Yamada Bimyō, and others who figure in this text. Knowing the contemporary Japanese discourses about poetry and translation allows us to understand and appreciate the problems confronted—in some cases overcome, in other cases left unresolved—by the poets and translators considered in the present study.

Before I begin the chapter summary, I should situate this book's overall project relative to other recent book-length scholarly works in the field of

Japanese literary studies. The protagonist of this book is neither a person nor a group of people nor an institution but is rather poetic form, both how it was imagined, debated, and reimagined, and how it was put into practice in actual poems. More narrowly, the book's focus might be described as a series of interactions between those who wrote poems and those who analyzed them (granting that both functions could be, and sometimes were, conjoined in a single person). That choice of focus is a matter of emphasis, and it makes this study different from others in the field. For contrast, many recent studies of the same period about which I am writing have focused on the individual poet as their primary unit of analysis—for example, Donald Keene's studies of Masaoka Shiki (2013) and Ishikawa Takuboku (2016), which might best be described as critical biographies. In a similar vein, there are poet-centered books that take a more theoretical approach, such as Robert Tuck's book about Masaoka Shiki, *Idly Scribbling Rhymers* (2018), which analyzes that poet's work in light of a prominent recent theory (Benedict Anderson's) about the interaction between print culture and nationalism. Other scholarly works of the past decade in English have focused less on individual poets and rather more on literary and cultural movements in Japan in the late nineteenth and early twentieth centuries. Some of these works, too, have included chapters about (among other subjects) poetry or poets—for example, Jeffrey Angles's *Writing the Love of Boys* (2011, 37–74) and Roy Starrs's *Rethinking Japanese Modernism* (2011, 229–320), two texts that examine a later period than the one I treat in this book. In still other kinds of studies, such as Takako Lento's translation anthology *Pioneers of Modern Japanese Poetry*, a survey of the turbulent formation of modern Japanese poetry is a necessary part of the introductory background (2019, 3–11).

Insofar as the present book can be categorized as a prehistory of free verse in Japanese, it bears comparison with Timothy Steele's *Missing Measures: Modern Poetry and the Revolt against Meter*, which "explores ideas and conditions that led to the development of verse without meter—of verse without the regularly measured units of rhythm that had, from pre-Homeric times onward, defined the structures of poetic lines" (1990, 4). Despite the breadth implied by "from pre-Homeric times onward," Steele's book treats the history of free verse primarily in English. There have been other accounts of English-language free verse, as well, by scholars such as Annie Finch (2000) and Chris Beyers (2001). Other languages, too, have had their historians of free verse: Clive Scott's work on French *vers libre* (1990) is foundational. As for the topic of the modern transformation of non-European poetries, other

comparable texts include the work of Ahmad Karimi-Hakkak on the forma-
tion of modern Persian poetry (1995), Maghiel van Crevel's (2008) and Lucas
Klein's (2018) studies of Chinese poetry, and Adriana Jacobs's work (2018) on
translation's role in the formation of modern Hebrew poetry. In a sense, the
various studies that I have just named are telling local versions of a global
story about how poetry has changed in the modern age; the present book
tells some of the principal Japanese episodes of that story.

Chapter Overview

During the reign of the emperor Meiji (1868–1912) in Japan there began to
appear translations of poetry in Western languages aimed at a broad public.
Chapter 1 inspects the premier of these, *Shintaishi shō* (New-style poetry
collection), an anthology that introduced to Japanese readers such writers
as Shakespeare, Tennyson, and Longfellow, while it also trumpeted the cre-
ation of a new poetic form: the *shintaishi* or new-style *shi*. The compilers
of *Shintaishi shō* claimed that other, extant varieties of Japanese poetry such
as the *haikai* (haiku), the *waka*, and the *chōka* were unsuited for express-
ing the complex thoughts and feelings of modern, up-to-date nineteenth-
century Japanese subjects: hence the necessity of inventing a new poetic
form. The *shintaishi* creators' statements did not escape the notice of poets
working in those other forms, and this chapter introduces the antitransla-
tion stance of the *waka* poet Ikebukuro Kiyokaze 池袋清風 (1847–1910),
a strident critic of the *shintaishi*. It also introduces another damaging cri-
tique of the *shintaishi* by a prominent Japanese psychologist, Motora Yūjirō
元良勇次郎 (1858–1912), who argued that the repetitive, insistent rhythm
of the *shintaishi*—which, like the *chōka*, was composed of recurrent fives and
sevens—was detrimental to the brains of Japanese readers, which needed
rhythmical variety (as Motora claimed) for healthy functioning.

What Motora did not know was that just one year earlier, in 1889, the
essayist and poet Kitamura Tōkoku had written poetry that can only be
described as free verse: his *Soshū no shi* 楚囚之詩 (The poem of a prisoner),
introduced in chapter 2. Tōkoku himself did not broadcast his poem's char-
acteristics effectively, and its metrical novelty went unremarked by the liter-
ary establishment. Later, in the last months of 1890 and the first months
of 1891, several poets and poetry critics became embroiled in a debate over
whether meter was an essential trait of poetry or not, a debate inspired by
the serialization of Yamada Bimyō's 山田美妙 (1868–1910) "Nihon inbun
ron" 日本韻文論 (On Japanese verse). Bimyō argued that any nation that
aspired to a high level of civilization must embrace a metrically regular

poetry, and to that end he advocated the adoption, by Japanese poets, of English prosodic structures (iambs, anapests, and the like)—a position that encountered much resistance from other poets and critics. As a result of the debate, the distinction between meter and rhythm in language came into much sharper focus. Just a few months after the *inbun ronsō* died down, Tōkoku published another text—a verse-drama in the manner of Goethe's *Faust* or Byron's *Manfred*—titled *Hōraikyoku* 蓬莱曲 (Song of Mount Hōrai), which included sections in prose and metrically free verse. This work, too, elicited from critics a puzzled reaction, at best, and Tōkoku's contribution to Japanese poetry sank into obscurity. Having appeared in not one but two works by Tōkoku, free verse still went unrecognized. For most Japanese readers and critics of the time, the link between meter and poetry was still very close, and Tōkoku's work did not have any well-positioned or articulate champions.

Chapter 3 considers the haiku's appearance on an international stage from the perspective of that form's first European-language translators, who had to grapple with the intractable problem of haiku's brevity. Haiku poets of the time regarded the same question with urgency: Would the haiku survive in the modern period? Beginning with essays he wrote in the late 1880s, the haiku poet Masaoka Shiki 正岡子規 (1867–1902) warned repeatedly that the haiku was doomed to imminent extinction unless a more catholic approach to poetic diction were adopted. As if to compensate for his withering attacks on one of the world's shortest poetic forms, Shiki proclaimed in a major 1895 text, his *Haikai taiyō* 俳諧大要 (The elements of *haikai*), that the haiku, no differently from other poetic forms, was literature. Shiki's assertion of haiku's literariness needs to be seen in a multinational frame, and so this chapter examines an exchange of articles between Ueda Kazutoshi 上田萬年 (1867–1937), a prominent Japanese linguist, and Karl Florenz (1865–1939), a professor of German at Imperial University in Tokyo, who had just published an anthology of Japanese poems in German translation. The Ueda-Florenz debate centered on the literary value of traditional Japanese poetic forms— are they literature or not?—with Florenz arguing that the *chōka* was superior to the far briefer *haikai* and the *waka*, and Ueda arguing that Florenz's translations had failed to convey what was worthwhile in those shorter forms. Florenz and other European translators, as many Japanese poets and critics were well aware, disparaged Japanese verse, insisting that brief poetry was incompatible with any fully evolved literature.

Chapter 4 approaches the crisis in early twentieth-century Japanese poetry through the work of the Japanese symbolist poet Kanbara Ariake 蒲原有明 (1876–1952). Critics had complained all along that *shintaishi* were metrically monotonous; other critics had just as consistently maintained that other meters, not just variations on 5-7, were possible. Ariake and other symbolists devised dozens of new forms of metrically regular verse, two instances of which are examined closely in this chapter. If the *shintaishi* was too familiar, then one prophylactic strategy would be to devise new meters—which Ariake did, prolifically. The Japanese symbolist movement, however, fell afoul of critics who objected not only to the abstruseness of the symbolists' vocabulary and subject matter, but also to the newness of the meters in which some symbolist poetry was written: critics perceived such poems as being chaotic and difficult to read.

Chapter 5 considers the free-verse poetry of Kawaji Ryūkō, which displayed one extreme of the naturalist aesthetic being advocated in Japanese poetry circles in the first decade of the twentieth century. As already mentioned, Ryūkō is the poet usually credited with writing the first free-verse vernacular-style poems in modern Japanese, and this chapter draws on the writings of the Soviet semiotician Yuri Lotman to explain why Ryūkō's poetry, not Tōkoku's, was recognized as the first Japanese free-verse poetry. Lotman writes of the relation between literature and literary criticism, arguing that cultural exchange drives cultural change: under certain circumstances, one culture's knowledge about another culture leads observers in the first culture to adapt the resources of the second. Something similar happened, I argue, in the case of Ryūkō's poetry: Ryūkō's free verse dovetailed with contemporaneous Japanese criticisms that were written both for and against the adoption of free-verse poetry in Japanese. (Tōkoku's free verse, by contrast, met with incomprehension or silence.) Soon after Ryūkō, other poets began writing free-verse poems in Japanese, and the form became one in which Japanese lyric poets were expected to write—unless, that is, they specialized in haiku and tanka. Although there were occasional exceptions, metrically regular longer lyrics in Japanese such as the *shintaishi* were eventually abandoned.

The epilogue returns to one of the compilers of *Shintaishi shō*, Inoue Tetsujirō 井上哲次郎 (1855–1944), who bemusedly acknowledged, late in the second decade of the twentieth century, that the *shintaishi* had all but disappeared from Japanese poetry. He seems to have been unaware of the literary-critical wrangling that had greeted or decried—and, earlier, had called for or hoped to prevent—the creation of meter-free poetry in Japanese. Likewise, he seems to have been unaware of the enormous expansion that had taken place in Japanese poets' familiarity with poetries abroad, especially English, French, and German. Certainly by the end of the 1910s, if not earlier, it was not at all uncommon for Japanese poets and critics to be fully up to date about happenings in literary publications and coteries in other countries. So much information was available that for ambitious poets, specialization had become the norm. Still, Inoue thought that Japanese poets of the time had forgotten their own recent history—or, to inflect the matter differently, had forgotten *him*. Inoue's reflections offer us an eyewitness view, biased as it was, of the episodes that had so rapidly transformed Japanese poetry—a history in which he himself had played a crucial role. What he could not acknowledge—what was almost unbelievable, for a pioneer—was that his character had been killed off during the first act.

I write this study, then, to dwell in a moment in poetry history quite removed from the present. I was trained as a scholar of comparative litera-ture, but in this study I have found myself in a position nearer that of literary historian, and the emphasis has fallen, I have often believed, on the history. Historians sometimes describe their work as a recreation of what it was like to live through some critical moment in the past—to bring to a reader today "the sensations of being alive in a different time," illustrating the thesis that "the past was once as real as the present and as uncertain as the future" (Damrosch 2019, 10).[13] When I began writing this study, I imagined it might become a means for such time travel; but as I worked my way further into the material, I felt more and more the divergence between constructing causal chains—one part of the historian's work—and experiencing the contingency of everyday life. I came to believe I could not, nor should I, hope to recreate what it was like to be a poet during the heady years of 1882–1907 in Japan; I cannot pretend to have no idea what happened after the point where I end my story. Nevertheless, I do hope to have avoided the kind of history writing that Philip Roth recently caricatured as "'History,' harmless history, where everything unexpected in its own time is chronicled on the page as inevi-table" (2013, 201)—and I hope I have conveyed something of the surprise many observers would have felt at the major developments during these piv-otal years in Japanese poetry history. Now, I am also aware of the possibility that such surprise can be an entirely retrospective creation. A character in a book by V. S. Naipaul, reflecting on the acts of reconstruction that underlie so much history writing, observes that "people doing research in university libraries, where everything is accessible, sometimes see progressions that didn't exist at the time" (1994, 108). This overly zealous unearthing—which is really invention—of past progressions, too, is something that I have tried to avoid, especially when the danger is greater now than ever before, when digitization makes available to me today materials that researchers a century ago, despite their greater temporal proximity, might have found impractical if not impossible to access. Yet I do not think I have imposed upon the material my own belated sense of surprise: I believe the heterogeneous evidence I have presented here does constitute a progression, a pattern, the importance of which was recognized in real time by the Japanese poets and critics whose works were what drew me to this subject in the first place.

CHAPTER 1

New Styles of Criticism for a New Style of Poetry

If it is true, as Ezra Pound wrote, that in literature "every allegedly great age is an age of translations," then the modern era meets that criterion for greatness as no other has done (1954, 34–35).[1]

Having read such a claim, a reader is likely to expect to be presented with statistics showing the vitality of the translation wing of the publishing industry—number of books translated per year and so forth. But the reader will, I hope, look tolerantly on my choice to omit such figures, which can rapidly become outdated in any case, and will accept in their place an observation about UNESCO's remarkable online resource about translation, the Index Translationum. The observation is this: the Index Translationum presents information about translations to and from "over 1,100 languages" (Index Translationum FAQ 2011). What I see in this statistic is that, today at least, the sheer number of languages being translated to or from is high in comparison with the number of working languages of any single scholar— or even any single university literature department.[2] Most of us, I would guess, cannot name anywhere near a hundred languages, let alone a thousand. To help visitors make sense of the material, the UNESCO site provides a wide variety of filters—source language, target language, and many others. There is even a separate section on literature and translation, with links to much more information than can be grasped in a single sitting. The current age is indeed one in which translation is so widespread, and published translations are so numerous, that computing technology is perhaps the most useful means for juggling the pertinent data.

Despite all of this, it is still possible to ask whether the present age is one that Pound would have recognized as "an age of translations." More recently, on the subject of poetry and translation Eliot Weinberger has written, in terms similar to Pound's, that "the great ages of poetry have been, not coincidentally, periods of intense translation. With no news from abroad, a culture ends up repeating the same things to itself. It needs the foreign not to imitate, but to transform" (1992, 227). If that is true, then American poetry is in trouble. The scholar of Chinese literature Lucas Klein, in an essay first published online in 2014, called attention to the paucity of literary translations published in the United States: "2013 was the first year ever," Klein wrote, "in which more than 500 new translations of poetry *and* fiction [emphasis added] saw publication in the US" (2014, n5; cf. 2017, 219n2).

That number obviously speaks loudest about the United States and cannot be taken as a reflection of "the age" at large. But the dearth of literary translation appearing in the United States may have something to do with the swell of voices—among critics and theorists not only in North America but also elsewhere—alleging the difficulty of translation. *Impossible* is a word sometimes used to describe translation: the philosopher Jacques Derrida, to name only one oft-cited recent writer on this subject, referred to translation as a paradoxically "necessary and impossible task" (1985, 171). Over the past century, at a time when the sheer number of available translations is higher than ever, many have proclaimed that translation is impossible, or at best profoundly and irremediably difficult.[3]

Whether a contradiction is lurking within this juxtaposition of statements depends very much on how one defines "translation" and "impossibility." For now, I would rather leave that tension unresolved, because I want to call attention to one subset of the claims about the difficulty of translation in general: claims about the difficulty of translating poetry. The futility of poetry translation has become a cliché, with the most famous example being probably the American poet Robert Frost's observation that poetry is what gets lost in translation.[4] To be fair, in the context in which Frost made this observation, he was offering a tentative definition not of translation but of poetry. Translation enters this definition circuitously, negatively, as a test of the degree to which a text is poetic: if nothing is lost in the transfer, then perhaps the text was no poem to begin with. (Or perhaps the translator was a poet.) Frost's observation may usefully be contrasted with a suggestion made by the Chilean novelist Roberto Bolaño, who proposed that one test of a work's quality is to see how well it survives translation: a work's merits, if they are sufficient, will be apparent even in another language. Bolaño wrote:

> How to recognize a work of art? . . . Easy. Let it be translated. Let its translator be far from brilliant. Rip pages from it at random. Leave it lying in an attic. If after all of this a kid comes along and reads it, and after reading makes it his own, and is faithful to it (or unfaithful, whichever) . . . , then we have something before us, a machine or a book, capable of speaking to all human beings. (2011, 241)

Whatever else Bolaño may be asserting about literariness, his disparagement of translators is evident. For Bolaño, a work of art will survive even a middling translation with its artistry intact.[5] Despite the seeming gulf that separates Frost's pessimism (translation obliterates poetry) from Bolaño's assuredness (not even a translation can erase the art), both writers pit the author against the translator, with manifest antagonism toward the latter.

If one were to read Bolaño against the grain, one might interpret him as suggesting that translation's limitations actually serve a potentially useful function: translation can pare away the non-art in a text, leaving only the art. That interpretation of his view exaggerates the so-bad-it's-good side of translation, but I want to use that revision of Bolaño to gesture toward a broader literary critical context, one in which the Chilean writer can be seen alongside other writers and critics who acknowledge the (hitherto insufficiently noticed, they would argue) potential merits of untranslatability. In hindsight, it seems inevitable that the alleged impossibility of translation, once a cause for distress at worst and resignation at best among literary theorists, would come to be reseen in an at least partially favorable light. For some recent examples one might consider Emily Apter's *Against World Literature: On the Politics of Untranslatability* (2013), or Barbara Cassin's *Vocabulaire européen des philosophies: Dictionnaire des intraduisibles* (2004), translated under the English title *Dictionary of Untranslatables: A Philosophical Lexicon* (2014)—texts that assert that an analysis of translation's difficulty can result in fruitful new ideas about the ethical and political valences of translated (or untranslated) language. Some translators, too, have claimed that they find translation alluring precisely insofar as it is challenging: for example, the poet and scholar Anne Carson has written that "there is something maddeningly attractive about the untranslatable, about a word that goes silent in transit" (2016). Carson has also written of "the benevolence of the untranslatable," viewing favorably a phenomenon that many others have treated as a problem.

If, with Pound and Weinberger, we grant that there are eras more ame-
nable to translation, we must also recognize that other periods and places
are less favored in that regard. Consider Japan before the second half of the
nineteenth century.

The Japanese Discovery of European Verse Forms

According to Hide Inada's annotated bibliography of translations from Japa-
nese, during the years 1593–1853—a span of 260 years—there were twenty-
two "important" translations into European languages (Inada 1971).[6] There
was a far greater number of translations of European-language texts into
Japanese—"in the thousands," according to Rebekah Clements (2015, 142).
The number of translations per year from European languages into Japanese
in the period 1700–1860 peaked at around sixty in the late 1850s (Clements
2015, 147). In Japan from the beginning of the seventeenth century to the
mid-nineteenth century, the impact and readership of texts translated from
European languages were limited, not only because of Japan's geographical
remoteness from Europe but also because of the policies in force during
what has sometimes been called the *sakoku* 鎖国 (closure of the country)
period.[7] By shogunal decree, starting in the early 1600s the only Europeans
who were permitted contact with Japanese people were the representatives
of the Dutch East India Company. Dutch–Japanese communication was
allowed only on the artificial island of Dejima, off Nagasaki, although excep-
tions to this geographical restriction were made—for example, when the rep-
resentatives of the Dutch East India Company were periodically required to
travel to the capital to pay their respects to the shogun. Few Europeans ever
stayed in Japan long enough to learn much Japanese; those few who stayed
any significant number of years had to contend with yet another regulation,
which required that the language of communication be Dutch not Japanese.
One of the results of these policies was that by the first half of the nine-
teenth century, despite almost two hundred years of exchange between the
Japanese and the Dutch, extremely little information was available to any
European who might have felt curious about the literary culture of Japan,
and vice versa.[8]

Beginning in 1853, then, when Japan began to be reintegrated into a
wider network of international communication, under pressure first from
the United States and then European countries seeking access to Japanese
markets, a broad population of educated Japanese came into extended con-
tact with the literatures of European languages for the first time in history.[9]
The fact that the greatest Japanese energies had previously been devoted to

learning Dutch meant that Japanese scholars' acquisition of other prominent languages of commerce in Europe—English, French, German, to say nothing of Russian—had to start virtually from scratch. Literature was not—at least, not at first—a priority, as Japanese society set about debating and deciding how it would forge its institutions in the radically altered post-1853 situation.

When Japanese scholars began learning about the literatures of the European powers in the second half of the nineteenth century, they did not regard poetry written in European languages as incomprehensibly alien. European-language poetries were perceived as having a strong resemblance to *kanshi* (poetry in literary Chinese): like poetry in Chinese, poetry in European languages could rhyme and had meter (Murata 1871, 18r–v; Toriyama 1873, 22v–23r). Comparisons to Japanese forms were also made. Nishi Amane 西周 (1829–97), an influential pro-Westernization philosopher, compared European poetic forms not to Chinese poetry but to various kinds of rhythmical compositions in Japanese: for example, the European *epic* resembled the *Heike monogatari* 平家物語, a medieval tale with passages in poetic meter; European *lyric* resembled songs for kabuki plays with koto accompaniment; *ballads* were similar to songs for shamisen accompaniment; the *drama* resembled the *jōruri* (1874, 2r). In Nishi's and other writings from the early 1870s, which were among the first published statements in modern Japanese about the poetries of Europe, no quotations were given to illustrate the precise nature of the imputed resemblances. There were no translations available.

To the Japanese readers of the earliest years of heightened European–Japanese exchange in the latter half of the nineteenth century, European-language poetries were strange, but familiarly strange: they resembled Chinese poetry in a few crucial points of poetic form. This did not mean, however, that there was a rush to translate European-language poems into *kanshi* for consumption by educated Japanese readers. Quite the contrary: despite a short-lived surge in *kanshi* composition during the Meiji period, there was no sustained attempt, on the part of Japanese translators, to bring European-language poetry into literary Chinese.[10] Would-be translators of European poetries for a Japanese readership hesitated to render such verses even into Japanese: it was not at all clear into which *form* of Japanese verse any given European-language poem should be translated. Take any sonnet in nineteenth-century English. Although a sonnet is nowhere near as long as an epic, it is far too long for easy adaptation as either a seventeen-*moji* haiku or a thirty-one-*moji* tanka.[11] Perhaps the *chōka*, with its flexible number of lines, could have been an option, but (as we will see below) the *chōka* was held in low esteem by many poets and critics who were eager to appear au courant. And no Japanese poet, as far as I have been able to determine, attempted to translate a sonnet as a fourteen-line poem in Japanese with ten *moji* per line, which would thereby have matched the syllable count of the original's iambic pentameter. Close adherence to European accentual meters was no easy feat for Japanese poetry translators to achieve.

Here it will be good to bring these generalizations into sharper focus by considering an example. I will cite the beginning of a poem that Japanese readers encountered for the first time in 1882, and then make a few observations about what those first readers would have found striking:

> Is it better to die? Is it better to live? Here indeed is cause for thought.
> The pitiless and poor fortune that piles sadness upon bitterness—
> I should be a man and endure it. Or, upon reconsideration, I should not.
> On the contrary: if I were to cut my sole dewdrop jewel necklace
> thinking death were merely sleep, and thereby summarily take leave of
> this bitter, painful world, would it not be a coward's deed?[12]

> *shinuru ga mashi ka / ikuru ga mashi ka*   *shian o suru wa / koko zo ka shi*
> *tsutanaki un no / nasake naku*   *ukime karakime / kasanaru mo*
> *koraeshinobu ga / otoko zo yo*   *mata mo omoeba / sa wa arade*
> *isso no koto ni / futatsu naki*   *tsuyu no tama no o / uchikirite*
> *shinde nemurite / soregiri to*   *karaki kurushiki / yo no naka o*
> *sarari to satte / kieyuku mo*   *hikyō no waza ni / aranu ka ya*[13]

> 死ぬるが増か生くるが増か   思案をするハこゝぞかし
> つたなき運の情なく   うきめからきめ重なるも
> 堪へ忍ぶが男兒ぞよ   又もおもへバさハあらで
> 一そのことに二つなき   露の玉の緒うちきりて
> 死んで眠りてそれぎりと   からきくるしき世の中を
> さらりと去つて消え行くも   卑怯の業にあらぬかや

(Toyama, Yatabe, and Inoue 1882, 40r)

In the first six lines of "A Scene from Shakespeare's *Hamlet*" (Shēkisupīru shi Hamuretto chū no ichidan シェーキスピール氏ハムレット中の一段), the professor of sociology Toyama Masakazu 外山正一 (1848–1900) presented in Japanese the beginning of a famous dramatic soliloquy: Hamlet's meditation on suicide, on human existence, and on thought itself. The first readers of this translation, however, would almost certainly not have known the narrative context from which the soliloquy was drawn: they would not have known, for example, *who* might be pronouncing these words, or why; nor would they have known that these words might be uttered by an actor on a stage.[14] Shakespeare was still a relative unknown in Japan, as to some extent were the conventions of European drama more broadly conceived.[15] Japanese readers encountered these lines in a manner altogether different from their contemporaries who were native readers of English.

There was also the soliloquy's subject matter. Wrested from its dramatic context, the soliloquy is elliptical even in the original English, describing suicide in rather metaphysical, metaphorical terms. Toyama's Japanese rendering of the text begins with a stark position of the central question whether it is preferable to live or die; but the question is framed impersonally, as it were, and relations between speaker and presumptive addressee are left unspecified. The verse proceeds rather on a rhetorical plane: the question about living and dying that is posed in the first half of the first line is described as a topic for reflection not action. The second line then introduces the abstraction *un* or fate; perhaps a reader is to infer that fate is bound up with the question that was posed in the first line. In the third line, enter an *otoko* or man, whose duty is to endure his *un* bravely. That is the freight of the first half, at least, of the third line; but the second half of the third line reverses the manly posture advocated in that line's first half. The *otoko* must choose, but the speaker now reflects that it would be a coward's deed (*hikyō no waza*) to choose the sleep of death, thereby suggesting that what had appeared to be a choice may in fact not be a choice at all. The verse seems to be undoing itself at every turn, even as it describes a speaker who hesitates over whether undoing *himself* is advisable.

By this point in the poem, the theme appears to be the behavior suitable to a brave man. According to the speaker's reflections in these early lines of the soliloquy, suicide would be an act of cowardice—contrary to any pronouncements that may have been made in Japan at the time about the nobility of suicide. Although no words specifically denoting suicide are used in the translation, the phrase "cut [the] dewdrop jewel necklace" brings the matter into high relief, invoking a vocabulary that many Japanese readers would have recognized from ancient poetry anthologies. The phrase *tama no o*, "jewel necklace," is used as a metaphor for human life in, for example, poem 12:568 of the enormously influential *Kokin waka shū*, a tenth-century imperially ordered *waka* anthology, and in poem 89 of *Hyakunin isshu*, a much-circulated thirteenth-century selection of *waka*. Hence, readers familiar with Japanese *waka* anthologies would almost certainly have understood the drift of the translation here. Such reuse of phrases from ancient poetry anthologies in translations of European verse was by no means limited to Toyama's *Hamlet*:

in fact, another contemporary version of the same soliloquy by a different translator, Yatabe Ryōkichi 矢田部良吉 (1852–99), similarly drew on a few handy poetic phrases to fill out the *moji* counts. Likewise, Yatabe's famous version of Thomas Gray's "Elegy Written in a Country Church-yard" (1751) drew on such familiar poetic topics as *aware* (the pathos of things), *ukiyo* (the floating world), and *mujō* (transience) even as it introduced names like Milton and Cromwell. (We will return to Yatabe's version of Gray below.) By incorporating familiar poetic diction in these translations of verses from an almost completely unknown tradition, the translators eased their readers into a new poetic world.

Yet the invocation of familiar and even ancient Japanese poetic vocabulary was directly opposed to one aspect of Toyama's stated aims in introducing poetry from abroad. The two versions of Hamlet's soliloquy, along with Yatabe's version of Gray's "Elegy" and sixteen other poems, were published in *Shintaishi shō* 新体詩抄 (New-style poetry collection, August 1882), the work of three translators and compilers: Toyama Masakazu and Yatabe Ryōkichi, the two translators who have already been named, and Inoue Tetsujirō 井上哲次郎 (1855–1944). This anthology had several ambitions. First and most obviously, it was an attempt to present Japanese translations of Western-language—actually, only English-language—poetry in an accessible way: fourteen of the nineteen poems in the anthology were translations. Important, too, were the brief prose commentaries that preceded or followed some of the poems, informing Japanese readers how poets and poetry were seen in Western countries. Second, along with the works of Shakespeare, Longfellow, Tennyson, and others, the anthology presented five original poems by the compilers: a demonstration that poetry on Western models could be written in Japanese, too. Third, and related to the previous two, the compilers hoped to bring Japanese poetry up to date: like other reformers in Japan who were attempting to place Japanese institutions on a more equal footing with comparable institutions in Europe and North America, the compilers of *Shintaishi shō* regarded Japanese cultural productions—in their case, poetry—as being disadvantaged, relative to those of European cultures, after more than two centuries of near-total, self-imposed isolation.

What the anthologists were attempting was a heavy conceptual lift by any measure. Just how heavy it was can be gauged from the many paratexts that they included in the anthology—the prefatory comments to the individual poems and to the collection as a whole. Those paratexts are a significant document in the story of poetry translation, and therefore in the next several pages I want to examine closely the translation theory espoused by the *Shintaishi shō* anthologists. Not only did their translations set the initial parameters for Japanese poetry translation, but also their translation practice had historical importance for all the later poets who will be appearing in the present study.

"Our long poems cannot equal them": Forging a Longer Japanese Lyric

Like all the translations in *Shintaishi shō*, Toyama's translation of Hamlet's soliloquy unfolded in lockstep meter: there was scarcely a deviation from five- or seven-*moji* phrases, alternating with perfect regularity; in this poem, there were initial and final doublets of 7-7. Metrically speaking, then, the *shintaishi* differed little from the *chōka*, leading the prefacers to anticipate that some readers might describe their "new-style *shi*" as not new at all.

The poems in the anthology, however, did include certain formal innovations. One of these was typographical: the division of poems into lines and stanzas. The prefacers of the anthology explained the phenomena of lineation and stanzification by recourse to the example of poetry in Western languages. Inoue wrote of these structural matters as follows, in one of the preliminary remarks to the collection as a whole:

> The form of long Japanese poems [Inoue means *chōka*] is the 5-7 or 7-5 *moji* pattern. The compositions in this book also employ the 7-5 *moji* pattern, but they are not bound by the old poetic rules. Moreover, our desire has been to seek out various new styles (*shintai*), and this is why we call our compositions New Style Poems (*shintaishi*).
>
> In dividing the poetry in this work into verses [*uberusu* 句] and stanzas [*sutanzā* 節] we follow the example of Western collections of poetry. (Toyama, Yatabe, and Inoue 1882, *hanrei*, 1v; Morrell 1975, 14)[16]

The use of lineation—dividing a poem into "verses"—was an important departure. Ordinarily, in earlier periods of Japanese poetry history, *waka* and haiku (that is, *hokku* or *haikai*) had appeared as unbroken strings of text with no marks to indicate the divisions between the five- and seven-*moji* phrases, which were known as *ku* 句. Those subdivisions were traditionally treated, however, as having an independent integrity, regardless of how they were presented on the page. *Waka* and haiku, then, could be regarded, as Hiroaki Sato has persuasively argued (1987, 356), as mono-linear poems that nevertheless are composed of syllabically determined subunits or *ku*.[17] The word *ku* was thus a suitable vehicle, Inoue evidently believed, for denoting the

シェーキスピール氏ハムレット中の一段

ゝ山仙士

死ぬるが増か生くるが増か
思案をするはこゝぞかし
つたなき運の情なく
うきめからきめ重なるも
堪へ忍ぶが男児ぞよ
又もおもへばさはあらで
一そのことは二つなき
露の玉の緒うちきりて
死んで眠りてそれぎりと
からきくるしき世の中と
さらりと去つて消え行くを
卑怯の業まあらぬかや
一眠りにてつもりこし
胸の焦れや現身の
萬の艱苦それぎりは
去りて去るゝものならば
それまゝされることなきも
死ぬる眠ると云ふものゝ
眠りて後は又や見ん
夢の行末おぼつかな
死んで眠りの肉身を
離れん離れ行くものゝ

FIGURE 1. *Shintaishi shō*. The first page of Toyama Masakazu's translation of the "To be or not to be" soliloquy from *Hamlet*. Source: Toyama, Yatabe, and Inoue 1882, 40r.

poetic *line* (or, as he put it, *verse*) in the English-language sense, as one can infer from the fact that he matched the gloss *uberusu* to the ideograph 句.[18] With the first publication of typeset *shintaishi*, lineation became a meaningful feature of Japanese poetry.

Shintaishi shō deviated from European practices of lineation in one important respect. In the late nineteenth century, the norm in European languages would have been to justify poetry along the left margin—that is, aligning the beginning of each line of verse—leaving the line-ends ragged and unjustified. *Shintaishi shō*, however, justified its margins at both the beginning and the end of every line—hence, at both the top and the bottom of the page (given that the lines were printed vertically, not horizontally).[19] Furthermore, the anthologists divided each long line into a top half and a bottom, with each hemistich containing twelve *moji* (or fourteen, at the very beginning or end of a poem)—so that the text of each poem formed two perfect rectangles of typeset characters.[20] As I have said, this typographical arrangement differed from the European norm, but it also differed from the formatting of Japanese poetry thereafter. The double-file presentation of verse was a short-lived feature of early *shintaishi*; later generations have embraced visible imparity of verse length on the printed page.

In addition to the new structural features I have just mentioned, there was a reimagining of the content of poetry—a new approach to the words with which poems were written. In the comment cited above, Inoue mentioned the "old poetic rules," by which he meant the rules governing acceptable poetic diction. Indeed, the prefacers insisted that what made the "new-style *shi*" different from earlier forms of Japanese poetry was its diction—the inclusion of a more up-to-date vocabulary—despite the fact that, as has been demonstrated above (with the phrase *tama no o* and other vocabulary drawn from classical poetry collections), *Shintaishi shō* was studded with poetic phrases of ancient vintage. But the prefacers were unanimous in insisting that Japanese poetic diction needed to be—as they would have seen it—modernized. In the prefatory comment to his translation of Gray's "Elegy," Yatabe wrote: "Since [Western poets] do not utilize the ancient vocabulary of a thousand years ago, even a child three feet tall understands the language of the country down to the last detail and is able to comprehend its poetry" (7r; 17). In a comment on one of his original poems, "Impressions on Visiting the Great Buddha at Kamakura" (Kamakura no daibutsu ni mōdete kan ari 鎌倉の大仏に詣でゝ感あり), Yatabe also wrote:

It is difficult to compose the traditional long and short Japanese poems to give full play to our feelings and thoughts with precision by using an ancient and elegant vocabulary which, since it is not in everyday use, is like a kind of rare foreign tongue.

This being so, I think that we should frequently mix in a few ordinary words to make a new style of poetry in order to adequately give vent to what we feel in our hearts. (25v; 19)

What Yatabe meant here by "ordinary words" can be seen by returning briefly to Toyama's version of Hamlet's soliloquy, in which the word *shian* ("cause for thought") is wrenchingly unpoetic, almost technical; *mata mo omoeba sa wa arade* ("Or, upon reconsideration, I should not") is a costly, twelve-*moji* way of prosaically saying "Then again, no." There was a hint of ambivalence in Yatabe's phrasing: he advocated "frequent" use of new diction in poetry, but the new diction should be limited to only "a few" words here and there. Even so, Yatabe's overall program for poetry reform was sweeping: it called for a kind of writing that was still recognizable as poetry, yet had pointedly innovative aims and was addressed to a wider readership than poetry had hitherto had.

The imperative to adopt a new poetic vocabulary had already been issued in sources that the compilers may have known, and some of those sources predated the Meiji reign by many decades. From Japan, for example, there were the writings of the influential *waka* poet Kagawa Kageki 香川景樹 (1768–1843).[21] In an 1811 text, Kageki enunciated an ideal of poetic spontaneity by invoking the *Kokin waka shū*, the preface of which had famously stated that poetry springs naturally from the heart. To write a spontaneous poem, however, a poet must not (over)use the diction of earlier poets: it was necessary, Kageki argued, to write in one's own contemporary idiom, not in a classical-contemporary patois. At base of such a view was an implicit belief that (written) language evolves. Kageki found objectionable those poets who hoped to resist the propulsive force of linguistic change over time:

> Contemporary poetry should be composed in current language using the style of the present. But since there is an inherent difference between poets, some poetry is naturally going to resemble the Man'yō style, Kokin style, or any number of other styles; however, the poet is not able to step outside his modern poetical style, so the poems he produces will vary from the styles in the age of *Man'yōshū* and *Kokinshū*, being naturally a part of the modern style. (Kagawa 2017, 274; [1811] 1975, 599)

Kageki's pronouncements, with their calls to update the vocabulary that poets had inherited from *Kokinshū* and *Man'yōshū* (an even older anthology of *waka* and other forms of poetry, compiled ca. 759 CE), anticipated by some seventy years the prefaces of *Shintaishi shō*. However, as later commentators have agreed, Kageki himself proved unable to follow his own prescriptions (Bentley 2017, 19; Keene 1976, 493).

The compilers of *Shintaishi shō* possibly also knew of an English-language precedent for their project of launching a new kind of poetry: the preface of *Lyrical Ballads* (1798), a poetry collection by the English poets William Wordsworth and Samuel Taylor Coleridge. *Lyrical Ballads* eschewed the rhyming couplets and elevated diction of the previous generation of poets, which had included figures such as Alexander Pope.[22] When *Lyrical Ballads* was reprinted in 1800, Wordsworth added a preface in which he explained his reasons for favoring what he called a "language really used by men" over an ostensibly more poetic diction. Such ideas certainly would have appealed to anyone hoping to justify a poetic revolution. Toyama and Yatabe might have encountered *Lyrical Ballads* during their years of study at American universities (the University of Michigan and Cornell University, respectively; Inoue, being younger, had not yet left for Germany at the time of *Shintaishi shō's* publication).[23] Whether the compilers of *Shintaishi shō* knew of Wordsworth in 1882 is difficult to determine conclusively—Japanese poets of a later generation, as we will see, certainly *did* know Wordsworth. In any case, the compilers' statements about poetic diction bore a resemblance to Wordsworth's program for bringing the language of poetry in line with the language of common speech.

More than that, the prefaces of *Shintaishi shō* shared an assumption with Wordsworth's preface and with Kageki's writings alike: namely, that language evolves over time, but at different paces for written and spoken language.[24] In the passages already cited from *Shintaishi shō*, the anthologists' belief that written style can (and even tends to) lag behind spoken language is evident. If a disparity between writing and speech is an inevitable feature of literate culture, however, then the imperative to modernize must constantly be reiterated; renovation must never end, as long as language continues evolving. Whether the *Shintaishi shō* compilers understood their program's implications of permanent revolution is not immediately apparent, but they persisted in seeing the gap between writing and speech as an obstacle that must be overcome. According to Inoue's account, his decision to become a *shintaishi* poet was brought about by his wish to help Japanese poetry overcome that obstacle:

Later, while reading his biography, I came upon this remark by [the philosopher] Kaibara Ekken (1630–1714): "In our country we should express our aspirations and relate our feelings only through *waka*. There is no need to provoke ridicule by composing clumsy poems in Chinese and making a fool of oneself." So I said to myself: "It is just as Master Ekken states. The people of our country should study *waka*, not Chinese poetry (*shi*). Compared with *waka*, Chinese poetry, even by a contemporary, is difficult to explicate. So why not cultivate *waka*?"

Then I entered college and studied the poetry of the West. Their short poems are comparable to our short poems, but their long poems extend to several tens of volumes; our long poems cannot equal them. Moreover, these Western poems change with the times, so that current poems employ current idioms and their comprehensiveness and elaborateness ensure that their readers will not become bored. Perhaps it was in response to this that I again remarked: "It is not enough to stick with the old *waka*. Why should we not cultivate a new-style poetry (*shintaishi*)?" (first *jo*, 1r; 13–14)

"These Western poems change with the times"—but, by implication, Japanese poetry, in Inoue's reconstruction, had not done so. One of the most quoted passages from *Shintaishi shō* is another comment by Inoue, written as part of the brief preface to the sole verse translation he contributed to the collection: "Meiji poetry should be Meiji poetry, not ancient poetry. Japanese poetry should be Japanese poetry, not Chinese. This is why we are creating a new style poetry. Now if only we can improve the methods of rhyming and the techniques of rhythm—but it cannot be done all at once" (15v; 15).

This last comment shows that while the compilers of *Shintaishi shō* never stated that poetry must be metrically regular, they likewise never evinced any awareness that poetry could be anything but metered. We have already seen the comment that "the compositions in this book also employ the 7-5 *moji* pattern, but they are not bound by the old poetic rules" governing a suitable poetic diction (*hanrei*, 1v; 14). Poetic diction, in other words, could and should be updated and brought into line with modern concerns, but meter (*moji* count) was seen as being an indispensable, nonupdatable feature of poetic language. At most, what the compilers of *Shintaishi shō* imagined was what they called an "improvement" of metrical arrangements at some unspecified point in the future.

It is worth dilating for a moment on the use of the term *shi* in the title *Shintaishi shō*, because it reveals much about where the compilers of that anthology located the boundaries between categories of poetry. The compilers were consciously attempting to redefine *shi*, as one of their prefatory remarks makes clear:

In China they refer to poetry as *shi*; in Japan we call it *uta*. But we do not yet have a common word for both *uta* and *shi*. The compositions in this book are not *shi* (i.e., not in the sense of Chinese poems), nor are they *uta*. Our sense of the word *shi* simply assigns a general term which includes both *uta* and *shi*, like the Western word "poetry." Ours are not the *shi* which have been so called since antiquity. (*hanrei*, 1r; 14)

The impulse to establish and propagate a "general term" (*sōshō* 総称) for a more capacious concept of poetry underlay the creation of *Shintaishi shō* itself.[25] To borrow vocabulary used by the translator and translation scholar David Bellos (2011, 26–27), what the compilers wished to do was to transform the word *shi* from a hyponym into a hypernym: from a word designating a subset (*shi* = poetry written in literary Chinese) into a word designating a superset (*shi* = poetry in general). Their ambition, they confessed, was to create a new kind of poetry, which could be designated *only* by the new term they had invented. This new poetry would have stanza divisions, lines of verse demarcated by typographic means, a smattering of words from current speech, and, not least, an openness to the possibility of new subject matter.

The success of this new type of poetry can be gauged in part by its effect on poets working in other verse forms. In the remainder of this chapter, we will examine the reception of the *shintaishi* in the first years after its invention, giving first consideration to the responses of writers of *waka* and *chōka*: it was they who felt the impact most keenly.

Waka and *Chōka* Poets Respond to the Challenge of the New

The influence exerted by *Shintaishi shō* on young readers in the 1880s and 1890s has become part of the lore of modern Japanese poetry history. The memoirs of Japanese writers who grew up in the Meiji period include fond recollections of the thrill of first encountering the new-style *shi* (Akatsuka 1991, 23–25). The vituperative reaction against *Shintaishi shō*, too, has been frequently mentioned; the scholar Akatsuka Yukio has suggested that the negative reaction was confined mainly to older readers (29). Perhaps it was the form's sheer novelty that stimulated a demand for so many *shintaishi* anthologies within months of *Shintaishi shō*. Five collections of *Shintai shiika* 新体詩歌 (New-style poetry) appeared in print before August of 1883; these were reprinted in May–August 1884; and in December 1884 *Shintaishi shō* was printed again (with the last ideograph of the title changed: 新体詩鈔). In 1886 another collection of *shintaishi* was published, this one titled *Shintai shisen* 新体詩選 (Selection of *shintaishi*); 1887 saw the publication of *Meiji shintai shisen* 明治新体詩選 (Selection of Meiji *shintaishi*) (Akatsuka 1991,

22–23). Yamamoto Kōji, a scholar of the *shintaishi*, has recently shown that counting only the anthologies titled *Shintai shiika*, twenty-seven such collections were published between 1882 and 1887 (2012, 80–84). In many of these anthologies, a sampling of the original *shintaishi* of *Shintaishi shō* were reprinted alongside newer compositions, so that the work of the original compilers, even if not always explicitly designated as such in these new publications, was kept prominently in view.

Most studies of the reception of *Shintaishi shō* have foregrounded the poets who would go on to write *shintaishi* themselves. One needs to keep in mind, however, the impression this new form of poetry made on those poets and critics who favored retaining the older kinds of poetry. The *Shintaishi shō* anthologists had written of other Japanese verse forms in disparaging terms, as has already appeared in the passages cited above. The most frontal attack on traditional Japanese verse forms was written by Toyama Masakazu:

> The methods of expression we use when we have been moved by something are the thirty-one *moji* [i.e., *waka*], *senryū*, and simple Tang-style poetry [i.e., *shi*]. We use them simply because they are not demanding modes of expression. But in the long run, when we view things through such simple modes of expression as this, without a doubt the ideas they encompass will also be simple. This may be a very rude objection to raise, but it seems to me that the ideas which we can exhaustively convey through such modes of expression as the thirty-one *moji*, or satirical verse, are those of a duration no longer than fireworks or shooting stars. When we get ideas in our head with the slightest continuity and try to enunciate them, such modes of expression are basically inadequate. (third *jo*, 1v; 23)

Despite Toyama's concern here to avoid impertinence, this was a direct attack on traditional Japanese poetics. The point about the brevity of *waka*, *senryū*, and even *shi* was a stark acknowledgment of a quite different—in this case, a European—perspective on poetic composition, one that exalted the achievements of long epic poems and dramas in verse. Toyama's point about the simplicity of Japanese verse emanated from parallel concerns. In combination with the other anthologists' statements about poetic diction, typographic arrangement, and other conventions of poetic culture, Toyama's forthright disparagement of traditional Japanese verse forms could not but elicit a reaction from poets working in those forms.

One of the first sustained post-*shintaishi* reflections on how—not whether, but how—to reform the *waka* appeared in "On the *uta*" (Kagakuron

歌楽論, 1884–85) by the writer (and later politician) Suematsu Kenchō 末松謙澄 (1855–1920), in which Kenchō—taking the term *uta* as meaning, literally, song—disparaged the Japanese *waka* as having lost its songlike quality. Kenchō had always in mind the example of Western songs: he singled out the chorus (*kōrasu*) as a feature of the European songwriting tradition that had been used with great effect in European poetries but was little in evidence in Japanese poetry (Suematsu [1884–85] 1975, 15). One of Kenchō's primary objections to the *waka*, referring particularly to the Heian period (794–1185 CE) and after, was that it had ceased to be song and had come to be literature (*bungaku* 文学) instead (22). (This deprecating use of the word *bungaku* forms a notable contrast with favorable claims that Masaoka Shiki would make only a decade later about the literariness of haiku.) Verbal artifice—represented most obviously by the survival of such poetic devices as pillow-words (formulaic epithets)—was one reason why long Japanese poetry was so seldom written after the time of *Man'yōshū* (24). In terms that recalled the prefaces to *Shintaishi shō*, Kenchō objected more generally that *waka* poets had continued using "the ancient language of eleven hundred years ago" (25). For contrast, Kenchō invoked the example of English poetry. Just consider the difference between English as Chaucer and Spenser wrote it, on the one hand, and as Byron and Shelley wrote it, on the other: the fact that these poets wrote in (what Kenchō regarded as) the different Englishes of their respective eras was proof, as Kenchō claimed, that they should so have written (24). Kenchō was unwilling to admit the possibility that written Japanese, in the *waka* as in other literary forms, had in fact undergone transformations since the time of *Man'yōshū*; his argument required a contrast between European culture—a relatively new culture (as Kenchō put it), but already advanced, highly amenable to change—and an older but more self-complacent, less advanced Japanese culture (12).

Yet Kenchō attempted to turn the antiquity of Japanese culture to advantage by observing that in ancient Japanese poetry, there actually was considerable metrical variety. Being older, Japanese culture had a wider range of native materials upon which to draw, Kenchō claimed, than did European cultures. A full investigation of the oldest Japanese poetry, including the *chōka* and the other forms of poetry extant during the *Man'yōshū* era, could bring about "a restoration of our ancient *waka* forms, many of which were not bound by [the prosody of] fives and sevens" (46; *goshichi ni kōdei sezaru mo ōshi waga katai no fukko ishin* 五七ニ拘泥セザルモ多シ我歌體ノ復古維新). This statement placed Kenchō in the vanguard of those who called for a loosening of metrical restrictions in Japanese poetry; it is not surprising that the proposal for change came in the same breath as a call for a return to ancient, unaffectedly Japanese practices.[26]

A few years later, the historian Hagino Yoshiyuki 萩野由之 (1860–1924) likewise asserted the need for *waka* reform. In March 1887 Hagino published his "Brief Comments" (Kogoto 小言), claiming that *waka* poets needed to adapt their art to the changed times—and had needed to do so for over a millennium. The verbal artifices of *waka* poetry—the setting of topics, the use of pillow-words, and so forth—all came in for Hagino's criticism: the poet's toolkit has not changed, even though the poet's heart—the very source of poetry, as the preface to *Kokinshū* had famously proclaimed—changes with the times. "The movements of the human heart," Hagino wrote, "inevitably undergo a myriad of changes. Therefore, one must not always use only thirty-one *ji* [in a poem]. One should write *chōka* or tanka in keeping with the meaning [one wants to express]—one should not always limit one's verses to 5-7-5 [*sic*]. The fact that we find, in antiquity, poems long and short alike is altogether as it should be" ([1887] 1975, 84). One of the most striking assertions here is that metrical strictures should be loosened—a suggestion that, as the *waka* poet and historian Kimata Osamu has observed, "distinguished those who advocated *waka* reform," such as Hagino, "from those who merely criticized the *waka*," among them the prefacers of *Shintaishi shō* (1965, 16–17). Reformers like Hagino wanted an update of the *waka* and the *chōka*, an update that could include the abandonment of certain conventions—even the conventional prosodic norm.

Later the same year (1887), Hagino's article was republished in a stand-alone volume titled *On Reforming Nation Studies and the "waka"* (Kokugaku waka kairyō ron 国学和歌改良論), which included one other essay about *waka* reform by the poet and literary historian Konakamura Gishō 小中村義象 (penname of Ikebe Yoshikata 池邊義象, 1861–1923). The study by Konakamura and Hagino elicited swift response, much of it negative. For example, there was the pointedly titled article by Taketsu Yachio 武津八千代 (d. 1931), "On the Impossibility of Reforming Nation Studies and *waka*" (Kokugaku waka kairyō fuka ron 国学和歌改良不可論), published in February 1888. "Let us not accept this vogue for reformism," Taketsu cried, "and thereby lose the basis for our characteristic style [*koyū no hontai*]" of poetry ([1888] 1975, 129). One month earlier, in January 1888, Hattori Motohiko 服部元彦 (dates unknown) published an essay critical of Konakamura and Hagino on several points. First, Hattori disagreed with how Konakamura and Hagino had used the word *waka* to mean metrical language of several varieties: their definition, Hattori alleged, allowed such forms as the *chōka*, the school song (shōka 唱歌), and the rhythmical songs sung by "farmers and men in the fields," all to be counted as waka ([1888] 1975, 91).[27] Hattori preferred instead to define waka as the body of poems found in Kokin waka shū, Man'yōshū, and other ancient texts. The point where Hattori disagreed with Konakamura and Hagino most strongly was on the nature of language evolution. Hattori conceded that language evolves, but he disagreed with Konakamura and Hagino's implicitly favorable view of that evolution. He preferred to see change as degeneration, which poets must resist: "Language worsened from the ancient times to the Middle Ages, and worsened even more from the Middle Ages to the recent past, and has worsened even more since then, so that now the language has approached an extreme of vulgarity" (94–95). By implication, poets who wrote in a classical style were helping to preserve what was best in the Japanese language. In this article Hattori did not deign to recognize the shintaishi by name, but we can imagine he would have interpreted its very existence as further evidence of (what he would have regarded as) the vulgarization of Japanese culture.

Aside from those who argued for or against waka reform, other writers took up the subject of chōka reform in its own right. Sasaki Hirotsuna 佐佐木弘綱 (1828–91), the forebear to many poets (his son and grandson were both waka poets; his great-grandson, Sasaki Yukitsuna 佐佐木幸綱 [b. 1938], remains active today), published in September 1888 an article, "On chōka Reform" (Chōka kairyō ron 長歌改良論), advising Japanese poets to write chōka: "a poet who cannot compose chōka," Sasaki claimed, "is no poet" ([1888] 1975, 161; chōka o eyomanu utayomi wa, utayomi ni arazu 長歌を得よまぬ歌よみは、歌よみにあらず). For evidence, Sasaki observed that many prominent waka poets in Japanese history had written chōka, although he also conceded that there were important works of Japanese literature in which no chōka appeared—for example, Tale of Genji (ca. 1000 CE) (161). Sasaki saw poetic forms as being relatively interchangeable, so long as they had meter (shirabe 調) to increase their affective appeal to the listener (160). Hence the chōka was not so very different, Sasaki claimed, from the dodoitsu, a poem in 7-7-7-5; nor was it so very different from the imayō, a four-line poem with twelve-moji lines (usually 7-5). His relatively relaxed stance toward poetic form led Sasaki to state, "From now on, let us write imayō instead of chōka" (161). To give the imayō greater flexibility, Sasaki suggested that the four-line imayō could be lengthened to eight lines, twelve lines, sixteen lines, or even more (161). Having recommended a renewed attention to the chōka, Sasaki overshot the mark and went so far as to recommend other forms altogether.

Sasaki's essay provoked critical responses from readers who thought he advocated too extreme a change, on the one hand, and from readers who thought he did not go far enough, on the other. Unagami Tanehira 海上 胤平 (1830–1916), a *waka* poet, critiqued Sasaki's essay phrase by phrase and word by word in a multi-installment article, "A Polemical Refutation of 'On *chōka* Reform'" (Chōka kairyō ron benbaku 長歌改良論辨駁)—more than five times as long as Sasaki's original piece. Evidently an opponent of efforts to modernize even Japanese prose, Unagami adopted a caustic, almost pedantically correct tone—at one point he objected to Sasaki's use of grammatical connectives ([1889] 1975, 179), at another to Sasaki's repetitive use of verb endings (175)—and concluded his essay with a curt, critical summary of Sasaki's article: "This essay isn't about reforming *chōka*. It's about eliminating *chōka*" (188). The fact that Sasaki had exhorted his readers to write *imayō* instead of *chōka*—thereby asserting, as one scholar has recently put it, "the irrelevance of the *chōka*" (Nakazawa 2008, 31)—clearly gave Unagami great displeasure.

A much younger scholar, Yamada Bimyō 山田美妙 (1868–1910), called attention to Sasaki's view of Japanese poetic meter, in particular to Sasaki's assertion that the 7-5 meter was the "meter of today" (Yamada [1888] 1975, 165). Against Sasaki, Bimyō asserted that, in fact, the "roots of meter" (*shirabe no ne* 調の根) were clusters of three, four, or five syllables (*gon* 言), which, when combined, added up to the various possible meters (165). Bimyō cited no authority in this matter; his analyses perhaps struck him as requiring nothing but simple addition. A six-syllable phrase might be composed of two three-syllable phrases, for example; a seven-syllable phrase might be composed of a three and a four, or a four and a three; and so on (165–66). Bimyō took a clear stand: "As for meter, I am of the opinion that you may use whichever you prefer"—as long as you used one (168). Mentioning the recent appearance of the *shintaishi*, Bimyō noted that "the great difficulty now is what language to use in poetry, what rhetoric" (168). All he could say with certainty was that he was in complete agreement with those who believed that the way forward for Japanese poetry lay not in the poetry of the past (167). Something else would be needed.

One *waka* poet's critique of the *shintaishi* took issue squarely with the *Shintaishi shō* anthologists' programs of reform and translation alike: Ikebukuro Kiyokaze's "A Criticism of the *shintaishi*," which is "representative," as the scholar Amagasaki Akira has written, "of the anti-*shintaishi* criticisms of the traditionalists" (2011, 166). There was much, Kiyokaze believed, to criticize.

Ikebukuro Kiyokaze's Self-Thwarting Translations

In his essay "The Task of the Translator," the German literary critic Walter Benjamin arrived at several conclusions about literary translation based on a premise about the reception of works of art. His essay began, "In the appreciation of a work of art or an art form, consideration of the receiver never proves fruitful. . . . No poem is intended for the reader, no picture for the beholder, no symphony for the listener" (1968, 69). With this antiexpressivist axiom as his foundation, Benjamin took exception to a commonplace view about translation: namely, the belief that translation should domesticate a foreign text, giving it a home in a new language. For Benjamin, domestication had the deleterious effect of alienating the text from itself, stripping it of its particularities. On this point Benjamin quoted the poet and philosopher Rudolf Pannwitz approvingly:

> The basic error of the translator is that he preserves the state in which his own language happens to be instead of allowing his language to be powerfully affected by the foreign tongue. Particularly when translating from a language very remote from his own he must go back to the primal elements of language itself and penetrate to the point where work, image, and tone converge. (81)

As we saw at the beginning of this chapter, Frost and Bolaño posited a fundamental and (for them) lamentably insuperable difference between the original author and the translator; Benjamin, for his part, defined the translator's task as one of overcoming that difference—which is not to say he regarded the task as a possible one.

Where a theorist like Benjamin would insist on the merit of a foreignizing translation, many early Japanese readers of the *shintaishi* regarded such translation as anathema. One of the most-cited critiques of the *shintaishi* was the *waka* poet Ikebukuro Kiyokaze's 池袋静風 (1847–1910) "A Criticism of the *shintaishi*" (Shintaishi hihyō 新体詩批評), serialized in three parts in January, February, and April 1889 in the thrice-monthly *Kokumin no tomo* 国民之友 (which carried a title in English: *The Nation's Friend*). In one sense, *Kokumin no tomo*—already well on its way to establishing a reputation for introducing authors from abroad, such as Dickens, Tolstoy, Hugo, and others (Pierson 1980, 164–77)—was a surprising venue in which to publish a nominally antitranslation screed. Kiyokaze, however, was asserting the superiority of rather a different style of poetry translation, he claimed, than had hitherto been attempted.

The first installment of Kiyokaze's essay ended with the attention-getting claim that "poetry [*shiika*] should not be translated" (Ikebukuro 1889, 15). The *shintaishi* had failed so miserably at its mission of translating poetic culture, Kiyokaze believed, that a cessation of poetry translation would be preferable to reading more examples of *shintaishi* versions of unfamiliar poems. He based these claims on an analysis of Yatabe Ryōkichi's translation of Thomas Gray's "Elegy Written in a Country Church-yard," which had appeared in *Shintaishi shō*. Kiyokaze cited the first stanzas of Yatabe's translation, criticizing it for deviating from the attested vocabulary of Japanese poetics—for doing, in other words, exactly what Yatabe and the other compilers of the anthology had set out to do:

> One must not alter the vocabulary that has appeared in Japanese poetry hitherto, nor can one simply use whatever diction suits oneself; one must write in accordance with the poetic language that has conveyed the sentiments of this country since antiquity. If one uses one's own words then [readers] will not understand at all. (14)

Those who are familiar with the topoi of Japanese poetry will indeed find much in Yatabe's translation that is untypical of *waka*.[28] The pastoral setting, with herd animals and farmhands peopling the scene, is quite different from the aristocratic poetics of cherry blossoms and kimono sleeves moistened by tears such as one finds in certain strains of classical Japanese poetry. Yatabe's translation of Gray's poem begins:

> mists in the mountains, and the evening / bell sounds as the cows in the field
> go walking slowly homeward / and the men working the fields, tired as well,
> also finally depart, and I alone / have remained here at the twilight hour[29]

> I look in the four directions: the evening / scenery so melancholy
> all that is heard now / [is] the sound of the wings of the insects in flight
> arriving to the stables in the distant pasture / the ringing of the bells on the sheep

yama yama kasumi / iriai no	*kane wa naritsutsu / no no ushi wa*
shizuka ni ayumi / kaeri yuku	*tagaesu hito mo / uchi tsukare*
yōyaku sarite / ware hitori	*tasogaredoki ni / nokorikeri*
yomo o nozomeba / yūgure no	*keshiki wa itodo / monosabishi*
tada kono toki ni / kikoyuru wa	*tobikuru mushi no / hane no oto*
tōki makiba no / neya ni tsuku	*hitsuji no suzu no / naru hibiki*

山々かすみいりあひの 　　鐘ハなりつゝ野の牛ハ
徐に歩み歸り行く 　　　　耕へす人もうちつかれ
やうやく去りて余ひとり 　たそがれ時に残りけり

四方を望めバ夕暮の 　　　景色ハいとゞ物寂し
唯この時に聞ゆるハ 　　　飛び来る蟲の羽の音
遠き牧場のねやにつく 　　羊の鈴の鳴る響

(Toyama, Yatabe, and Inoue 1882, 7v–8r)

For comparison, here are the first stanzas of Gray's "Elegy" in the original:

> The Curfew tolls the Knell of parting Day,
> The lowing Herd wind slowly o'er the Lea,
> The Plow-man homeward plods his weary Way,
> And leaves the World to Darkness, and to me.
>
> Now fades the glimmering Landscape on the Sight,
> And all the Air a solemn Stillness holds;
> Save where the Beetle wheels his droning Flight,
> And drowsy Tinklings lull the distant Folds.

(Tillotson, Fussell, and Waingrow 1969, 943)

Yatabe's version of this famous poem retained many of the images present in Gray's original: the pasturing animals, the dusk, the quiet so pervasive that the only sound is that of insect life. The conclusion of the second stanza in the Japanese version reversed two metonymies that had appeared in the original, with the translator inferring that "Tinklings" implied the presence of *bells* and "Folds" (sheepfolds) the presence of *sheep*.[30]

The newness—sheep, pasture, lowly shepherd—was unacceptable, as Kiyokaze thought, in poetic language. Kiyokaze regarded not only Yatabe's version of the poem but also Gray's original as emanating from so different a poetic tradition as to be maladapted for a Japanese audience. (Never mind that poor fisherwomen and woodcutters had appeared, similarly weary, in very early Japanese literary texts—Gray's poem did not have enough in common with those writings, or so Kiyokaze seemed to think.) Where Benjamin would have the translator disregard the audience's expectations, Kiyokaze maintained that the reader's expectations were of first importance. And if poetry could not meet a reader's expectations—as English-language poetry would not meet a Japanese reader's—then it would be better, in Kiyokaze's view, to leave that poetry untranslated.

It is truly surprising, then, that Kiyokaze provided not one but two translations of his own, to suggest how poetry ought to be translated into Japanese.

Kiyokaze's first translation rendered the same stanzas of Gray's "Elegy" into a series of tanka (he does not use the word *waka* here):

> how mournful—the evening bell of Asuka Temple, tolling the end of day
>
> in the distance the sound from the darkening field: the farmer's cow, too, comes home now
>
> even the lowly man is tired: see him coming home quietly on the path through the fields
>
> on [*ashihiki no*] Tōyama [the far mountain], too, the light has faded: who is that person standing in the field?
>
> field and mountain are peaceful and dark: the sounds of insects under the grass
>
> the bell, too, of the sheep in the distant pasture has sounded faintly: autumn evening

> *kanashikute / kyō mo kurenu to / tsuguru nari / asuka no tera no / iriai no kane*
>
> *kurewataru / nozue haruka ni / koe su nari / nogai no ushi mo / ima kaeruran*
>
> *shizu no o mo / tsukarehateken / shizuka ni mo / kururu nomichi o / kaeri yuku miyu*
>
> *ashihiki no / tōyama no ha mo / kage kiete / kureyuku nobe ni / tatsu hito wa tare*
>
> *no mo yama mo / shizumari hateshi / yūmagure / asaji ga moto ni / mushi no ne zo suru*
>
> *hitsuji kau / tōki makiba no / suzu no ne mo / kasuka ni narinu / aki no yūgure*

> 悲しくてけふもくれぬと告る也あすかの寺の入相のかね
> くれ渡る野末はるかに聲すなり野かひの牛も今歸るらむ
> 賤の男もつかれはてけんしつかにもくるゝ野道を歸り行見ゆ
> あし曳の遠山の端も影消へてくれ行野邊に立つ人は誰
> 野も山もしづまりはてし夕まくれ浅茅かもとにむしの音そする
> 羊かふ遠き牧場の鈴の音もかすかになりぬ秋の夕くれ

(Ikebukuro 1889, 14, voicing as in the original)

Before commenting on the particulars, I want to present Kiyokaze's second translation, which recreated the first two stanzas of Gray's poem as a *chōka*. Commas, present in the original text, indicated the divisions between five- and seven-*moji* phrases:

> あし曳の、遠山寺の、入相の、鐘のひゞきハ、かへりこぬ、け
> ふの別を、告にけり、野末はるかに、うちむれて、野かひの牛

の、歸り行、聲もあはれに、聞えつゝ、畑をたかへす、賤の男
も、つかれはてけん、とり／＼に、廣き野中を、しつ／＼と、
家路さしてそ、歸りける、なほ立とまり、なかむれハ、遠山の
端も、影消ゑて、くれ行のへに、ふく風も、しつまりハてし、
草むらに、むしのなく音も、聞えつゝ、遠き牧場の、ねやにつ
く、羊の鈴の、音さへも、今ハかすかに、なりにけり

(14, voicing as in the original)

ashihiki no, tōyamadera no, iriai no, kane no hibiki wa, kaeri konu, kyō no wakare o, tsuginikeri, nozue haruka ni, uchimurete, nogai no ushi no, kaeri-yuki, koe mo aware ni, kikoetsutsu, hata o tagaesu, shizu no o mo, tsukare-hateken, toridori ni, hiroki nonaka o, shizushizu to, ieji sashite zo, kaerikeru, nao tachidomari, nakamureba, tōyama no ha mo, kage kiete, kureyuku nobe ni, fuku kaze mo, shizumari hateshi, kusamura ni, mushi no naku ne mo, kikoetsutsu, tōki makiba no, neya ni tsuku, hitsuji no suzu no, oto sae mo, ima wa kasuka ni, narinikeri

An English prose translation suggests that Kiyokaze's *chōka* translation of Gray is not so different from the tanka version:

> From [*ashihiki no*] Tōyama Temple there comes the echo of the evening bell: it has announced this day's end. Gathering in the distant fields, the farmer's flock comes home, lowing mournfully. Even the lowly men who till the soil are fatigued, and one by one, quietly, through the expanse of the fields they make their way home, now pausing. Even on the distant mountains the light has vanished; and the wind blowing over the darkling fields dies down. In the grasses the sounds of insects can be heard, and the ringing, too, of the bells on the sheep arriving to the pasture can be heard, now, faintly.

Readers who encounter these three versions of Gray—Yatabe's *shintaishi*, Kiyokaze's tanka sequence, and Kiyokaze's *chōka* version—may think the differences between them, at least in the English translations, much of a muchness. The three renderings do share many words and expressions in common, and those commonalities reveal something about Kiyokaze's dislike of *shintaishi* translations. Let us call Yatabe's *shintaishi* version Poem A, Kiyokaze's tanka sequence Poem B, and the *chōka* version Poem C. Poems A and B share the words *shizuka ni* (quietly), *tsukare* (tired / tiring), and *yūgure* (evening), along with variations on such basic verbs as *kaeru* (return) and *iku* (go). Poems A and C share the words *tagaesu* (work in a field), *neya ni tsuku* (arrive at the stable), and *hibiki* (sound, echo). Poems B and C—the two that, being written by the same translator, we might expect to share the greatest number of phrases—have in common the words *kyō* (today), *tsuguru / tsugu* (announce), *nozue haruka ni* (fields at a distance), and *nogai no ushi* (the farmer's cow); the phrases *shizu no o mo tsukarehateken* (even the lowly man is exhausted) and *ashihiki no tōyama* (the faraway mountain); the whole phrase *tōyama no ha mo kage kiete kureyuku nobe ni* (even on the distant mountain the light has died down, and on the darkling field . . .); and *shizumari hateshi* (. . . has quieted down), along with many adverbs and other common connectives. The words *iriai no kane* (evening bell), *mushi no . . . ne* (sound of the insect), *tōki makiba* (the distant pasture), *hitsuji* (sheep), and *suzu* (bell) appear in all three versions.

Although one might expect even highly divergent translations of a single source text to share much in common, a comment about these points of shared diction is in order, precisely because Kiyokaze opposed the introduction of new vocabulary. Kiyokaze's most striking invocation of tradition came with his use of the pillow-word (that is, conventional poetic epithet) *ashihiki no*, which appears more than one hundred times in *Man'yōshū* alone, at least twenty-six of which are in *chōka*. Kiyokaze's mention of the toponym Asuka similarly drew on associations with ancient poetry: Asuka appears in at least nine poems in *Man'yōshū*, five of them *chōka*. There is no need to go further into Kiyokaze's diction here; the point is that Kiyokaze, despite his protestations, evidently felt no qualms about translating Gray, in more than one sense: he transposed the scene of the poem altogether, whisking the reader away from the English countryside and setting them down within earshot of one Japanese temple or another. About Kiyokaze's strikingly localized versions of Gray, the poetry scholar Amagasaki Akira has commented: "These [renderings] may very well be the outcome of a fusion of Japan and the West, but insofar as they have remained in the world of the traditional *waka* they have done nothing more than borrow new elements from the West"—for a construction that does not look Western at all (2011, 178).

Something similar can be said, however, of Yatabe's version, the very text against which Kiyokaze was supposedly reacting. If it is true, as Kiyokaze held, that "one must write in accordance with the poetic language that has conveyed the sentiments of this country since antiquity," it must be admitted that that is exactly what Yatabe's version did. It began with the ringing of an *iriai no kane*, the evening bell that also tolled in well-known anthologies (for instance, *Shinkokinshū* poem 2:116 and *Shūishū* poem 20:1329); it described a scene during the time of day known as *yūgure*—one of many words for the end of the day, familiar for centuries as a poetic word connoting melancholy;[31] the *neya* or "stable" (a more literal rendering would be "sleeping room") appears, for instance, in *Kokinshū* poem 14:693 and in *Shinkokinshū* poem 14:1274; sounding insects are the subject of several dozen poems in *Kokinshū*. Yatabe's version even included another evening-related word, *tasogaredoki* (twilight), present in (for instance) *Shinkokinshū* poem 3:208, that did not appear in either of Kiyokaze's versions.

If the diction of the tanka and *chōka* versions of Gray was so little different from that of the *shintaishi* translation, then what was Kiyokaze's complaint? The answer, I think, relates to form—the very forms named in the question I have just posed. Kiyokaze could accept the tanka and the *chōka* as poetic forms, but not the *shintaishi*: I think the matter is as simple as that. Notably, Kiyokaze's *chōka* version of Gray evoked typographic practices that would have been familiar to Japanese readers from before the time of the *shintaishi*: in contrast with the *shintaishi*, with its typographically distinct formal units at the level of the line and the stanza alike, Kiyokaze's *chōka* version of Gray was printed without line breaks (albeit with commas). The tanka version, likewise, presented each line as a single, unbroken string of text, unlike *Shintaishi shō* with its blocks of lineated verse. Kiyokaze's resistance to the typographic subdivision of the poem manifested itself even in his citation of Yatabe's translation: as the poetry scholar Kakuta Toshirō has pointed out, Kiyokaze's article actually removed the space in Yatabe's translation that divided the first and second stanzas, misrepresenting the two tercets as a sextain (1966, 25).[32]

Kiyokaze called his own translations *iyaku* 意訳, "translations of the meaning." Kiyokaze himself did not regard either of his translations very highly, if we take his comment about them at face value:

> I improvised these translations, letting my brush run freely, and they do not deserve to be called poems [*uta*]. . . . A paraphrase [*iyaku*] into our language must be longer [than the original]; if a translation were to remain as brief as [the text] in the other [original] language, it would not be a poem [*shiika ni wa arazu*]—only the skeleton of the meaning would remain. That is why I have added the flesh of sentiment, by expanding the poem with the elegant diction of our language and thereby giving it, for the first time, the form of an *uta*. (Ikebukuro 1889, 15)

With reference at least to Kiyokaze's versions of Gray, the numbers bear out his observations about the telescoping nature of translation: there are 221 *moji* in Kiyokaze's *chōka* and 186 in his tanka sequence, but only 144 in Yatabe's *shintaishi* version of Gray. Kiyokaze added, however, that translating from Japanese into English would be just as cumbersome: translating in that

direction, too, would require verbal amplification (15). It is the prolixly addi-
tive nature of localizing translation, as he saw it, that led Kiyokaze to declare
that poems should not be translated.[33]

Kiyokaze's antitranslation stance reveals something about the position in
which some protradition Japanese poets found themselves during the early
years of reform. Kiyokaze was associated with the Keien-ha 桂園派 group
and thus was nominally a follower of the precepts of Kagawa Kageki, men-
tioned above as a poet who earlier in the nineteenth century had promoted
the use of nontraditional, "ordinary" language in *waka* (without, however,
practicing what he preached).[34] Confronted with the poetics of *Shintaishi
shō*—which aspired to adapt poetic diction for contemporary readers—
Kiyokaze opted for a position that was more conservative than the one that
Kageki had espoused more than seventy-five years before.[35]

The *shintaishi* made a complex impression on Japanese poets working in
traditional verse forms. The compulsion to reform was felt by *waka* and *chōka*
poets alike, but some commentators cautioned against a too-quick rejection
of familiar poetic practices. In the next section, we will see a critique of
the *shintaishi* emanating from a different quarter altogether: experimental
psychophysics. This critique, far from advocating gradual change, argued in
favor of a change as rapid as possible—the health of Japanese brains was at
stake.

Prosody on the Brain: Motora Yūjirō's Scientific Argument for Metrical Variety

One of the most important early critiques of the *shintaishi* originated outside
the literary establishment, in the new field of psychology. Motora Yūjirō 元
良勇次郎 (1858–1912), known as Japan's first experimental psychologist—
he earned his doctorate at Johns Hopkins in 1888—and a pioneer in the use
of laboratory methods for psychological research, published in 1890 a pair
of articles on Japanese prosody under the title of "'Rhythm': Psychophys-
ics" ("Rizumu" no koto: seishin butsurigaku 「リズム」ノ事：精神物理
学), in which he asserted that, based on a statistical application of certain
principles of the psychology of stimulus, the traditional view of Japanese
prosody was wrong.[36] The fundamental building blocks of Japanese poetry
were not, Motora claimed, groups of five or seven *moji* as one might expect
based on traditional Japanese poetics, but rather of one, two, or three (rarely,
four or five).[37] Motora's essay set off a debate among poets and poetry critics
that would last for over a year, with repercussions even a decade later. What
interests me here is not the validity of Motora's claims, but rather the literary

critical context in which a psychologist's statements about prosody could be seen as inflammatory. Why was a psychologist writing about poetic rhythm? Why did the literary establishment take a psychologist's statements about poetry so seriously?

While Motora had not yet attained the prominence he enjoyed later in his career, he spoke with the authority of science and objectivity. One of the topics he broached in his essays on poetic rhythm was *thought*, which was squarely inside the territory marked out by the prefacers of *Shintaishi shō*. Above, I have already quoted Toyama Masakazu's assertion that the shorter forms of Japanese verse were "basically inadequate" for expressing continuous thought.[38] While the compilers of *Shintaishi shō* had implied that the *shintaishi* was *not* defective as a medium for expressing continuous thoughts, however, Motora claimed otherwise: the rhythm of the *shintaishi*, according to Motora, was repetitive, and the *shintaishi* itself was useless and even harmful.

Motora's article was motivated, it appears, by a desire for a poetic form that improved on the *shintaishi* and (what he saw as) its monotonous meter. At the end of his essay Motora stated,

> I derive no pleasure whatsoever when I peruse the recent new-style verse [*shintai no inbun*] or the translations of Western verse. Why, I know not. It might be just my amateur taste; yet I think it might also be that a layman like myself cannot derive pleasure when our country's poets, in their pursuit of beautiful language, do not choose a *rhythm* that serves for auditory delights suited to the *rhythmical* nature of the mind. ([1890b] 1975, 458)

Motora espoused an overtly hedonic evaluative criterion: poetry should give pleasure. But what gives pleasure? For Motora, any understanding of how poetry gives or fails to give pleasure must be undergirded by a science of the sensations, a matter that lay adjacent to Motora's researches into the physiology of stimulus and response. Hence Motora's emphasis on mental phenomena: the right evaluation of poetry must entail an understanding of the evaluating mind itself.

It is necessary here to say a few words about Motora's psychological views, which related to his studies in the field called psychophysics. Motora viewed the mind as an open stimulus-response system—open inasmuch as the mind had at least some freedom actively to choose which stimuli it passively received. The faculty of attention (*chūi*) therefore was crucial for Motora's researches into mental phenomena: he believed, following the German physician and philosopher Wilhelm Wundt (1832–1920), that a subject's attention span could be quantified using variables such as the duration or intensity of a given stimulus. The quest to quantify mental experience led psychophysicists around the world to create laboratory "setups combining a human subject and a variety of inscribing and calibrating devices" (Saussy 2016, 121). It is significant, however, that Motora based his findings on the impressions of one human subject: himself. Rather than testing a number of readers in a controlled setting, Motora simply stated the results of his one-man experiment, implicitly asserting the mental sameness of all readers of Japanese poetry.

While it may seem surprising that Motora would base such broad conclusions on what were, from a certain perspective, merely the impressions of one man, nevertheless from another perspective his experiment was not atypical of psychophysics at the time. For example, in another famous psychophysical autoexperiment, conducted in the late 1870s and early 1880s, Hermann Ebbinghaus first tested his ability to memorize and recite passages of a certain number of carefully selected nonsense syllables, and then repeated the test using lines of verse, discovering that, syllable for syllable, nonsense was much more difficult to memorize than was meaningful verse. From this finding, Ebbinghaus derived various conclusions about the function of human memory in general.[39] What this suggests is that there was in psychophysics a foundational assumption about the generalizability of particular results in matters of the mind. Thus, Motora's reliance on a one-man data set implies his familiarity with the standards of his field. However, his self-generalization does *not* mean, as we will see, that Motora asserted the sameness of *all* reading minds. His results were valid for an educated reader of Japanese, as he supposed, but he also assumed (realistically enough) that this hypothetical reader would belong to *waga kuni*, "our country," and would have attained a certain level of standardized education. A reader—a mind—belonged to a nation and had received a particular kind of training.

Motora's approach to questions of prosody invited a sweeping reevaluation of poetic standards: his essay called for nothing less than a revolution in Japanese verse. It based its revolutionary call on an examination of some of the earliest Japanese poetry: Motora compared the poems appearing in *Kojiki* (ca. 712 CE), the earliest chronicle of Japanese imperial history, with the poems in *Kokin waka shū*, the tenth-century *waka* anthology. Drawing on verses from these two sources, Motora provided several pages of charts showing distributions of *moji* patterns to reveal that the *Kokinshū* poems are (by his criteria) prosodically more consistent than the *Kojiki* poems. In particular, the *Kokinshū* poems tend to group their units of sense so that they

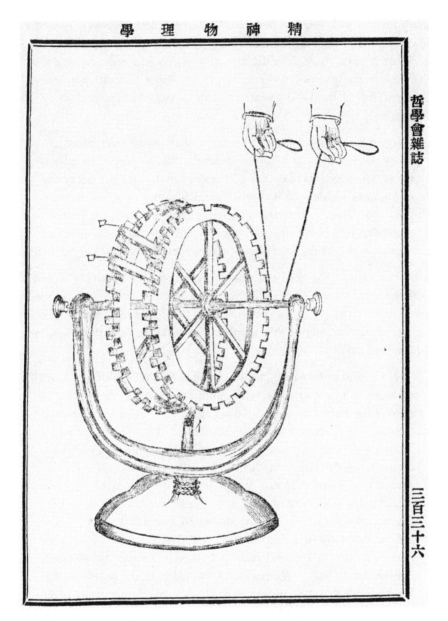

FIGURE 2. Motora Yūjirō's study of rhythm. An illustration in Motora's essay on poetry shows an instrument for investigating the perception of rhythm. The experimenter turns the wheel, which is fitted with metal strips (marked as 口) that pass over a quill at the base of the instrument (marked as イ), making audible clicks. Source: Motora 1890a, 336 for the illustration, text on 334–35.

add up to five or seven *moji* per phrase, while the *Kojiki* poems vary wildly in comparison, having as many as eleven or as few as two *moji* per phrase.

What Motora then did with this information was unprecedented: he related it to the qualities of the mind (*seishin*). From Motora's perspective, the flexibility of the *Kojiki* poems made them more suitable for conveying thoughts:

> When we analyze *Kokinshū* it appears already to have been more nar-rowly bound to the rule of a 5-7 meter. Hence the purpose of the poems became not that of sufficiently giving voice to thought but rather one of linguistic elaboration and ornamental diction. Conversely in *Kojiki* it was possible to express thoughts freely, so that, although in point of regularity [the poetry in] *Kojiki* appears highly erratic, one is not infre-quently struck by the level of conception. ([1890b] 1975, 453)

Motora concluded that the centuries-long dominance of *Kokinshū*'s 7-5 pros-ody was regrettable but scientifically explicable. The monotony of Japanese prosody, Motora claimed, can be ascribed to two factors: what he alleged to be the limited capacity of the Japanese brain, and the poverty of Japanese educational customs. Motora wrote,

> The five- and seven-*moji* meter was not bad in and of itself, but I find it greatly to be regretted that this meter was the only one to develop, preventing others. Yet when we think about it, do we not find the rea-sons for this development in the deficiencies of the Japanese people? Not only with regard to poetic [*uta no*] meter but in all things our ideas do not advance proportionally in all four directions but always biased toward one direction alone—and is this not the consequence of our small brain capacities? Nor, because of the simplicity of our education, can we do anything to expand our brain capacities. Even so, I have created these charts, as you see above, categorizing and cataloging the various meters to be found in the poems [*uta*] in *Kojiki* and *Kokinshū*, despite the difficulty and trouble of the work, in the belief that the work here undertaken might influence even slightly the future devel-opment of our nation's literature, revealing the extent to which one rhythm, the five- and seven-*moji* meter, has, of all the possible meters, come to dominate, and promoting henceforth a greater variety in rhythms. (454)

Motora's statements about the brain capacity of "the Japanese people" and the inadequacy of Japanese education were not contested by poetry crit-ics, but his statements about prosody were intensely debated. (Both points suggest his readers' acceptance of Western standards, broadly conceived, or perhaps their reluctance publicly to oppose allegedly Western ways of thinking.)

Here I think it fruitful to cite an essay by the comparatist Haun Saussy on similar experiments conducted by European psychophysicists. Saussy's essay begins from a question: How is rhythm learned? One of Saussy's approaches to this question is to ask under what conditions a person finds learning a rhythm difficult, an approach that leads Saussy to consider text-related and body-related discourses alike. Drawing on Marcel Mauss's notion of the "socialized body," Saussy writes:

> The question hanging over these investigations is whether rhythm is necessarily a physical thing or an intellectual thing. Posed in these terms, the alternative is false, for a socialized body, as Mauss would have said, is a physical thing that performs cultural work on itself and its environment. The body attentive to rhythm is, we can say without too much metaphorical exaggeration, a transformer. It takes a flow of energy (sonic pulses) and packages it into a specific form of current that is best able to travel in its particular cultural milieu. (2019, 116)

As I understand him, Saussy uses the word "transformer" in an electronic sense (hence the mention of current). I am willing to take the matter a step further and say that the "body attentive to rhythm" in poetry is also, in a certain sense, a translator, constantly enacting a double reformulation of text into prosody and prosody into text. Confronted with a metrically regular poem, the reader or hearer is on the lookout for how words add up to longer, iterable units of rhythm—such as the iambic pentameter, or the five-*moji* or seven-*moji* phrase. But the reader is simultaneously attending to how pregiven larger forms arrive at a compromise, on a text-by-text basis, with the material at hand, sometimes sacrificing a prosodic rule to achieve a remarkable image or turn of phrase. I will grant that this process is not translation in the linguistic sense, but it is what we might call a process of in-formation—"packag[ing]" a text "into a specific form." Motora hoped to see Japanese readers in-forming their poems in a new way—and, by extension, Japanese poets *composing* poems according to a (putatively) more sophisticated prosody.

One early critique of Motora's work, the scholar of Japanese literature Haga Yaichi's 芳賀矢一 (1867–1927) "On the Form of Japanese Verse" (Nihon inbun no keitai ni tsukite 日本韻文の形体に就きて), for example, made no mention of Japanese educational practices or the presumed traits of Japanese anatomy—Haga's critique centered on prosody. One of Motora's foundational assumptions had been that a reader's or hearer's attention was restimulated with each successive word (Motora [1890b] 1975, 440).[40] Haga held that Motora had not thought through the implications of that assumption: if a reader's attention were restimulated at each word boundary, with no regard for recurring clusters of fives and sevens, then what, Haga wondered, would distinguish poetry from prose ([1892] 1975, 486)? Haga contended, further, that Motora had not adequately accounted for the pauses (*pōzu*) that a reader would add when intoning a line of poetry: for Haga, such pauses were what distinguished poetry from (pause-free) prose (487). In response to Haga's essay, Yoneyama Yasusaburō 米山保三郎 (1869?–1897?) contended that in fact each five- or seven-*moji* phrase should be counted as a single unit, and pauses should be added only between such units ([1892] 1975, 511–12).[41] Yoneyama conceded that perhaps what Haga was describing was what in English could be called (according to Yoneyama) a "secondary pause"; but a secondary pause should never separate the constituent parts of a single unit of meaning (512). Like the articles I have just summarized here, other responses to Motora's essay generally fixated on the accuracy of his claims about Japanese meter.

A skeptical 1890s reader of Motora's essay *might* have objected to it on taxonomic grounds—by arguing that the verses in *Kojiki* were not strictly comparable with those in *Kokin waka shū*.[42] The poems of *Kokin waka shū* are almost all *waka*; there are indeed *waka* in *Kojiki*, but there are many other kinds of rhythmical language in that myth-historical chronicle as well: short lyrics, songs, hymns. Motora's vocabulary for referring to versified language was loose: following no pattern I have been able to determine, he used the terms *waka* and *uta* interchangeably to designate the poems of *Kokin waka shū* and *Kojiki* alike. Motora preferred variety in poetic rhythm, as has already been indicated. In support of his view, Motora cited Aristotle, according to whom there are many kinds of rhythms in language: "a rhythm suited to declamation is not suited for ordinary speech. A rhythm suited for ordinary speech is unfit for ceremonial utterances. And there is still another rhythm, suitable for dramatic performance" ([1890b] 1975, 455). That, at least, was the situation in ancient Greek language; but in Japanese poetry, a single rhythm, alternating fives and sevens, had come to predominate—to the detriment, as Motora saw it, of Japanese poetry. Furthermore, musicology in the West had reached a high level of refinement in the study of sung rhythm, Motora claimed, but in Japan such studies had had only the most uncertain of beginnings (456–57). Motora held that the specialization of rhythms was an improvement to be sought; "and if I have not yet been able to determine which [kind of rhythm] is suited for this purpose or that one, I can say with certainty that a rhythm like that of the Japanese *chōka* in fives and sevens is unsuited for composing anything like a compelling expository essay" (458). Motora concluded by calling for the improvement of Japanese literature through better and further study of music and prosody.

Motora's way of seeing the verses of *Kokin waka shū* and *Kojiki* as comparable members of a class—for which he seemed not to have a consistent name—would scarcely have been possible without the influence of *Shintaishi shō*. But Motora was thinking of the future. Although he did not say it in so many words, he hoped to see a new kind of Japanese poetry, prosodically irregular, matching the varied rhythms (as he would have described them) of the brain by means of variation at the level of prosody. What Motora evidently did not know was that just a year earlier, poetry that might have satisfied his hopes had been written, and in Japanese.

CHAPTER 2

"This Dead Form, Begone"

The Shi of Kitamura Tōkoku and the Debate over Meter

With greater ease of transportation and communication in the modern era, the intensified intercultural circulation of literary forms and motifs has unsettled the concepts of authorship and authenticity on what I will venture to say is a global scale. In many literary geographies, originality came to be thought of as occurring on a gradient: if there was a local and therefore lesser criterion for originality, it became possible to imagine a greater-because-more-global originality, as well. Writing the first novel in Tagalog was a feat, but writing *the first* novel—the global first novel—was taken to mean something different altogether. Not all originalities are equal, according to such a view. Of course, determining which sorts of literary production merited such competitive evaluation became itself a matter for dispute.

Such inequalities arise because there are inequalities in international and interliterary relations. Is the first Tagalog novelist less worthy of acclaim because of the attribution "Tagalog"? Is the first Japanese free-verse poet less worthy of acclaim because other free-verse poets had already shown the way in other languages? Which varieties of invention are legitimate, and which are to be subjected to the varieties of critical disapproval? Christopher L. Miller's *Impostors: Literary Hoaxes and Cultural Authenticity* (2018) approaches such questions by examining debates concerning authorship and authenticity in Francophone colonial and postcolonial literatures. Miller observes, "Intercultural literary hoaxes are almost always premised on *inequality*, and most of them, in their creative pretense, cross a boundary from a realm of greater privilege to one of lesser privilege. . . . Hoaxing almost always follow[s] that trajectory rather than its opposite" (2). What Miller is referring to are instances of literary production in which writers from the metropole "usurp . . . colonized, oral, or minority cultures" (51). Miller distinguishes such top-down intercultural "usurp[ation]" from "plagiarism," which, in Miller's analysis, "tends to reach 'upward,' from colonized to colonizer" (50–51). For Miller, what makes intercultural usurpation and intercultural plagiarism worth examining closely is the unevenness of the playing field, an unevenness rendered visible in the quite different consequences for the authors involved.

One could observe that the concern over authenticity, as Miller is describing it, dwells on matters of content, not form. In this sense the distinction between form and content is indisputably clear, no matter what might be said by critics who insist that form and content are inseparably intertwined. In contemporary literary cultures where European ("Western") norms apply, an author who appropriates another's words or experiences without avowing the appropriation in advance is seen as having perpetrated a fraud, while an author who appropriates a literary form has not necessarily done anything discreditable. To give examples of appropriations involving Japanese literary culture, we can contrast the American poet Kent Johnson (b. 1955) and the Swedish poet Tomas Tranströmer (1931–2015). In the 1990s Kent Johnson published poems that were, he claimed, translations of poems by one Araki Yasusada, allegedly a Hiroshima survivor; but it turned out that, by all appearances, the poems were Johnson's own, accepted for publication and published under what struck many readers as false pretenses—an episode that provoked a sharp reaction from critics.[1] Conversely, Tomas Tranströmer, who wrote and published a number of haiku in Swedish (2010, 54–61), never elicited so much as a raised eyebrow: to my knowledge, no one has ascribed to Tranströmer a desire to avail himself of Japanese cultural properties unfairly, to say nothing of his wanting to become somehow Japanese through writing haiku. As the contrast between Johnson and Tranströmer suggests, to borrow content without permission is subject to censure if not outright punishment; to borrow a form is not only acceptable but is even praised as evidence of wide competence.

I mention these questions of interliterary circulation and appropriation because they matter for our understanding of a debate that arose in Japanese poetry circles in 1889–91 over the meaning and use of poetic meter—the so-called *inbun no sensō* or versification war. The principal figures of this debate, as I reconstruct it in this chapter, were Yamada Bimyō 山田美妙 (1868–1910), who held that meter was an essential feature of Japanese poetry and that Japanese poets should follow English prosodic rules, and

Kitamura Tōkoku 北村透谷 (1868–94), whose long poems during these years assayed new metrical techniques even as they drew liberally from the work of European-language precursors such as Johann Wolfgang von Goethe and George Gordon, Lord Byron. Both were intercultural appropriators: Bimyō advocated the adaptation of English prosodic forms to Japanese content; Tōkoku, for his part, silently incorporated English and German verse content into radically unstable new Japanese verse forms. As we will see, both writers met with stiff resistance. That resistance tells us much about how poetic form was constructed and imagined at a critical turning point in the history of modern Japanese poetry and poetics.

Kitamura Tōkoku's Debut

Like many Japanese writers of his generation, Kitamura Tōkoku came to the English language relatively young. By 1883, Tōkoku was "spen[ding] his free time working as a [bell]boy at the Grand Hotel in Yokohama, with the intention, it seems, of *improving* his English"—meaning that, by the age of fifteen, he had already acquired some of the language (emphasis added, Mathy 1963, 9–10).[2] When he began his studies in 1885 at the Tokyo Senmon Gakkō (founded in 1882, later renamed Waseda University), his course in English covered such materials as John Stuart Mill's *On Liberty*, Shakespeare's *Macbeth*, and Samuel Johnson's *Rasselas* (Schamoni 1983, 51–52). Tōkoku learned the language well enough to become an English teacher in 1890. When a traveling theater troupe presented Shakespeare's *Hamlet*—in English—at a theater in Yokohama in the summer of 1891, Tōkoku was one of two Japanese in the audience: the other was Tsubouchi Shōyō 坪内逍遥 (1859–1935), the novelist and noted translator of Shakespeare's works into Japanese (Irokawa 2007, 25). Tōkoku's readings had acquainted him with English poets who had been active earlier in the nineteenth century, among them Byron. I mention Byron here because Tōkoku's long 1889 poem *Soshū no shi* 楚囚之詩 (The poem of a prisoner), of which the first stanza is quoted below, bears a distinct resemblance, as many readers and critics have noted, to Byron's long poem *The Prisoner of Chillon* (1816). In Byron's poem, a speaker recalls a time of captivity following his activities of protest against oppressive authorities; in Tōkoku's poem, the speaker is in a similar plight. Tōkoku's poem began:

> Once, going astray, I broke the law
>   and was seized as a political prisoner.
> Several activists and I had made a life-and-death pact,
>   and of their number I was the leader.
>   Inside [this prison], [there was] my beloved,

a young woman, a budding flower—
both of us, the bride and groom,
[in prison] together for our country's sake.

曽つて誤つて法を破り
　　政治の罪人として捕ハれたり、
余と生死を誓ひし壮士等の
　　数多あるうちに余は其首領なり、
　　　　中に、余が最愛の
　　　まだ蕾の花なる少女も、
国の為とて諸共に
　　この花婿も花嫁も。

(Kitamura 1950–55, 1:5; [1889] 1968, 1;
indentations and *rubi* reflect the 1889 version)

While Byron's poem *The Prisoner of Chillon* may have been one of the thematic inspirations for Tōkoku's May 1889 poem, Byron's poem differs from Tōkoku's in one key respect: the prosody.[3] Byron's poem is rhymed; although the number of feet per line varies, the meter is predominantly iambic, as the first lines of the first stanza of *The Prisoner of Chillon* reveal:

My hair is grey, but not with years
　　　　Nor grew it white
　　　　In a single night,
As men's have grown from sudden fears:
My limbs are bowed, though not with toil,
　　　But rusted with a vile repose,
For they have been a dungeon's spoil,
　　　And mine has been the fate of those
To whom the goodly earth and air
Are bann'd, and barr'd—forbidden fare.

(Byron 1816, 10)

Tōkoku's poem, conversely, has no predictable metrical scheme. In the transliteration that follows, slashes have been added to indicate conjecturally the most likely positions of the caesuras:

katsute ayamatte / hō o yaburi	[8, 6 = 14]
seiji no tsumibito toshite / torawaretari,	[11, 6 = 17]
yo to seishi o chikaishi / sōshira no	[10, 5 = 15]
amata aru uchi ni / yo wa sono shuryō nari,	[8, 9 = 17]
naka ni, / yo ga saiai no	[3, 7 = 10]

mada tsubomi no hana naru / shōjo mo,	[10, 4 = 14]
kuni no tame tote / morotomo ni	[7, 5 = 12]
kono hanamuko mo / hanayome mo.	[7, 5 = 12]

In this stanza, the even-numbered lines rhyme: lines 2 and 4 end in *ari*, while lines 6 and 8 end in *mo*. (If 少女 in line 6 is read not as *shōjo* but as *otome*, then that strengthens the rhyme between lines 6 and 8: *otomemo, hanayomemo*.) The most striking feature, though, is the syllabic contour of this poetry: consecutive lines tend to have different numbers of *moji*, varying from ten *moji* to seventeen. The stanza ends with two lines in 7-5, a typical *shintaishi* distribution. With their more familiar prosody, those two lines come almost as a shock, contrasting as they do with the preceding lines, in which it is seldom clear where to locate the caesuras—if there are caesuras at all. The impulsiveness of the meter finds an analogue in the formatting of the poem, whose margins, far from being justified, vary according to no apparent rule.

Tōkoku's poem did not fit the *shintaishi* mold, but it was described as a *shintaishi* nevertheless. An advertisement written about this supposed *shintaishi* emphasizes the text's novelty:

> *The Poem of a Prisoner* by Kitamura Montarō. Price 8 *sen* plus postage.
> This book represents a new phenomenon in modern *shintaishi*.
> This book uses poetic form, rhythm, rhyme, and the like in a completely new way.
> This book plumbs the feelings of a prisoner of the state while imprisoned. (Kitamura 1950–55, 3:275)

It is believed that Tōkoku wrote this advertisement (Kitamura 1950–55, 3:677). Whoever the author, the advertisement was calling attention to the poem's formal innovations. Moreover, the price was reasonable: the twenty-four-page poem, at eight *sen*, cost a little more than a magazine (Pierson 1980, 168).[4]

While the advertisement for *Soshū no shi* insisted on the poem's novelty, Tōkoku's brief preface to the poem rather situated the text with reference to extant, familiar literary forms. "[The verse in] this collection [*Soshū no shi*] is neither our country's so-called *waka* [*uta*] nor [Chinese] poetry [*shi*]," Tōkoku wrote in the preface; "instead, it resembles narrative [prose] [*shōsetsu ni niteoru*]. Yet even so it is poetry [*shi*]" (Kitamura 1950–55, 1:4; [1889] 1968, unpaginated preface).[5] Beyond this brief comment, Tōkoku's preface to the poem doled out the relevant details sparingly or not at all. The preface did not mention, for example, that Tōkoku's poem included stanzas of rhyming verse—a feature of the poem that assuredly would have been a point of distinction, given that the vast majority of *shintaishi* did not rhyme (Schamoni

1983, 101–3; Higashinaka 1995). As for the text's prosodic qualities, perhaps it is no great surprise that Tōkoku did not go into specifics about the metrically irregular (or "free") verse of his poem—because he would have needed to devise a new vocabulary for doing so. The term *vers libre* had come into general circulation in France only a few years earlier, in 1886—the same year in which, according to later commentators, the first poetry in *vers libre* had been published (Dujardin 1922, 28–29).[6] The calque "free verse" was created in English by as early as 1890 (Steele 1990, 3–28; Scott 1998, 73–81), so there is little chance that Tōkoku would have known of the existence of free verse either in French or in English. He was probably unaware of the poetry of Walt Whitman, who would be introduced to a wider Japanese readership in an 1892 article by a young Natsume Sōseki 夏目漱石 (1867–1916) (Natsume [1892] 1995). As for the comparison Tōkoku drew between his poetry and the *shōsetsu* (narrative prose fiction), the comparative literature scholar Kenmochi Takehiko has surmised that Tōkoku had a particular model of the *shōsetsu* in mind: the psychologically realistic narrative fiction described by Tsubouchi Shōyō (mentioned above), whose *Shōsetsu shinzui* 小説神髄 (*The Essence of the Novel*) had been published only a few years earlier, in 1885 (Kenmochi 1973, 177–78). However, it is also possible that Tōkoku wanted to acknowledge that *Soshū no shi* might strike some readers as being prose-like because of the absence of meter.

Another signal example of the taciturnity of Tōkoku's preface lay in its seeming refusal to acknowledge one of its debts: the preface made no mention of Byron. The fact that Tōkoku modeled *Soshū no shi* on *The Prisoner of Chillon* has become so well known that it may be difficult to imagine how the affinities between Tōkoku's work and Byron's must have struck whoever first detected them.[7] To be clear, to most readers *Soshū no shi* would not appear to be a *translation* of Byron's poem: it is a different text, on the whole, as a comparison of the first stanzas alone suggests. But individual lines of Tōkoku's poem closely evoke phrases from Byron's. The scholar Masuda Michizō (1954, 35–36) indicated several passages in Tōkoku's poem that are nearly word-for-word renderings of *The Prisoner of Chillon*. Consider the following parallel—first, Byron:

> There are seven columns massy and gray,
> Dim with a dull imprison'd ray,
> A sunbeam which hath lost its way
> And through the crevice and cleft
> Of the thick wall is fallen and left.

> (ll. 29–33)

Now, Tōkoku:

> O prison! The prison in which, pitiably, I am confined
>> has separated me from the world with <u>a wall two layers thick,</u>
> but <u>working its way in through some crevice in the wall, some fissure,</u>
>> <u>even a sunbeam, rushing in thus, has no egress,</u>
> and comes down the wall trying to brighten
>> the pallor of my arms, and comes up as far as my knees.

> *hitoya! tsutanaku mo yo ga mayoiireru hitoya wa,*
>> *<u>futae no kabe</u> nite sekai to hedatareri,*
> *saredo <u>sono kabe no suki mata ana o mogurite</u>*
>> *<u>nigeba o ushinai, kakekomu nikkō mo ari,</u>*
> *yo no aozametaru ude o terasan tote*
>> *kabe o tsutai, yo ga hiza no ue made ayumiyoreri.*

> 獄舎！つたなくも余が迷入れる獄舎は、
>> 二重の壁にて世界と隔たれり、
> 左れど其壁の隙又た穴をもぐりて
>> 逃場を失ひ、馳込む日光もあり、
> 余の青醒めたる腕を照さんとて
>> 壁を傳ひ、余が膝の上まで歩寄れり。

(beginning of stanza III)[8]

One thing Tōkoku did state in his preface to the poem was that he had for years tried to write poetry, but the difficulty of composition prevented him from publishing anything earlier: "I tried my hand at translations and original verses alike," Tōkoku wrote, "and all I have to show for my efforts is this poem" (Kitamura 1950–55, 1:3; [1889] 1968, unpaginated preface). The implication is that Tōkoku discarded his earlier efforts. The glance toward translation is intriguing, but it is no more than a glance: by omitting any mention of Byron's work, Tōkoku suppressed the usual paratextual indicators of his text's rootedness in another text. One may speculate that *Soshū no shi* was the outcome of a process of translation and variation, the final draft in a series of earlier drafts that had started with a quite close rendering, perhaps, of Byron's poem, then—in a process just the opposite of an asymptotic approximation—moved further and further away from the original. One might describe the echoes of Byron in the published version of Tōkoku's poem as leftover traces of that process; but unless earlier drafts of *Soshū no shi* are found, such a claim must remain speculation.

Because Tōkoku did not identify Byron as a precursor, I treat *Soshū no shi* as being something other than an adaptation. In late nineteenth-century Japanese literature, adaptation was a common means for bringing foreign literature into Japanese in a localized way, freely changing the matter of the source text, altering character names, even dropping, adding, or reordering major episodes. Such texts were called *hon'anmono* 翻案物. As J. Scott Miller has argued, these *hon'anmono* were distinct from *hon'yaku* 翻訳, which were nearer to what readers today might recognize as translations, insofar as *hon'yaku* retained (more of) the original's meaning. What distinguished *hon'an* from *hon'yaku* were the contexts in which they were practiced: as Miller puts it, "in early Meiji Japan literal translation prevailed in the sphere of diplomacy, law, and the sciences, while in the arts adaptive translation was the rule" (2001, 12).[9] In literature, adaptive translations were indeed numerous: Miller lists some seventy-seven such adaptations being published between 1868 and 1888 (18–20). As a rule, such adaptations made clear their origins in a text written first in another language: indeed, that was much of their appeal (21). As I have indicated, though, Tōkoku suppressed the origin story of *Soshū no shi*.

What Tōkoku was doing with his *Soshū no shi* is a variation, one might say, on the phenomenon called pseudotranslation, which the translation theorist Gideon Toury has defined as the practice of presenting an original text as a translation (Toury 1995, 40–46). Transposing the original and the translation in Toury's definition, we might rather call Tōkoku's *Soshū no shi* a pseudo-original: a loose adaptation-cum-translation presented as an original text. Summarizing the intent behind many pseudotranslations, the literary translation scholar Thomas Beebee has written, "Pseudotranslation is . . . a device for innovating within the literary system without claiming responsibility for doing so" (2016, 64), it being safer, as some writers might think, to risk a radical departure from local literary norms under the guise of foreignness. A pseudo-original, on the other hand, would be a means to claim credit for a novelty not actually of the author's own devising.

Tōkoku's *Soshū no shi*, however, is not exactly a pseudo-original, either. If Tōkoku was reticent about those elements of his poem that owed a debt to Byron, he seems also to have been reluctant to flaunt his text's novelty. As we have seen, the poem's advertisement and preface could have insisted much more strenuously on the text's newness: *Soshū no shi* did incorporate many formal features that would have seemed most novel to the poem's first readers. For whatever reason, Tōkoku was content, it appears, to let his audience respond as it would.

For most readers at the time, poetry without a predictable meter was unthinkable, but metrically nonregular verse is exactly what we find throughout *Soshū no shi*. As a later commentator put it:

For Tōkoku's contemporaries, who assumed that poetry [*shiika*] was anything in fives and sevens [*goon shichion*]—or rather to put it more

extremely, who held that anything in fives and sevens was poetry . . .—
for [them], [*Soshū no shi*] was almost certainly beyond anything their
standards of evaluation could accommodate. (Sasabuchi 1959, 325)

An unsigned early review of *Soshū no shi* exemplifies the puzzlement the text
provoked in its first readers. The review began: "Perhaps it is a *shintaishi*. . . .
If one were to sing it, which meter would one choose? If I had to describe the
text, I would say it is prose laden with poetic sentiment [*shijō aru no sanbun
nari to*]" ([Iwamoto] 1889, 21).[10] The reviewer's ambivalence as to the text's
generic designation did not differ so much from that of Tōkoku himself—
except that Tōkoku insisted his text was a *shi* above all.

It is typical in discussions of formal novelty in the arts to tell origin stories.
However, scholars have not been able to trace Tōkoku's metrical innovation
back to an earlier model. One candidate is Goethe's *Faust* (part I, 1808; part II,
1832), a play written in a wide range of rhyme schemes and meters, includ-
ing sections in which the meter is altogether unpredictable (perhaps even
free).[11] Tōkoku, as will be seen below, certainly knew of *Faust* by the
time he was writing his 1891 *Hōraikyoku* 蓬莱曲 (Song of Mount Hōrai).
Sasabuchi Tomoichi, the author of an influential study of Tōkoku, suggests
that Tōkoku would have been familiar with *Faust* in the metrically faith-
ful 1887 English translation of John Anster (1959, 81). Assuming Tōkoku
did read that translation, the crucial question for our purposes is, When?
As Sasabuchi would have it, the timing and extent of Tōkoku's reading of
Goethe's work cannot be determined precisely (81). What is certain is that
by 1890 at the latest, Tōkoku regarded *Faust* as the great masterpiece of the
nineteenth century (Kitamura 1950–55, 1:248). But 1890 would be too late
for a connection between *Faust* and *Soshū no shi*. Wolfgang Schamoni has
speculated that Tōkoku's work might have been influenced by other kinds
of prosodically irregular texts that would have been known to him—Japa-
nese translations of Christian hymns in meters other than 7-5, the prose-like
Japanese pronunciations of *kanshi* (1983, 98 and 105)—but Schamoni's study
does not attempt to recreate the specifics whereby Tōkoku arrived at the
metrical looseness of *Soshū no shi*. If one takes the poetry scholar and poet
Kitagawa Tōru's 北川透 (b. 1935) advice and treats *Soshū no shi* as a whole
(1974, 95–96), then one must admit that as far as prosody is concerned,
Tōkoku's work attempted something different from any single one of the
text's identifiable precursors.

Tōkoku's work was a practical application of the dictum—never stated
by him in so many words—that poetry need not be metrically regular. That
dictum would soon become the focus of a debate among Japanese poets and

critics over the function of rhythm in poetic language. This debate peaked in intensity in late 1890—more than a year after the publication of *Soshū no shi*—and continued well into 1891, with aftershocks lasting until the late 1890s. No clear winner emerged, but one consequence was, arguably, a refinement in critical terminology, especially as it related to *form* and *content* in poetry. The controversy eventually died down and had little tangible effect on poetry composition in Japan, for reasons that we will examine at the end of this chapter when considering the reception of another prosodically hard-to-classify text by Tōkoku, his 1891 *Hōraikyoku*. First, though, the debate itself merits a closer look.

The Versification War (*inbun no sensō*)

In her study of the political underpinnings of the discourse on poetic meter in England in the decades before the Great War, Meredith Martin refers in passing to a study by the American poetry scholar C. E. Andrews, who used the phrase "prosodic wars" to describe a dispute over terminology (Martin 2012, 98). The dispute was anything but passing: it was about the dominance of Greco-Roman terms for describing poetic feet in *English* poetry. Even today in English we say *iambic pentameter* instead of *five ta-tums per line* or some other seemingly more Anglo-Saxon locution. In the "prosodic wars" recalled by Martin, "the foreign names for classical feet were called into question and students were taught to feel English poetry according to 'natural' accents (traced to an Anglo-Saxon past) divorced from the valueless and hegemonic classical system of iambs and trochees" (98). These wars were part of a far-reaching transformation, whereby poetic culture, as Martin argues, became inseparable from concerns over English national identity.

At the end of the previous section I alluded to a debate over poetic form and content in Japan starting in 1890, and that debate, too, posed questions about Japanese national identity, even as some of the debate's participants sought to wage it on an aesthetic plane. The Japanese debate, like the contemporary English-language one, "enlisted . . . those committed to moving the concept of [Japanese] meter away from its classical origins . . . into a more capacious metrical system" (98).[12] But there the resemblance ends. The writer who instigated the Japanese debate, Yamada Bimyō, aimed to transform Japanese prosody into the same, English, classically inflected prosody—iambs, pentameters, and all—that the English-language prosodic wars called into question. While the "capacious metrical system" of the English-language prosodic wars would debouch, according to Martin, into the free rhythms of modernism, the new prosodic system proposed by Bimyō was intended to promote a stricter regularity. For these reasons, I avoid translating *inbun no sensō* as "prosodic wars" and render it as "versification war" instead.

Bimyō laid out his position in an eight-part essay, "Nihon inbun ron" 日本韻文論 (On Japanese verse), which was serialized in the magazine *Kokumin no tomo* 国民之友 (*The Nation's Friend*) from October 1890 to January 1891.[13] During its serialization it provoked many rejoinders, with eight responses appearing in the week beginning on November 22, 1890, alone. By the time the controversy started dying down in February 1891, the versification war had spread to half a dozen other Tokyo periodicals (Chiba Shinrō 2006, 282–83n1). Bimyō's "Nihon inbun ron" can be seen as a continuation of *Shintaishi shō's*

Table 1 Principal articles in the debate on poetic rhythm (inbun ronsō)

DATE	AUTHOR'S NAME (AND OTHER NAME, IF USED)	TITLE	PUBLICATION
1890.10.3	Yamada Bimyō	"Nihon inbun ron 1"	*Kokumin no tomo*, no. 96
1890.10.13	Yamada Bimyō	"Nihon inbun ron 2"	*Kokumin no tomo*, no. 97
1890.10.18	Isogai Unpō (Unpōshi)	"Ikkahyō: inbun"	*Jogaku zasshi*, no. 235
1890.10.23	Yamada Bimyō	"Nihon inbun ron 3"	*Kokumin no tomo*, no. 98
1890.11.13	Yamada Bimyō	"Nihon inbun ron 4"	*Kokumin no tomo*, no. 100
1890.11.22	Uchida Roan (Rokō shoshi)	"Gaikei ronsha"	*Kokumin shinbun*
1890.11.23	Yamada Bimyō	"Nihon inbun ron 5"	*Kokumin no tomo*, no. 101
1890.11.23	Mori Ōgai (Ikan koji)	"Rokō shoshi to iu hennaru gaikei ronsha"	*Kokumin shinbun*
1890.11.24	Uchida Roan (Aru otoko)	"Kore wa hyōban no inbun ron"	*Kokumin shinbun*
1890.11.25	Ishibashi Ningetsu (Bi tengu)	"Inbun ron o azakeru"	*Shigarami zōshi*, no. 14
1890.11.25	Yamada Bimyō	"Bi tengu shi ni"	*Shigarami zōshi*, no. 14
1890.11.26	Ishibashi Ningetsu (Ningetsu)	"Shi (poejii)"	*Kokkai*
1890.11.27	Yamada Bimyō	"Ningetsu kun e"	*Kokumin shinbun*
1890.11.28	Ishibashi Ningetsu	"Bimyōsai ni kotau"	*Kokkai*
1890.12.3	Yamada Bimyō	"Nihon inbun ron 6"	*Kokumin no tomo*, no. 102
1890.12.5	Biyōshi (? = 眉楊子)	"Ningetsu sensei ni tei su"	*Iratsume*, no. 75
1890.12.10	Ōnishi Hajime	"Shiika ron ippan"	*Nihon hyōron*, no. 19
1890.12.12	Ishibashi Ningetsu (Mushi mo korosanu otoko)	"Inbun ron no shūki o tou"	*Kokkai*
1890.12.23	Yamada Bimyō	"Nihon inbun ron 7"	*Kokumin no tomo*, no. 104
1891.1.3	Uchida Roan (K.U. sei)	"Shiben: Bimyōsai ni atau 1"	*Kokumin no tomo*, no. 105
1891.1.10	Uemura Masahisa	"Yo ni iwayuru inbun 1"	*Nihon hyōron*, no. 21
1891.1.13	Uchida Roan (K.U. sei)	"Shiben: Bimyōsai ni atau 2"	*Kokumin no tomo*, no. 106
1891.1.23	Yamada Bimyō	"Nihon inbun ron 8"	*Kokumin no tomo*, no. 107
1891.1.24	Uemura Masahisa	"Yo ni iwayuru inbun 2"	*Nihon hyōron*, no. 22
1891.1.24	Yamada Bimyō	"Shiben kai: K.U. sei ni ichigen su"	*Kokumin shinbun*
1891.2.14	Uchida Roan (K.U. sei)	"Bimyōsai ni ichigen su"	*Kokumin shinbun*
1891.10.25	Mori Ōgai (unsigned)	"Bimyōsai shujin ga inbun ron"	*Shigarami zōshi*, no. 25
1892.8	Hatano Shirō (different first name)	"Muin hika ron"	*Waseda bungaku*, nos. 21, 22
1892.12	Yoneyama Yasusaburō	"Kokushi ni tsukite"	*Tetsugaku zasshi*, vol. 7, no. 70

conjoint projects of improving Japanese poetry, on the one hand, and justifying the introduction of a hypernym for Japanese verse, on the other.

For Bimyō one important improvement for Japanese verse would be the adaptation and adoption of the metrical patterns of English verse. Fully half of "Nihon inbun ron" was dedicated to explaining how Japanese poetry could be adapted to fit "Western" prosodic norms. By "Western," Bimyō actually meant English, as is clear from the names of the poetic feet he introduced: the *aiamubasu* (iambus), the *torokii* (trochee), the *anapesuto* (anapest), the *dakuchiru* (dactyl), and so on. (Had Bimyō drawn on a different language for the names of his meters, he would have derived different katakana spellings.)

Bimyō's explanation of his proposed overhaul of Japanese metrics involved a brief comparative analysis of the Chinese, European, and Japanese languages. His comparison amounted to a hierarchical ranking of cultures, with Europe at the top, China at the bottom, and Japan occupying the perilous middle position—ascent was possible and to be hoped for, but backsliding equally had to be guarded against. In Bimyō's description of Chinese prosody, he identified the language's tonal quality as being foundational for its poetry: arranging the tones according to fixed patterns had been, Bimyō pointed out, one of the principles of Chinese versification since the Tang period. The allegedly transhistoric constancy of Chinese verse came in for critique on Bimyō's part, who disparaged later Chinese poets as simply "conserving the ink" (*bokushu* 墨守) left to dry by their forebears in the Tang era (Yamada [1890–91] 2014, 116). China was not the place to look for progress.

What Japanese poets should do instead, Bimyō suggested, was learn the prosody of European languages. European poems, like Chinese ones, were created by assembling words to fit given prosodic arrangements; but the European arrangements were, "in comparison with the Chinese, much more elaborate" (117). The units of European prosody—syllables—were of only two varieties: one denominated high or long or stressed, the other low or short or unstressed. But the possible prosodic arrangements were numerous when one considered all the different metrical feet. An iambus, for example, is a short syllable followed by a long one; in Japanese an iambus would be a word such as *yume*, with its low-pitched *yu* and its high-pitched *me* (117). Bimyō gave examples of Japanese words to match the other varieties of feet, as well, admitting that the difficulty of using Japanese pitch patterns to recreate the attested English prosodic patterns "was not slight" (118). One feature of the Japanese language, however, made it uniquely amenable to the new prosody Bimyō was proposing: its relative paucity of homophones, or, as Bimyō put it, its freedom from pitch constraints. In Chinese, if one changes the tone of a word, one changes its meaning altogether. In English, the stress pattern of a word is a relatively fixed thing; one cannot stress the word "battle" in English on the second syllable and expect to be understood (119). In Japanese, however, it is generally possible to alter the pitch without loss of meaning: the word *yanagi* means "willow" no matter where one situates the high-pitched syllable, as Bimyō claimed, and it would be easy for a poet to anticipate and avoid the few cases where an ambiguity could arise from a shifted pitch (119–20).

The reason to adopt a more European-like prosody, for Bimyō, was partly aesthetic and partly related to international relations. Judging from word count alone, the aesthetics of the matter were clearly Bimyō's first concern: the Japanese prosody that characterized the *waka* and the *hokku* hitherto, based on counting *moji*, "could not by any means be called satisfactory," Bimyō wrote. Traditional Japanese poetry had been, according to Bimyō, "prose-like verse [*sanbunteki inbun*]," in other words not poetry at all, if one looked at it from an English-language prosodic standard (123). To make this point, however, Bimyō adduced a political example: the poem known as "Kimi ga yo" 君が代 (Thy reign), which had recently (in 1888) been set to music as an unofficial national anthem for Japan. It was a mere "stroke of luck" that the poem had been set to good music, Bimyō claimed; there was no reason to believe that all the tens of thousands of other *waka*, with identical metrical profiles, could survive the transition into music (123). By such an indirect slight, Bimyō here posited an intersection between the poverty of Japanese poetry and customs of governance—both of which, Bimyō implied, should emulate, for their benefit, the analogous institutions in allegedly more advanced nations abroad.

For Bimyō, the creation of a hypernym for (Japanese) poetry would be only one plank of a much broader program of improving the terminology used to discuss poetry: as he put it, he was "for convenience's sake giving names to phenomena [in poetry] that either had no names at all [in Japanese] or had names that were unsuitable for specialized discussions" (82). In the second installment of "Nihon inbun ron," Bimyō took aim at the term *shi* itself, declaring it unfit as a general term because it still held too strong an association in readers' minds with *kanshi* or Chinese poetry and therefore did not yet comfortably apply to other forms such as the *waka*, the *chōka*, the *renga*, or the haiku (88). Bimyō rejected the term *shintaishi* for the same reason: it contained the character *shi* (88). A host of other terms came under Bimyō's scrutiny—even *poetorī* itself—and each was rejected as being insufficiently general, leading Bimyō finally to plump for *inbun* as being the most serviceable term: it evoked the parallel but opposed term *sanbun*, "prose."[14]

Bimyō, granting that *inbun* was not an ideal label, added that he would happily use a more suitable term if one ever came to his attention (88–89).

Bimyō construed *inbun* as a category that would encompass all forms of metrically regular writing that had been produced in Japan, including the following: the *waka*, the *shi* (which meant *kanshi* in this context), the *chōka*, the *saibara* (a kind of court song with instrumental accompaniment), the Nō chant, the *jōruri* (song for a puppet play), and other varieties of *shinchō inbun* (new-rhythm *inbun*—a circumlocution for *shintaishi*) (89–90). There is no reason to interpret this list as exhaustive—as excluding, for example, the *senryū* or the haiku, which are in any case mentioned elsewhere in "Nihon inbun ron"—because Bimyō, in the very next section of the essay, shifted his attention to British theorists and practitioners of *inbun*: Milton, Tennyson, Matthew Arnold, and others. *Inbun* referred to poetry in other languages, too.

Bimyō's reasons for exploring poetry in English were clear: he wished to examine the link, if there was one, between the status of a nation's verse art and the status of the nation itself, with England being, in his view, the paradigmatic advanced nation. Here Bimyō was invoking the language of *kaika* or "enlightenment" and *bunmei* or "civilization," calling on a discourse of progress that would be familiar to all Meiji-period readers.[15] Bimyō paraphrased with disapproval Thomas Babington Macaulay (1800–1859), the British historian who had written, "As civilization advances, poetry almost necessarily declines."[16] In reaction to this, Bimyō asked, "Shall we agree with Macaulay's thesis?" (Yamada [1890–91] 2014, 90). The answer was no, obviously. But the next step in Bimyō's argument is noteworthy: based on a selection of examples, he deduced that a nation's *inbun* does not necessarily lag behind its level of civilization. There remain two possibilities: either *inbun* does (or, is able to) keep pace with a civilization's advancement, or it is ahead of the civilization's state of advancement (96). "To say that *inbun* is ahead of the level of civilization would be claiming too much for it," Bimyō went on, "so it is enough to state that [the level of] *inbun* keeps pace with the level of civilization" (97). Bimyō thus squarely aligned his project with that of Japanese enlightenment.

He evidently believed that enlightenment, as a national project, could be supported by a rigorous analysis of questions of aesthetics. The first section of Bimyō's essay, titled "On the Difference between Prose and Poetry," foregrounded the term *sessō*, "rhythm," making it the identifying feature of poetry: poetry had *sessō*, prose did not.[17] As Bimyō put it very early in "Nihon inbun ron," "The basis of the distinction between verse and prose lies in rhythm [*sessō*] alone" (83). He rephrased this assertion in various ways: later in the text he claimed that the difference between verse and prose was one of "form" (*taikei*) (85). For the duration of the versification war Bimyō never resiled himself from the claim that what distinguished poetry from prose was the presence of an identifiable, recurring rhythm.

One part of Bimyō's argument was his insistence that content was independent of form. He maintained that a thought could be expressed as either prose or poetry without changing its content: "I would like to ask," Bimyō wrote, "how a thought in prose would differ from a thought in verse. . . . If we come to fundamentals, a thought is the same whether [expressed] in prose or in verse: it is the form [*taikei*] [alone] that differs" (85). Bimyō's examples were sensational: Hamlet's soliloquy would express the same thought if it were rewritten as prose; the American Declaration of Independence, if it were rewritten as verse, would still declare America's independence (85). In other words, according to Bimyō, knowledge about a text's content alone would not enable one to predict whether that text were poetry or prose.

This position could be attacked from many angles, and it was. The first writer to inveigh against Bimyō's essay was the critic (and, later, prolific translator of Western literature) Uchida Roan 内田魯庵 (1868–1929). As the title of Roan's first essay in the debate suggests, he viewed Bimyō as a *gaikei ronsha*, a "theorist of externals." In Roan's view, Bimyō had arrived at a superficial definition of poetry, which not even Plato had been able to define (Uchida [1891a] 1984, 260–61). The eminence of the thinkers who had been incapable of defining poetry did not prevent Roan himself from taking a position: for Roan, a poem must be a record of inspired thinking—the kind of thinking to which an elevated diction is likewise suited. In support of this view Roan drew on Kada no Arimaro's 荷田在満 (1706–51) "The Origins of the *uta*" (Kagenron 歌源論), Yan Yu's 厳羽 (1191–1241) *Canglang Poetry Talks* (*Canglang shihua* 滄浪詩話), Thomas Carlyle's (1795–1881) description of "musical thought" in *Heroes and Hero Worship* (1841), and Ralph Waldo Emerson's (1803–82) essay "Poetry and Imagination" (1836), among others (265–69). The range of Roan's references—Japanese, Chinese, English, American—suggests that he, like Bimyō, understood *poetry* to have a wide scope, applying to texts from any period or language. In a later article, Roan claimed that Bimyō's insistence on the equation *poetry = metrical language* led to absurdities: Roan criticized, for example, Bimyō's claim that a law (or a Declaration of Independence) written in verse must be counted as poetry (Uchida [1891b] 1984, 281).

Another opponent of Bimyō's position was the literary critic Ishibashi Ningetsu 石橋忍月 (1865–1926), who entered the fray with a short article titled "Mocking [Bimyō's] 'On Verse'" (Inbun ron o azakeru 韻文論を嘲る)

in late November 1890. Ningetsu was steeped in German philosophy, to the point that he was nicknamed Lessing Ningetsu after the German thinker (Irokawa 2007, 6). Ningetsu agreed with Bimyō that the Japanese language needed a hypernym for designating a generally conceived category of *poetry*; but he did not approve of the term *inbun* "as a translation of the Western term 'poetry'" (Ishibashi [1890a] 1995, 198). Ningetsu objected most strongly to Bimyō's definition of poetry as metrical language: "Bimyō regards poetry superficially and doesn't know how to look at it with an eye to human intention, thought, nature, or feelings" (197). In another article, Ningetsu advanced a definition of poetry based "not on outer form but on inner essence" (Ishibashi [1890b] 1995, 199; *gaibu no keishiki yori sezu shite, naibu no honshitsu yori suru*). Poetry, Ningetsu claimed, was "artistic [beautiful] writing" (*bijutsuteki no moji* 美術的の文字), and for that reason he proposed that the general term for poetry be *bibun*, "beautiful writing," instead of *inbun* ([1890a] 1995, 198).[18] To this proposal he added the following definition of poetry: "Poetry is that which artistically expresses the *Seelenleben* [*zēre seikatsu* 性情(ゼーレ)生活 (soul-life)] and the *Geistesleben* [*gaisuto seikatsu* 意思(ガイスト)生活 (spirit-life)] of humanity in words" (199). In these articles, Ningetsu was joining the many eighteenth- and nineteenth-century critics who had written on aesthetics in terms of form and content, including such figures as Shaftesbury, Schelling, Goethe, Hegel, and Carlyle.

Behind Roan's and Ningetsu's criticisms lay an understanding of poetry that both echoed Bimyō's and differed from it. Bimyō, Roan, and Ningetsu alike viewed poetry as a general category of literary creation: it included the varieties of Japanese verse as well as verse in other languages. They further agreed that poetry had both content and form. But they disagreed which of the two—content or form—was more important for poetry. For Bimyō, as we have seen, form was all: meter (*moji* count, in the Japanese case) was what identified a poem. For Roan and Ningetsu, content was what mattered. Roan, who would go on to be known primarily as a writer of prose, pointed out that "a man might write ten thousand verses and not be a poet," just as a person might be a poet without ever writing a line of verse (Uchida [1891a] 1984, 269). Ningetsu, for his part, made it clear where his interest lay: given an opposition between the supposedly outward and inward parts of poetry—between the poem's formal qualities (meter, rhyme, stanzaic profile, etc.) and its content—he always privileged the content. Hence it is no surprise that Ningetsu attacked Bimyō for attending to form alone. Ningetsu wanted poetry to be beautiful; he feared that if poetry were equated with meter, there would be too much room for unbeautiful poetry.

The positions that have been outlined here are only some of the views advanced by the combatants in the versification war. Bimyō's essay, in particular, is too long and too various in its coverage to be easily summarized: it touched on a wide range of topics, from the possible uses of poetry in education to the incorporation of scientific discourses in aesthetic ones. In a literary critical milieu that fostered so searching a debate over the definition of poetry, Kitamura Tōkoku was publishing long poems that broke with the *shintaishi* orthodoxy—as we have seen with his *Soshū no shi*—and we now return to his poetry.

Tōkoku's *Hōraikyoku*

The critics who took part in the versification war made no comment about Tōkoku's *Soshū no shi*. This is most likely due to the extremely small number of copies of *Soshū no shi* that Tōkoku allowed to circulate (Kitamura 1950–55, 1:414–15; Schamoni 1983, 92–93).[19] Even if the poem had circulated more widely, however, the writers who participated in the versification war would probably not have referred to it. In all the pages of the debate, only one living Japanese poet was quoted—Bimyō himself—when Uchida Roan cited two brief extracts from a *shintaishi* by Bimyō as ironic evidence against the claims made in "Nihon inbun ron" (Uchida [1891a] 1984, 260, 270). The versification war was fought using weapons made of abstractions, not of specific textual examples. It was unusual to see mention made even of Japanese poems of the past: Bimyō's long explication of a *waka* from *Shinkokinshū* was the only such occurrence in this debate (Yamada [1890–91] 2014, 100–101). The poem that was mentioned by title most frequently in the debate was Milton's *Paradise Lost* (1667): Bimyō's opponents brought Milton's unrhymed epic as evidence that even a poem that goes against a received poetic orthodoxy (in Milton's case, rhyme) can still be poetry. Bimyō's opponents in the versification war could also have cited Tōkoku's recent *Soshū no shi*; whether they would have done so if they had known of the poem is of course a question we cannot answer. In October 1890 Tōkoku, who had otherwise published only a few short translations and articles, was still a relative unknown in the Japanese literary establishment.

In May 1891, only a few months after Bimyō ceased adding new installments to "Nihon inbun ron," Tōkoku self-published a long work titled *Hōraikyoku*. In some passages *Hōraikyoku* is formatted as prose; in others it looks like poetry, with the lines ending before reaching the margin. At the same time it has many features that would seem to identify it as a drama. There are stage directions; the text is divided into acts and scenes; the names of the characters precede the speeches they utter. Indeed some later commentators have called *Hōraikyoku* a *gekishi* 劇詩 or "drama in verse" (Kenmochi 1973). It is, by any standard, a generic chimera. Anticipating that the text might puzzle his readers, Tōkoku wrote a preface to *Hōraikyoku* in which he described the text in relation to generic and stylistic conventions:

> My *Hōraikyoku* is in the form of a drama, but I have no ambition to stage it. Nor have I any great interest in whether my rather disorderly and varied poetic style be termed poetry or not: as for the versification war, the world already has the outstanding generals of the literary establishment. (Kitamura 1950–55, 1:42; [1891] 1977, 1)

From this prefatory comment it would appear that Tōkoku saw the text as comparable to not one form but two, the "form of a drama" (*gekkyoku no tei* 劇曲の体) and that of poetry (*shitei* 詩体). The text is, we might now say, a *Lesedrame*, a drama to be read not staged, in the manner of plays such as Goethe's *Faust* or Byron's *Manfred*, both of which Tōkoku knew of and drew on when composing *Hōraikyoku* (Higashinaka 1990). As for the poetic style, Tōkoku disparaged *Hōraikyoku*'s as "disorderly and varied," so much so that he supposed it might not be regarded as poetry at all. On this point, however, Tōkoku added that "as for the versification war, the world already has the outstanding generals of the literary establishment," suggesting that he was not one of them: it was not his fight.

When Tōkoku referred to the "versification war" (*inbun no sensō*), he was almost certainly alluding to the controversy caused by Yamada Bimyō's "Nihon inbun ron." By implicitly refusing to recognize the distinction between prose and poetry, Tōkoku's preface to *Hōraikyoku* issued a demurral to the whole debate. Tōkoku used the term "war" probably as a humorous exaggeration—as an acknowledgment that, inside the teapot of critical discourse, the *inbun* controversy might have felt like a tempest. But Tōkoku's intervention, if we can call it that, was anything but trivial: his *Hōraikyoku* can be seen as a resounding rebuke to a critic like Yamada Bimyō who insisted that poetry must be metrically regular. When Tōkoku wrote that *Hōraikyoku* was "disorderly and varied," he must have suspected that its amalgamation of prose and new-style verse—a prosodically unusual variant of new-style verse, at that—would deviate considerably from its readers' generic expectations. The text was thus very much oriented toward the topics debated in the versification war.

The plot of *Hōraikyoku* is convoluted, with a cast that includes humans, supernatural beings, and even deer, in a drama "some two thousand lines" long (Brownstein 1981, 91). Yet the inwardness of the drama invites comparison with the plight of the solitary, imprisoned speaker of *Sōshū no shi*: in *Hōraikyoku* the prison in which the protagonist finds himself is that of his consciousness. To summarize very briefly the plot of the poem (which is how I designate the text despite the many questions it raises about generic categories), the protagonist of *Hōraikyoku*, a biwa player named Yanagida Motoo, is a young man whose circumstances make him believe that suicide will solve his difficulties. Convinced that he will find enlightenment if he dies on Mount Hōrai, which is inhabited by various spiritual beings, he climbs the mountain, reaches the summit, and dies. In an appendix to the play, Tōkoku added a scene in which the protagonist sails in a little boat with the spirit of his dead wife to the Western Lands: he has found peace in death.

In light of the versification debate, what is most interesting is that the protagonist of *Hōraikyoku* insists that he himself is composed of two related but opposed principles, a spirit and a body:

> Within me there seem to be two unreconciled essences—one is human, one divine. Within me, these two essences
> wage war continuously; for as long as I live, they will bring me distemper, exhaustion, and unease.[20]

> *omoeba waga uchi ni wa, kanarazu yawaraganu futatsu no saga no aru rashi,*
> *hitotsu wa kami, hitotsu wa hito, kono futatsu wa waga uchi ni,*
> *koyami naki tatakai o nashite, waga shinu inochi no tsukuru toki made wa,*
> *ware o yamase tsukarase nayamasuran.*

> おもへばわが内には、かならず和らがぬ兩つの性のあるら
> し、ひとつは神性、ひとつは人性、このふたつはわが内に、
> 小休なき戰ひをなして、わが死ぬ生命の盡くる時までは、わ
> れを病ませ疲らせ悩ますらん。[21]

(Kitamura 1950–55, 1:141–42; [1891] 1977, 52)

Earlier in the play a demon tries to tell the protagonist that it is impossible for a human, composed as he is of physical matter, to ascend Mount Hōrai. The protagonist rejoins that since he is also at least partially spirit, he is able to ascend the mountain:

> Although I am a child of dust, I also have a soul that is not dust. It is in order to purify this soul that I am climbing this sacred mountain.[22]

> *ware chiri no ko nari to iedomo, chiri naranu tama o mo moteri, kono tama o*
> *araikiyomen tame ni, ide miyama ni noboran.*

> われ塵の兒なりと雖、塵ならぬ靈をも持てり、この靈を洗ひ
> 清めんために、いで御山に登らん。

(Kitamura 1950–55, 1:129; [1891] 1977, 46)

(I indent this passage to emphasize that it is prose, with the line breaks being determined by the margins of the page.) Later in the same scene, Motoo states, in lineated verse, that what he desires is to purify his spirit by ridding himself of his body—his form—altogether:

> This dead form, this dead form, begone!
> With its mountains of disgrace to be washed away,
> with its sky-vast illusions to be dispelled,
>
> . . .
>
> this dead form, this dead form, begone!

nugisarashite yo, / kono mukuro, / kono mukuro!	[7, 5, 5 = 17]
sosogubeki / haji no yamatakami,	[5, 8 = 13]
haraubeki / mayoi no sora hiromi,	[5, 9 = 14]
. . .	
nugisarashite yo, / kono mukuro, / kono mukuro!	[7, 5, 5 = 17]

脱去らしてよ、この形骸、この形骸！
雪ぐ可き恥辱の山高み、
拂ふ可き迷の虚空廣み、
. . .
脱去らしてよ、この形骸、この塵骸！

(Kitamura 1950–55, 1:134; [1891] 1977, 49)

(I add slashes to the transliteration to mark conjectural phrase boundaries, and in brackets I give the *moji* counts.) In a text that itself incorporated formal features from a number of genres and was at odds with other *shintaishi* being written at the time, Tōkoku had his protagonist pray for the passing of an old form. The speech ends, moreover, with an ideographic pun. The word "corpse," *mukuro*, is written in two ways in a single line: 形骸 and 塵骸.

A further comment on this pun is in order, because it exemplifies what Tōkoku was doing with the opposition between form and content, between matter and spirit.[23] It is in the nature of puns to resist translation; this pun, simultaneously graphical and aural, draws on a tension between ideographic and phonetic writing for its effects. In modern Japanese, *mukuro* (corpse) is usually written with one kanji: 骸. In the passage cited above, however, the pronunciation *mukuro* is assigned to not one kanji but two: in all but the final instance in this speech *mukuro* is written as 形骸, in which the first ideograph means "shape" or "form." These two kanji together, meaning "bare skeleton" (literally "form-corpse"), are pronounced *keigai* in modern Japanese, but the pronunciation gloss given in Tōkoku's text imposes the reading *mukuro*. The use of this two-kanji compound has the effect of emphasizing the (visible) form of the (lifeless) body, which Motoo is addressing as a dead

thing of which he would gladly rid himself. Then the last line adds a compli-
cation: the second and final occurrence of the word *mukuro* in the last line of
the speech is written not as "form-corpse" but as "dust-corpse" 塵骸, with
a different first kanji (which had figured, not incidentally, in the protago-
nist's earlier speech about being a "child of dust"). The two-kanji compound
"dust-corpse" is not attested in standard reference works and appears to be
Tōkoku's invention. If a reader pronounced these words aloud, the differ-
ence between these two ideographic spellings of *mukuro* would be inaudible:
this rhetorical stroke is for the reader's eyes only. Two different words, 形骸
and 塵骸, despite the difference in orthography, can have the same
pronunciation—can have the same "content": *mukuro*. This pun is achieved
through an implied parallel between 形, "form," and insignificant 塵, "dust,"
a comparison that assumes another layer of meaning when considered in
light of the recent versification debate.

Tōkoku's contemporaries could make little sense of his experiments,
which seemed to destabilize prosody, genre, and orthography all at once.
The poet Isogai Unpō 磯貝雲峰 (1865–97), reviewing *Hōraikyoku* in June
1891, called attention to the text's mystifying form:

> Is it an *uta*? I couldn't say. Is it a *shi*? I couldn't say. Is it a drama?
> I couldn't say. . . . I understand that this work hasn't been written as a
> drama; but since there is no meter I find it difficult to call this a work
> in verse [*inbun*]—neither is it everyday prose. . . . In the end, *I cannot
> say clearly what manner of text this is or for what purpose it was written.*
> (Isogai [1891] 1989, 252)

Another review by the critic Nagasawa Betten 長沢別天 (1868–99) charac-
terized Tōkoku's text as a "prose poem" (*purōzu poimu* 散文的詩篇 [sic]): it
was not poetic enough to be a poem yet too poetic to be prose (quoted in
Hiraoka 1967, 143). For these and other reasons Nagasawa concluded that
the text was a "failure" (*shippai*) but that, with time and diligence, Tōkoku
might become a great "poet or dramatist" (quoted in Hiraoka 1967, 144).

The Japanese literature scholar Hiraoka Toshio, surveying these bewil-
dered first reviews of *Hōraikyoku*, writes, "How should the incomprehen-
sion of these critics be interpreted? It would be easy to chalk it up to the
low critical standards of the time. But would Tōkoku have written without
keeping an eye on the contemporary literary establishment? Of course not;
naturally he would have wanted to be understood" (1967, 144). Given the
resonances between Tōkoku's text and the debate over the nature of poetry
that had recently shaken the Japanese poetry world, it seems to me that
Tōkoku was indeed writing for his contemporaries. I grant that there are

many other ways to situate *Hōraikyoku*: for one, a most obvious alternative reading of the poem would be to interpret it autobiographically as a harbinger of Tōkoku's own eventual suicide in 1894—a reading that would not be incompatible, in any case, with the interpretation I am proposing here. There is a close and relevant parallel between the terms that are explored in *Hōraikyoku* and the terms that poets and critics had been debating in Japan in the months immediately preceding its publication. The protagonist of Tōkoku's text is praying for the extinction of a *form* that prevents him from achieving contentment; when he does bring about the death of that form, it is revealed that his spirit still exists, purified and improved in the Western Lands. If one wanted to read the text allegorically, one might interpret the text as asserting that the spirit of the artist (Motoo is, let us recall, a biwa player) can survive even when the artist's form has undergone an apparently total transformation. The spirit of poetry need not inhabit the body that it had inhabited before. Given a greatly revised understanding of the concept of poetry—such as the one that had come into focus over the course of the versification debate—even a text as multiform and as atypical as *Hōraikyoku*, Tōkoku and others believed, could be denominated a poem. Tōkoku's contemporaries, however, were unwilling, in the main, to countenance such latitude in verse composition, in their belief that civilized poetry must adhere to a standard of metrical regularity.

CHAPTER 3

A Disaster Averted

Masaoka Shiki and the Value of Brevity

Octavio Paz's Spanish-language version of the haiku poet Matsuo Bashō's 松尾芭蕉 (1644–94) travel narrative *Oku no hoso-michi* 奥の細道 (posthumous, 1702) contains haiku translations that I admire very much. Paz translated the text in collaboration with Hayashiya Eikichi, publishing their *Sendas de Oku* (Paths of Oku) in April 1957, whereupon "it was received with the usual indifference," as Paz recalled ([1970] 2005, 9). Theirs was the first complete version of Bashō's text in a Western language, to be followed by four others in the 1960s—three in English, one in French. Paz and Hayashiya republished *Sendas de Oku* in a revised and expanded version in 1970, and a further updated version of that revision was published in 2005, with the addition of the Japanese text on facing pages and illustrations by the famous painter and haiku poet Yosa Buson 与謝蕪村 (1716–84). This lavish treatment reveals something of the haiku's status, in the ascendant in the latter half of the twentieth century. It also reveals Paz's long-standing esteem for the haiku as a poetic form, and for Bashō's work particularly.

What I admire about the Paz-Hayashiya version of Bashō is the deployment of Spanish prosodic rules to recreate, in an intriguingly altered way, the prosody of the original haiku. For just one example, here is a haiku by Bashō:

五月雨の降り残してや光堂

(Matsuo B. 1979, 41)

samidare no / furinokoshite ya / Hikaridō

This haiku is a standard 5-7-5. My English translation:

the May rain has held off, here, for now: Golden Hall

(The Golden Hall, *Hikari-dō*, is a structure at Chūsonji Temple in Iwate Pre-fecture.) My provisional English version makes no attempt at a meter or syllable pattern.

Paz and Hayashiya revised their translation of this poem, bringing the meter of their Spanish version into closer alignment with that of the original Japanese—according to Spanish counting rules. In the first edition of *Sendas de Oku*, the poem about Golden Hall was given as

Las lluvias de mayo
no te atacan ya,
Templo de Oro.
      (Matsuo B. 2005, 213)

In Spanish prosody, consecutive adjacent vowels are usually elided, a con-vention called *sinalefa* (or, when employed within a single word, *sinéresis*); a stressed syllable at the end of a line counts as two syllables. These two rules, applied to this version of the poem, yield a syllable count of 6-6-4.[1]

The later revision achieves a match on the 5-7-5 of the original through a strategic application of the two rules I have just mentioned:

Terco esplendor:
frente a la lluvia, erguido
templo de luz.
      (Matsuo B. 2005, 127)

Although the first and third lines appear to have four syllables each, in fact each line would be scanned as having five syllables: the final *or* of *esplendor* is stressed and therefore adds an inaudible fifth syllable; the same applies to *luz* at the end of the third line. As for the second line, two *sinalefas* reduce the syllable count to seven exactly: *frente a* becomes two syllables, and *lluvia erguido* only four.[2]

Paz took pains to revise the poems for the second edition, explaining that he "tried to adapt [him]self to the meter of the originals" ([1970] 2005, 29). He gave no reason for wanting to do so, but his reason is easy to imagine: Paz was adhering to the principle that metrical fidelity is itself a crucial expres-sion of fidelity in poetry translation.

Metrical fidelity would be one among several possible varieties of formal fidelity; another would be fidelity in point of rhyme, for instance. The merits of formal fidelity have long been a matter for debate; certainly not all translators insist on adhering to the formal qualities of their original texts. Paz himself took a flexible approach. In his essay on translating the French poet Stéphane Mallarmé's (1842–98) "Sonnet en -yx" (Sonnet in -ix), Paz admitted that "it would have been impossible to retain the -ix rhymes in Spanish," and settled for unrhymed fourteen-syllable lines instead (1971, 47). He retained, however, the stanza structure of the sonnet: two quatrains and two tercets.

There are poetry translators whose translation practice suggests they believe that the greater the number of formal fidelities one can achieve, the better one's translation. Put differently, if two translations of a poem attain a similar level of semantic accuracy, then (for these translators) the better translation will be the one that exhibits greater formal fidelity. It is easy to find translators and critics in this camp: Paz is one, and I mention others over the course of this chapter. Conversely, some translators and theorists view formal fidelity to the original as a detriment: replicating the form in the target language can require, those translators would say, undesirable misrepresentations of the original's content. The hexameters of ancient Greek, for example, had little success in English translation; in the nineteenth century (to say nothing of the twentieth), the view that classical meters need not be exactly replicated in the contemporary target language gained wide acceptance.[3] There are even famous examples of free-verse translations of comparatively recent, formally regular originals: the novelist Vladimir Nabokov, for instance, in his translation of Aleksandr Pushkin's *Evgeny Onegin* (1833), insisted that the best way to render Pushkin's intricately rhymed stanzas in English was to ignore the rhyme altogether and convey the poem's semantic effects alone.[4]

What of the translator who, despite ascribing importance to poetic form in general, does not acknowledge the value of a particular form? What of the translator whose sensibilities are even affronted in some way, or who imagines that readers' sensibilities will be affronted, by the original's formal features? Such questions arise at some level, I believe, whenever any translation is attempted, but they become especially acute when a translator is translating poems from a literary tradition that has been little explored in the target language. Consider the example of Edward Fitzgerald (1809–83), whose adaptive translation of the *Rubáiyát of Omar Khayyam* (1859) reflected the translator's "conflicted views of Persian poetry and of [the British] empire," as Annmarie Drury has persuasively explained (2015, 162).

Fitzgerald's avowedly "very unliteral" approach to translation led him to "mash . . . together" Khayyam's verses (quoted in Drury 2015, 148)—a liberty he felt justified in taking because, as he explained in a letter to a friend, "these Persians . . . are *not* poets enough to frighten one from such excursions, and really *do* want a little *Art* to shape them" (Terhune and Terhune 1980, 261).

It took time for a haiku translation like Paz's to become possible. When translators were first bringing the Japanese haiku into European languages, the great obstacle with which they had to contend was the form's brevity. In many senses this is the obverse of the problem that was confronted by the compilers of *Shintaishi shō* 新体詩抄 (New-style poetry collection, 1882): while the compilers of that anthology had to make a decision about how to represent lengthy originals to readers whose poetic culture had for many centuries conferred the greatest prestige upon much shorter forms, the first translators of haiku into European languages had to persuade readers that brief poems could be worth reading.[5]

Even as European translators were first confronting these questions, Japanese poets, informed by ideas from abroad, were seeing their poetic forms in a new light. For Japanese poets, brevity became not a premise of versification but a problem, a quality that could no longer simply be assumed to confer merit upon a composition. After becoming acquainted with a European literary culture that, on the whole, regarded brevity as a mark of inferiority,[6] how did Japanese poets revise their understanding of the haiku as a form?

In this chapter I examine the problem of brevity from several different angles and will not be following a chronology or making a single claim. Although this chapter does have what we might call a principal character—the haiku poet Masaoka Shiki 正岡子規 (1867–1902)—we nevertheless will frequently be diverting our attention away from him: the theme here is the significance of brevity for poetic form. It was a theme about which Shiki himself cared deeply. He was a haiku poet of unquestioned importance; moreover, in his criticism he grappled directly with the brevity of the haiku, applying to that question a variety of methodologies, even as he continued to write haiku throughout most of his short life. Shiki pronounced that the haiku, a poetic form constrained most of all by its brevity, would not outlast the Meiji reign. That pronouncement is one of the most famous Shiki ever made, but Shiki's opinion of brevity as a feature of poetic form changed over the span of several years, to judge from the diversity of his published thoughts on the matter. It must be admitted, however, that Shiki as a critic can appear strikingly different from Shiki as a poet: the critic castigated haiku, while the *haijin* continued writing them.

The vast majority of studies of Shiki approach him in a Japan-only frame-work, and thus one of the aims of the present chapter is to juxtapose Shiki's understanding of the haiku's brevity with that of European critics. I do this not because Shiki was in colloquy with non-Japanese critics of Japanese literature—he was not[7]—but precisely because the extent of his engagement with ideas from abroad can be hard to pin down. Even more famous than his pronouncement that the haiku was doomed to extinction was his pronouncement that haiku is literature—a pronouncement Shiki made even as scholars and critics abroad, upon encountering short Japanese verses for the first time, were expressing doubts as to the value of Japanese literature, and of short Japanese poetry in particular.

Here we come again to an important question about translation: the question of how translators decide for or against translating a given work. As any translator can report from firsthand experience, the reasons for nontranslation can be hard to locate, because a never-completed—or even never-begun—translation might leave no trace. A decision not to translate a text can spring from any number of causes: imponderables of personal taste; one's feel for the preferences of the reading public; or one's writing schedule, whether feasting or famished. Conversely, a decision to translate a text need not be interpreted as an endorsement—indeed, there are reasons why a translator might even feel reluctant to make a translation public. The reasons for that reluctance, if stated, reveal much about the translator's notions of literary worth. All the poetry translations I cite in this chapter are—with the meta-exception of my own translations—previously published work; but many of those, as we will see, were published with warnings and disclaimers, priming the reader to approach the texts with lowered expectations. The translators evidently felt some compunction at the thought that, through their works, they were translating not only literary texts but also literary values.

Shiki on Finitude

The following two haiku by Masaoka Shiki date from 1889, published two months apart:[8]

the birds at their song
deep in the mud-nestled flowers

tori naku ya / nigori tatasumu / hana no oku

鳥なくや濁りた丶すむ花の奥[9]

(Masaoka 1975–78, 1:15)

as far as the eye can see
up to the base of Fuji
rice planting

miwataseba / Fuji made tsuzuku / taue kana

見渡せば富士迄つゞく田植哉

              (Masaoka 1975–78, 1:419)

As haiku go, both poems share many standard features of the form. Each poem is a straightforward 5-7-5, with no *jiamari* or *jitarazu*. Each has a *kireji* or cutting word: *ya* ends the first *ku* of the earlier poem; *kana* ends the later poem. Likewise, each has a suitable *kigo* or seasonal word: the poem about the birds includes *hana* (flowers), a spring word; the second poem is about *taue* (rice fields), a summer word. As a point about their publication history, both poems appeared in *Masago no shirabe* 眞砂の志良邊, a magazine that until recently had been under the editorship of Ōhara Kijū 大原其戎 (1812–89), who had died earlier that year. Kijū had mentored Shiki in haiku composition; it was during Kijū's editorship that, two years earlier, Shiki had published his first haiku.

The two haiku cited above share these various traits of prosody, diction, and distribution. What leads me to juxtapose them here, however, is simply this: one of them was published before and one after the April 1889 publication of an essay by Shiki in which he stated, with what he claimed was mathematical certainty, that the haiku was doomed to extinction. Yet the post-extinction-theory haiku bears no trace of any great change in Shiki's practice of haiku composition; indeed, the fact that the later haiku was published at all suggests that Shiki was not terribly concerned about the form's imminent obsolescence.

In his April 1889 essay "The Origin and Development of Poetry" (Shiika no kigen oyobi hensen 詩歌の起源及び変遷), Shiki invoked an idea that he derived from the English philosopher Herbert Spencer: the "economy of mental energy" as expressed through literary style. By arguing that the haiku was the most efficient literary form for the communication of mental energy, Shiki shaped his essay as a praise of the haiku—albeit a qualified praise. The haiku's compression came with what Spencer's phrase invites us to think of as being quite literally a price:

And in poetry [*shiika*], as human feelings and thoughts become more complex, the verses [that express those feelings and thoughts] become, by necessity, longer, as has been explained above; but ever since Bai Juyi's verses there have been in *kanshi* no long works, and ever since

Man'yōshū it has been uncommon to write *chōka* in Japan. In [such texts as] the *uta* with its thirty-one *moji*, it is difficult, undoubtedly, to shoehorn more than a single meaning into the ambit of one work; it would be the height of absurdity for a poet today to imagine writing something as good as or better than the best poems of antiquity, pure and flavorless as they are. In comparison with these, the haiku, with its fewer *ji*, is far more profound. Keeping in mind Mr. Spencer's notion of the "economy of mental energy," which of the following has the greater interest: the deep meaning contained in the seventeen *ji* of Bashō's poem about the frog, or the single point expressed by the many verses of Hitomaro's poem about the tail of the mountain bird?[10] . . . But unfortunately the *hokku*, too, has its maximum of just over ten *ji* [*sic*]; . . . If we look at a table of logarithms then we see with perfect clarity that, by the law of permutations, the total number of haiku written in [the] words [of this language] does not exceed a certain limit. (Masaoka 1975–78, 9:386)

The haiku's brevity, according to this account, is simultaneously its best feature and its death sentence. One of the reasons for the latter is the law of mathematical permutations, which dictates that the number of possible haiku is finite. With this argument, Shiki indirectly underscored the claims made by the compilers of *Shintaishi shō*: not only was the haiku too short for expressing complex thoughts, as that anthology's compilers had claimed, but also it was too short a poetic form to survive indefinitely.

Below, we will return to Shiki's use of mathematics for intensifying his argument's rhetoric; for the moment I want to examine Shiki's reference to Spencer. The works of Herbert Spencer (1820–1903), the English philosopher and popular author, had appeared in Japanese translation as early as the 1870s. According to the scholar Narita Tatsuo, "The Spencer boom in Japan started in the second decade of Meiji [1878–87], when virtually all his major writings were translated into Japanese one after another" (1988, 71). Certain of Spencer's works were used as English language texts for university courses; the epicenter of Spencer reception in Japan was Imperial University (later Tokyo Imperial), where the American art historian Ernest Fenollosa (1853–1908) taught philosophy and where other figures such as Toyama Masakazu 外山正一 (1848–1900) and the politician Itō Hirobumi 伊藤博文 (1841–1909) were also lecturing on Spencer's ideas. Although Shiki did not enter the university until 1890, he had been enrolled since 1884 in the university's affiliated preparatory school, where Shiki, as Narita has written, "could not have been oblivious to the Spencer boom" (72).[11] As Seth Jacobowitz has noted, "It is remarkably refreshing to think that Shiki's concepts of brevity and concision derived not from the purportedly minimalist essence of Japanese poetry or language, but from Spencer" (2015, 234).

Shiki's "economy of mental energy" was adapted from axioms spelled out in Spencer's 1852 *Philosophy of Style*. The foremost of these was: "A reader or listener has at each moment but a limited amount of mental power available" (1892, 3). Spencer's other axioms included assertions regarding learning and memory—for example, "the earliest learnt and oftenest used words, will, other things equal, call up images with less loss of time and energy than their later learnt synonyms" (5). This rule justifies Spencer's favoring words of Anglo-Saxon origin as being less wasteful of the reader's or hearer's effort than Latinate words. While Spencer did acknowledge exceptional cases— for example, the occasional effectiveness of a long Latinate word, because "a long word . . . allows the hearer's consciousness a longer time to dwell upon the quality predicated" (6–7)—in general, anything that shortens an utterance or a text will, in Spencer's view, tend to reduce the effort required of its audience. Spencer's was, as the Japanese poetry scholar Mark Morris has observed, "perhaps the most Gradgrinderly of nineteenth-century poetics" (1985, 276), but Shiki found Spencer's conclusions agreeable. And while *Philosophy of Style* did devote a section to poetry—including such features of poetic language as metaphor, simile, elision, inversion, and so on (30–35)— Shiki ignored that part of the text. His interest lay primarily in the benefits of brevity.

In his 1889 essay, as already noted, Shiki acknowledged that the haiku's brevity had certain advantages. Over time, however, Shiki took a more pessimistic view of the haiku's chances of survival, as for instance in his *Talks from the Otter's Den* (*Dassai shooku haiwa* 獺祭書屋俳話), serialized in the Tokyo newspaper *Nippon* from June through October of 1892 in thirty-eight instalments and published as a book in May 1893. Shiki's tone in this later series of essays was almost apocalyptic:

> A certain contemporary scholar conversant with mathematics has said: "It is evident from the theory of permutations that there is a numerical limit to the tanka and haiku of Japan, which are confined to a mere twenty or thirty syllables [*jion*]." In other words, sooner or later the tanka . . . and haiku will reach their limit. (Masaoka 1975–78, 4:165; translation at Beichman 1982, 35)

Here again Shiki invoked the notion of permutations: given that the haiku is, normatively, seventeen *moji* long, and given that there is only a finite number of possible *moji* in Japanese, then one need only calculate the number—the exact, finite number—of possible haiku in Japanese to see that the haiku form was not an inexhaustible resource. However, because of conventional constraints on poetic diction, the number of admissible haiku was even lower than a straightforward calculation would suggest, leading Shiki to predict the haiku's imminent demise:

> Though one may place the blame on people, part of it must certainly be assigned to the intrinsically narrow confines of the tanka and haiku. You may ask, "If that is so, when will the end come for the haiku and tanka?" And I reply: "I can't, of course, predict the time of their total extinction but *speaking approximately, I think the haiku has already played itself out. Even assuming that the end is yet to come, we can confidently expect it to arrive sometime during the Meiji period.*" (Masaoka 1975–78, 4:166; translation at Beichman 1982, 36)

By predicting that the haiku would die even before the emperor—who was born in 1852 and was therefore forty-one years old by the Oriental count when Shiki published the passage just quoted—Shiki gave urgency to his predictions of the haiku's endangerment.

To put Shiki's predictions in perspective, I have done a few calculations to estimate the number of possible haiku. One way to approach the matter is to calculate the number of possible seventeen-*moji* sequences in Japanese. If we say that there are forty-seven *moji* in Japanese,[12] then the number of such sequences is much larger than standard pocket calculators can display on their screens: 2.6647937×10^{28}. Even if all 127 million Japanese now alive did nothing every day but compose these seventeen-*moji* sequences, each individual Japanese person's share of that total would be 2.0982627×10^{20} sequences. If that number of texts were distributed equally over fifty years (a rough estimate of the span of a literate person's adulthood), then each Japanese person would need to write, if my calculations are correct, 1.149733×10^{16} texts per day.

These numbers are clearly beyond any writer's capacity, so let us approach the question again from a more human scale. Over the course of one day in 1684, as subsequent accounts had it, Ihara Saikaku 井原西鶴 (1642–93) famously wrote some 23,500 haiku (or *haikai*, as they would have been called at the time). How many years would a Saikaku need to maintain that pace before reaching the total possible number of seventeen-*moji* strings of Japanese? At the rate of 23,500 per day, the answer comes to 3.1067253×10^{21} years. That is 3.1067253×10^{18} *millennia*. For contrast, consider this number: 1.7, which is approximately how many millennia Japanese writing has existed. It is expected that the earth's sun will become

A DISASTER AVERTED 85

a red giant in 5.0×10^6 millennia, which would occur long before our Saikaku could complete his assignment.

These calculations do not yet incorporate what many take to be a crucial component of the haiku as a form: its meter. In a typical haiku, there should be a caesura after the fifth *moji* and another after the twelfth. How many seventeen-*moji* strings are eliminated by that stipulation is something I have not calculated; I suspect the total number would be considerably reduced. The total expands again, however, if haiku with *jiamari* or *jitarazu* are added to the sum. Setting aside for a moment the thorny question of how actually to compute the total number of possible haiku, let us acknowledge that the numbers involved are enormous. And I am considering only metrically regular haiku; if we include free-verse haiku (which began appearing in the 1910s) then the number expands further still.

Shiki evidently was not greatly concerned with the mathematics of the issue. Nor have I seen any indication that he ever ran the numbers. To return briefly to the two haiku by Shiki mentioned above, it is worth pointing out once again that despite Shiki's having recently published a prediction of the haiku's imminent demise, the second one was written and published. Having concluded that a literary form is doomed to extinction—an extinction that will be hastened precisely by the production of new instances of that form—what does a writer do? Continue writing and publishing? Forswear the form, in the hope of extending its life even by a little bit? After claiming in 1889 that the haiku's end was rapidly approaching, and even after reiterating that assertion in 1892 in even stronger terms, Shiki continued writing haiku.

Later in the same year as his *Talks from the Otter's Den* (1892), Shiki wrote in his notebook 102 haiku on the theme of beggary. These were among the first haiku he wrote after publishing the installment of *Talks from the Otter's Den* that included the prediction of the haiku's extinction. One of these haiku was the following:

wrapping around the beggar
rolling him up
autumn gusts

kotsujiki no / fukimakuraruru / nowake kana

乞食の吹きまくらるゝ野分哉

(Masaoka 1975–78, 3:518)

Far from seeming a poem by a poet who believes the form in which he is working is soon to be irretrievably lost, this verse displays the many arrows still remaining in Shiki's quiver. The *kigo* and the *kireji* alike are saved for the final five *moji*: *nowake* (or *nowaki*), as suggested by the translation "autumn gusts," indicates the season; *kana* cuts the poem off. The middle seven *moji* of the poem are occupied entirely by the sole verb, *fukimakuraruru*, a passive form of *fukimakuru*, which can mean "blow incessantly, bluster." (*Fukimakuru* is a combination of two verbs: *fuki* from *fuku*, meaning "blow" as of wind; and *makuru*, which can mean "roll something up.") There are two nouns in the poem, one before and one after the verb: in the first five *moji* there is the noun *kotsujiki*, "beggar"; in the last five *moji* there is the noun *nowake*, literally "the meadow-splitter," a word meaning a powerful and relentless late autumn wind.[13] The passive verb in the middle of the poem modifies the noun *nowake*, yielding a literal translation somewhat like the following:

> O autumn gusts by which the beggar is buffeted/enveloped

The use of the possessive particle *no* instead of the (grammatically also possible) particle *ga* after *kotsujiki* seems, at least to this reader, to tighten the bond between the beggar and the meadow-splitting wind: it is as if the wind itself were his primary, his identifying possession.

Shiki was not the only writer to assert the finitude of the haiku form. The haiku poet and politician Mori Mukō 森無黄 (1864–1942), writing in *Yomiuri shinbun* in August 1890 as Mori Sankei 森三渓, also invoked the notion of a mathematical limit on the number of possible haiku (Tuck 2018, 238n3). In the same month, and in the same publication, the poet Maeda Ringai 前田林外 (1864–1946) wrote the multi-installment "A Description of the Incompatibilities between *kanshi*, *waka*, and *shintaishi*, Including a Consideration of *haikai*" (Kanshi waka shintaishi no aiirezaru jōkyō o joshite haikai ni oyobu 漢詩和歌新体詩の相容れざる状況を叙して俳諧に及ぶ). Ringai, too, asserted that he was aware of claims that the *waka*, being allegedly out of joint with the times, was doomed to extinction (Maeda R. [1890] 1973, 427). Ringai took a more sanguine view of the *haikai*, which, he claimed, was "the poetry of the present time" (428; genzai no shifu 現在の詩賦). For contrast, Ringai explained, the *waka* and the *kanshi* had remained unchanged for generations, and as such could not be "a poetry of commoners, a universal poetry, a Japanese poetry, a uniquely Eastern poetry" (428).[14]

Robert Tuck has analyzed the idea of "a poetry of commoners"—*heiminteki shifu*—as a notion that had unstable and contested outlines in the 1890s. Tuck quotes several writers who, despite their disagreements over the details, "all shared the view that *haikai* was, for better or worse, a genre with a special connection to the common people of Japan" (Tuck 2018, 121). However, Tuck adds, "for Shiki, the notion of 'commoner literature' was a contradiction in terms; if everyone could compose and appreciate haiku, then it would become diluted to the point where it ceased to be literature" (122).

The word *literature* in that pronouncement has a particular freight: as many commentators have noted in recent decades, the notion of literature was undergoing a sea change in late nineteenth-century Japan.[15] This could be seen, for example, in the new genre of scholarly texts known as *bungakushi*, histories of literature (*bungaku*)—a prominent early example of which was Mikami Sanji 三上参次 (1865–1939) and Takatsu Kuwasaburō's 高津鍬三郎 (1864–1921) *History of Japanese Literature* (*Nihon bungakushi* 日本文学史, 1890). Mikami and Takatsu defined the field of Japanese literature capaciously, lumping together medieval tales, ancient poetry anthologies, several varieties of writing for the stage, and many others in a single broad category.[16] That category (*bungaku*) unambiguously included the haiku (or *haikai*), but Mikami and Takatsu acknowledged that skeptics might question its inclusion ([1890] 1982, 400). Putting such questions to rest in his *Haikai taiyō* 俳諧大要 (The elements of *haikai*), serialized in October–December 1895 in *Nippon*, Shiki pronounced unequivocally that the haiku was literature.[17] After a brief introductory note, Shiki began his text with the proclamation:

> Haiku belongs to literature. Literature belongs to the arts. Therefore, the standards of beauty are the standards of literature. The standards of literature are the standards of haiku. That is, painting, sculpture, music, drama, poetry and fiction—all should be judged by the same standards. (Masaoka [1895] 2001, 262; translation at Morris 1985, 289)

The standards Shiki mentioned here, as Tuck persuasively argues, excluded all but a relatively small number of privileged, educated readers. As Shiki and other writers presumed, a *heimin*, a "common citizen," should know and admire Japanese literature (*bungaku*). But what was literature? Public debate centered, too, on the place of *bungaku* or "literature" in Japan as a modern nation. That debate over literariness in Japan was being conducted even as foreign critics were, for the first time, evaluating the merits of Japanese literature.

A Transnational Dispute over the Literary Worth of Short Japanese Poetic Forms

In the months leading up to the publication of Shiki's *Haikai taiyō*, two writers—one Japanese, one German—had published an exchange of essays, "the first controversy in comparative literature in Japan" (Tsuji 2012, 715), in which they disputed the value of haiku as literature. The terms of this debate illuminate how Japanese literature was perceived abroad, as well as how writers in Japan were marshalling their resources to mount a defense of Japanese literature against the disparagements of critics (Japanese but also European). Early in 1895 a literary journal called *Teikoku bungaku* 帝国文学 (Imperial literature) began publication under the auspices of the College of Letters of Imperial University (later, Tokyo Imperial).[18] It was in the pages of this journal that Ueda Kazutoshi 上田萬年 (1867–1937), then a professor of linguistics at Imperial University, and Karl Florenz (1865–1939), a German who had been teaching German language and literature at Imperial University since 1889, conducted their debate, which hinged on their differing notions of literariness.[19]

In late 1894, Florenz had published a translation anthology of Japanese poems titled *Dichtergrüsse aus dem Osten: Japanische Dichtungen* (*Poetical Greetings from the Far East: Japanese Poems*). In his translation, Florenz gave nearly every poem a title; nearly every line is in iambic pentameter, sometimes hypercatalectic (with an extra syllable at the end of the line); and his German versions rhymed. The anthology began with a prefatory comment about the principle of selection: the main difficulty of selecting Japanese poems to translate, for Florenz, lay not in the poetic vocabulary—although that did pose a difficulty, he acknowledged—but in the strangeness, for a European reader, of the entire Japanese poetic culture. Florenz's text began:

> Japanese poetry is extraordinarily rich in productions of the most varied kind, and one might therefore think that it is only necessary to put one's hand upon what is considered good by the Japanese themselves, and then to arrange the material with very little trouble into an anthology. But this is not so. The great majority of Japanese poems is of such a kind that very little remains if they are divested of their specifically Japanese expressions, especially as most of them have the brevity of aphorisms. The form outweighs the contents. . . . The translation is on the whole as accurate as the fundamental differences between the spirit of the Japanese and German languages would allow; the notes contain only such information as is absolutely necessary. (1896, 5–6; [1894] 1896, 3–4)

What Florenz might have meant by "specifically Japanese expressions" is not entirely clear—one would imagine that *all* the words in the originals were Japanese expressions. His use of that phrase is of a piece, I would say, with his assertion that there existed "fundamental differences between the spirit of the Japanese and German languages": he seems to have believed, with many nineteenth-century nationalists, that languages were repositories of national traits. As a German, therefore, Florenz should expect to be puzzled by the Japanese language.

Ueda published a brief review of Florenz's anthology, faulting it for misrepresenting the original texts on multiple grounds. Ueda offered two specific examples, in which he compared Florenz's German version with the Japanese original. The first was the following:

Florenz translates the haiku "The fallen blossom returns to the branch: a butterfly" [rakka e ni / kaeru to mireba / kochō kana 落花枝にかへる と見れば胡蝶かな] as

> Augentäuschung
> Wie? schwebt die Blüte, die eben fiel,
> Schon wieder zum Zweig am Baum zurück?
> Das wäre fürwahr ein seltsam Ding!
> Ich näherte mich und schärfte den Blick—
> Da fand ich—es war nur ein Schmetterling.
> (Ueda K. 1895, 98)[20]

Ueda noted with disbelief that the haiku had been expanded into a poem five lines long. Ueda then retranslated the German into a Japanese prose paraphrase, to comical effect. Ueda followed this example with another—a haiku that Florenz had expanded to a *six*-line poem in German—and commented in exasperation: "Is not this translation far removed from the poor, unfortunate original? . . . I humbly ask the translators of the world whether there is no way to translate this poem as two lines" (99).

In the following issue of *Teikoku bungaku*, in March 1895, Florenz published in Japanese a rejoinder to Ueda's review titled "A Comparison of the Spirit of Japanese Poetry and the Spirit of European Poetry" (Nihon shiika no seishin to ōshū shiika no seishin to no hikaku kō 日本詩歌の精神と欧州詩歌の精神との比較考). Florenz's apologia ran to seventeen pages, explaining his method of translation and defending his choices, while at the same time impugning the quality of Japanese poetry. Near the beginning of the essay, Florenz mentioned the successes of the Japanese navy—there was no need to specify that these successes were against the Chinese, in what is now called the First Sino-Japanese War (1894–95)—and asserted that Japan's military victories had rightly earned the world's admiration (1895a, 1). He went on, however, to lament the fact that Japan's military fame far outstripped its reputation for culture: "Despite the [Japanese people's] antiquity and the abundance of their erudition, they have occupied hitherto but an extremely low rank in world literature [*sekai bungaku*]" (2). The first reason for the low regard in which Japanese literature was held, Florenz claimed, was the Tokugawa-period policy of *sakoku* or isolationism: Japanese literature had not been circulated outside Japan, and therefore European readers could not be expected to understand Japanese literary standards—or to appreciate Japanese literature. The second reason, according to Florenz, was the difficulty of translating Japanese into European languages—a difficulty that stemmed from features of the Japanese language.

Florenz then raised a question about translation, probing the very possibility of rendering Japanese literary language in another tongue:

> Here a question arises: Can a Japanese poem [*nihon shiika*], by means of a suitable translation into a European language—say, German—call up in a German person the same sentiments as the original does in a Japanese? I would answer yes and no. (3)

To explain his ambivalence, Florenz provided a brief overview of his philosophy of translation. Following the German poet Johann Wolfgang von Goethe, Florenz held that there are three types of translation: the first is a prose paraphrase; the second tailors the source text for the comprehension of the target language audience; the third, which approaches a word-for-word, literal translation (*chikujiyaku* 逐字訳), aspires to "take the place of" the original.[21] To achieve the third variety of translation, the translator must "discard the predilections of nationality" (*waga kokumin no tokusei o sutsuru*) in their own language and create "a new style, of sorts," to represent the original text as nearly as possible (4). Florenz concluded that "of these three methods of translation, only the third perfectly conveys the thought of the original" (4).

Having explained his views of translation, Florenz mounted a critique of Japanese poetry. He acknowledged that Japanese poetry is filled with wordplay—*jiguchi rōgo* 地口弄語 (which referred, as the context suggests, to *kakekotoba* or "pivot words," i.e., puns)—but asserted also the following: "Westerners do not enjoy wordplay less than do the Japanese, but they certainly do not treat it as poetic language, and in fact avoid it altogether in the best literature [*kōtō bungaku* 高等文学]" (6). The next great problem that beset Japanese poetry, in Florenz's view, was its brevity. Florenz pronounced forcefully on this point:

> The tanka and the *tanku* [i.e., haiku] have restricted the range of Japanese poetry, and that has been the single worst disaster for Japanese literature [*nihon bungaku no ichidai saiyaku* 日本文学の一大災阨]. . . . I say this with the utmost conviction: the reputation of Japanese literature

would gain far more from the translation of a hundred *chōka* than from the translation of ten thousand tanka. (6)

Florenz's anthology did provide translations of *chōka*, and in his tanka translations he amplified and lengthened the poems seemingly wherever possible, to the point that, as Judit Árokay has written, it is "almost impossible to identify which Japanese poem" was the original of any given translation (2017, 16).

For Florenz, brevity posed a fundamental difficulty: it was incompatible with poetry. He held this to be true of German verse, too, as he made clear in his later "Response to Professor Ueda" (Ueda bungakushi ni kotau 上田文学士に答ふ). In this article Florenz acknowledged that although in his initial rejoinder to Ueda he had suggested that Germans did not write short poems, in fact there existed in German a form of verse called *Klapphornvers* (four-line rhyming poems). But Florenz insisted that the *Klapphornvers*, although it had been recognized in "ordinary literary histories," tended to be "indecent" and, as such, had not been highly esteemed and would eventually, and deservedly, fade from view (1895b, 71). By contrast, Ueda, as we have seen in his first review of Florenz's anthology, deemed Florenz's translations too long to give the reader an accurate impression of the originals. Ueda had not elaborated on his reasons for wishing the translations shorter; he had not, for example, invoked a criterion such as the economy of mental energy to which Shiki had alluded in his description of the haiku. Against Ueda, however, Florenz asserted that a poet in a Western language simply would not write such short poetry:

> If we think of the implications of Goethe's third type of translation, we must ask whether it would be necessary to translate a short original as a short poem. . . . I acknowledge that a translation [of a short original] should be as brief as the spirit of the [target] language allows [*kokugo no seishin no yurusu kagiri*]. But I cannot agree with the objection Ueda has raised. The reason is that in Western literature, strictly speaking, such short poetry does not exist. There are verses that are composed of linked couplets, but poems of this sort tend to fall into the narrow category of didactic verse: moral proverbs, aesthetic maxims, apothegms, satirical epigrams. The majority of critics do not regard such verses as true poetry. (Florenz 1895a, 7)

Florenz then alluded to an earlier German translator of Japanese *waka*, Rudolf Lange (1850–1933), who had rendered the Japanese originals into distichs (*disuchikku* ヂスチック): in Florenz's opinion, Lange's translations were failures, not simply because Lange lacked poetic genius (*shisai ni kakuru tokoro* 詩才に欠る所) but precisely because he had translated the *waka* into two-line poems (8).[22] This was the length (two lines) Ueda had proposed as a better rendering of the Japanese haiku; Florenz believed, though, that translations as brief as Lange's were exposed to the very criticisms he had leveled against the originals.[23]

Here I should say something about the lineation of Japanese poems in translation, a matter that informs the debate between Florenz and Ueda. In chapter 1, I mentioned the term *ku*, which names any five- or seven-*moji* subdivision of a metrically regular Japanese poem. For example, a regular haiku, then, has three *ku* (5-7-5). Sometimes, however, *ku* assumes another meaning, as seen in the phrases *kami no ku* 上の句 (upper *ku*) and *shimo no ku* 下の句 (lower *ku*). *Kami no ku* refers by convention to the 5-7-5 beginning of a *waka*, while *shimo no ku* refers to the concluding 7-7 doublet.[24] To Florenz's displeasure, Lange had translated *waka* as distichs, as we have seen. Lange's reason for doing so, as he stated in the preface to his translation, was precisely to render visible each poem's division into *kami no ku* and *shimo no ku* (1884, xviii). Now, haiku, too, are sometimes said to be divided into a *kami no ku* (the first five-*moji* phrase) and a *shimo no ku* (the remaining 7-5), but neither Florenz nor Ueda mentioned that convention in their exchange. Ueda's above-cited recommendation that haiku be translated into couplets was probably motivated not by the structure of haiku but by a belief—which Ueda did not state explicitly—about poems in European languages: a text that does not have at least two lines is not a poem. Florenz, for his part, seems to have been working from a different assumption: the fewer the lines, the worse the poem.

Ueda had concluded his original review of Florenz's anthology with a recommendation: readers should consult Basil Hall Chamberlain's 1880 text *The Classical Poetry of the Japanese*, which offered, Ueda suggested, more satisfactory translations of Japanese poetry. Chamberlain (1850–1935), a professor of Japanese languages at Imperial University in Tokyo (Ueda had been one of his students), played an important role as a shaper of the Anglophone reception of Japanese literary culture. *The Classical Poetry of the Japanese* begins with a long prefatory essay, the first sentence of which is: "The current impression that the Japanese are a nation of imitators is in the main correct" (1). Chamberlain recognized one exception to this generalization: Japanese poetry, which struck him as being the "one original product of the Japanese mind" (2). Even so, that original product, as Chamberlain believed, had "preserved down to our own times the unaltered form and the almost unaltered substance of the earliest manifestation of Japanese thought"—in other words, without subsequent development or further originality (2).

Ueda did not explain why he preferred Chamberlain's anthology to Florenz's. Given that Ueda deemed fidelity (at least as regards length) an important criterion of translation quality, we might expect to find, based on Ueda's preference, that Chamberlain's translations tended to be shorter than Florenz's. It is generally the case that Chamberlain's renderings were shorter than Florenz's, but apparently not because Chamberlain approved of brevity. Chamberlain himself wrote unfavorably of the "lilliputian limits" of Japanese poetry (Chamberlain 1880, 4n), offering an example of a *waka* transliterated into roman letters:

Momiji-ba wo
Kaze ni makasete
Miru yori mo
Hakanaki mono ha
Inochi nari keri.

(4n)

As this sample shows, Chamberlain lineated his transliterations according to divisions between each five- or seven-*moji ku*. Chamberlain's translation appeared later in the text:

One thing, alas! more fleeting have I seen
Than wither'd leaves driv'n by the autumn gust:
Yea, evanescent as the whirling dust
Is man's brief passage o'er this mortal scene!

(129)

(This is *Kokinshū* poem 16:859.) The four lines in iambic pentameter of Chamberlain's English translation came nearer to matching the thirty-one *moji* of the Japanese original than did Florenz's translation of the haiku about the leaf and the butterfly, and on the whole Chamberlain's versions did tend to be brief. Perhaps this was why Ueda preferred Chamberlain's English versions of the Japanese originals.

The fact is that when Ueda and Florenz were debating matters of Japanese poetry translation, there existed few book-length collections of Japanese poetry in European languages.[25] The bulk of available translations, few as they were, had included *waka* almost exclusively.[26] One early translator who went unmentioned in the Ueda-Florenz debate was Frederick Victor Dickins (1838–1915), a physician who lived a number of years in Japan and rendered into English such Japanese works as *Chūshingura* and *Taketori monogatari* (*Tale of the Bamboo-cutter*) (both in 1875).[27] In his 1866 translation of another noted work, the thirteenth-century *waka* anthology *Hyak Nin Is'shiu* (that is, *Hyakunin isshu*)—"the first Japanese book translated in its entirety into English" (Horton 2018, 124)—Dickins called the poems "odes" but did not dwell upon their brevity. Dickins did, however, disparage the Japanese originals as "pretty" and "popular":

> The Odes of which the following translation is offered in no way lay claim to any high poetic merit, and are but prettily and somewhat cleverly-rendered metrical expressions of pretty but ordinary sentiments. But, whatever their intrinsic value may be, they are extremely popular with the Japanese, and on that account rather than for any literary merit they may possess, have I ventured to offer this English version of them to the public. (1866, viii–ix)

Dickins's translations varied in length—some as short as four lines, some as long as eight—and tended to rhyme, as in the following translation of *Hyakunin isshu* poem 56:

> Ere long for me this world shall end,
>   Thus doth my mind to me foretell;
> Ere long to other world shall wend
>   My soul that thee hath lov'd so well.
>   Ah! would that thou
>   But once more wer't beside me now.
>
>   (30)

The addenda to Dickins's *Hyak Nin Is'shiu* included a vocabulary and a transliteration of each poem into roman letters. Dickins also provided what he called "literal versions" of the poems, in case a meaning had been lost in the rhymed and metered version. These translations were in unlineated prose, as in the following "literal version" of the same poem:

> The thought arises in me of going to a world other than this, which shall soon be not. O that I might once more now meet thee.
>
>   (Appendix, xi)

This version of the poem, we might observe, happens to have thirty-one syllables.

Dickins did not anticipate a warm reception for his anthology. The originals themselves, Dickins asserted, did not have "any high poetic merit." Yet the ubiquity of the poems among Japanese readers was something Dickins granted outright, as Dickins's preface to the collection averred: "The Odes of

which I have endeavoured in the following pages to give an English render-
ing are familiar in every Japanese household, high and low" (1866, v). The
assertion that "every Japanese household" knew the poems was, apparently,
Dickins's whole justification for undertaking the translation.

While Dickins disparaged Japanese poetry as pretty, Chamberlain dispar-
aged the *waka*'s brevity, describing the poetry of *Kokin waka shū* in the fol-
lowing terms:

> It consists almost entirely of the short thirty-one-syllable stanzas. . . .
> This stanza, after having, during the ages that witnessed the produc-
> tion of the poems contained in the old histories and in the "Myriad
> Leaves" [i.e., *Man'yōshū*], struggled against the longer form which was
> then also in common use, drove the latter out of the field, and has ever
> since remained the favourite metre of a people, who, in every species
> of composition, consider brevity to be the soul of wit. (1880, 12)

The "longer form" to which Chamberlain referred was the *chōka*; the eclipse
of the *chōka* by the *waka* had dealt a blow to Japanese poetry, in Chamber-
lain's view. Where Dickins had ranked the verses of *Hyakunin isshu* low in
"literary merit" and "intrinsic value," however, Chamberlain counseled
against hasty conclusions: he asserted that Japanese poetry "has been more
often judged than studied" (2). Chamberlain's opinion, significantly, was that
"Japanese poetry" was a branch of "Japanese literature" (8). That the poetry
should be regarded as literature was not in doubt, for Chamberlain.

Among the early European translators of Japanese poetry, it was perhaps
the French scholar Léon de Rosny (1837–1914)—a noted anthropologist and
ethnographer of East Asian as well as South American cultures—who took
the most favorable view of his source texts. In the preface to his 1871 *Antholo-
gie japonaise: Poésies anciennes et modernes des insulaires du Nippon* (Japanese
anthology: ancient and modern poems of the islands of Japan), Rosny wrote
of how he came to appreciate Japanese poetry:

> On reading the works of Japanese poetry that I have in my collection,
> my first impression was that this otherwise so abundant literature was
> completely lacking in poetry, and that what they called "poetry" was
> only anthologies of more or less tasteless wordplays. . . . [But my]
> further studies have led me to grant that, in general, Japanese poetry
> should not be compared with Indo-European poetry, which differs in
> the most essential traits—form, spirit [*génie*], even purpose; and that, in
> its most outstanding exemplars, [Japanese poetry] does not deserve to
> be disparaged as mere trifling wit; and that it is suitable for expressing

the soul's great feelings, and that it expresses them in a fashion that is
no less powerful and convincing for being short [*laconique*]. (1871, i–iii)

The *waka* was described by Rosny in the following terms:

> The Japanese national verses, called *uta* or "songs"—not to be confused
> with the poetry called *shi*, which are composed according to the Chi-
> nese system—are merely simple distichs. These distichs, which may
> not include foreign words, must develop a complete idea in thirty-one
> syllables made up of two lines. (xv)

About the passages I have just cited, I will make two observations. First,
Rosny, like Lange after him, regarded the division into *kami no ku* and *shimo
no ku* as an important structuring principle of the *waka*. As we will see in an
example below, Rosny's concession to this conventional division quite liter-
ally shaped his renderings of the poems. Second, Rosny evidently anticipated,
and wished to forestall, the comparison a translator like Florenz would later
make, between Japanese and European forms of poetry. On the basis of such
a comparison, a translator would likely disparage Japanese verses as being
too brief for adequate poetic expression, and therefore Rosny advised against
making such comparisons in the first place.

In a brief 1878 selection of his new *waka* translations, Rosny commented
that his 1871 *Anthologie* had met with unexpected acclaim. Unexpected
because, as Rosny put it, "these distichs, so esteemed in the Far East, were
endowed with few of the traits we seek in the verses of all times and places"
(1878, 3). What he meant by "traits we seek in the verses of all times and
places" ("qualités que nous recherchons dans les compositions versifiées de
tous les temps et de tous les climats"), Rosny did not specify. He never sug-
gested that the poems were in need of padding, nor does he appear to have
added to his translations the sought-after poetic traits to which he alluded.
In his 1871 *Anthologie* and in his shorter 1878 pamphlet alike, he presented
each poem as follows: first, a title; then the poem in Japanese hiragana, with
a break to show the division between the *kami no ku* and the *shimo no ku*;
then a transliteration, divided into two lines—again showing the division of
the *ku*; then an unlineated prose translation. These textual features may have
been aimed at students of Japanese—Rosny did teach Japanese language—
but they were also a means of conveying the original clearly. Each *moji* was
represented (albeit at the expense of the ideographs); the lineation showed a
crucial structural principle of the poem; the transliteration conveyed vowel
lengths and other elements of pronunciation; and the translations generally
hewed closely to the meaning of the originals. Improving on Japanese poetry

SUR LA LUNE

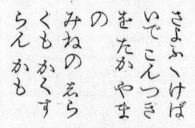

Sayô fukeba ide-koṇ tsŭki-wo taka yama-no
Mine-no sira kumo kakusuran ka mo [1] ?

 E blanc nuage qui passe sur le pic de la haute moṅtagne cachera-t-il donc la lune qui apparaît au milieu de la nuit?

Cette petite pièce de vers a été composée par *Kaki-no Moto-no Asoṇ ʎito-maro.*

---

1. *Man-yô-siù ryak-kaï,* vol. X, part. 2, fᵛ 43.

FIGURE 3. Léon de Rosny's *waka* anthology: Rosny's prose French translation of *Man'yōshū* poem 10:2332 happens to be a thirty-one-syllable match on the original. A translation of Rosny's French would read "And so is the white cloud that passes over the peak of the high mountains going to hide the moon that appears in the center of the night?" The text underneath provides the name of the poet, using special symbols to convey nuances of pronunciation. Source: Rosny 1871, 24.

was not on Rosny's agenda.[28] I have not ascertained whether Ueda knew of Rosny's work, but I wonder whether Ueda would have been pleased with it. Florenz would not have been.

If the poets of *Shintaishi shō* had known of Rosny's work and had critically engaged with his favorable views of Japanese poetry, might the history of Japanese poetry have unfolded differently? I beg my reader's patience as I indulge in a paragraph's worth of speculation. Contrary to claims made by Chamberlain and reiterated in different terms by Florenz, Rosny asserted that Japanese poetry should not be compared with the poetries of European languages. Japanese poetry, Rosny claimed, should not be expected to supply European readers with what it was never intended to supply. From a claim such as Rosny's, it is not far to arrive at the assertion that Japanese poetry should not be expected to provide even Japanese readers anything other than what it had already been providing them. The *Shintaishi shō* anthologists' dissatisfactions with the shorter forms of Japanese verse shaped the tone of subsequent discourse about Japanese poetry. But the anthologists might have set a different tone. Instead of taking the existence of a different kind of lyric poetry in the putatively more advanced West as evidence that Japanese poetry was intrinsically defective, the *Shintaishi shō* compilers might have placed greater emphasis on the sheer excitement of discovering a new method of poetry composition: a form to supplement the already attested forms of Japanese poetry, not to supplant them.

There is no evidence that Shiki himself knew of the debate between Florenz and Ueda, or knew Florenz personally (M. Satō 1995, 60–64). Nevertheless, the Florenz-Ueda debate clarifies one of the meanings of Shiki's assertion that haiku was part of literature: he was asserting that the term *bungaku* (literature), newfangled as it was, could be applied to very short texts of ancient provenance.[29] Seen in a multinational context, that assertion, applied to the haiku, was most unusual. Recent commentaries have emphasized the novelty of Shiki's assertion that the haiku was *literature*,[30] and I agree that the shift toward a new understanding of the term *literature* was one of the pivotal episodes in modern Japanese cultural history. For our purposes, though, it is important to imagine that Shiki would have emphasized a different word in that assertion: even *haiku* was literature. For Shiki, it was crucial to secure a place for brevity in any notion of literariness. There were observers, some of them in positions of authority (such as Florenz, with his professorship at the premier Japanese university), who argued otherwise. Against those who maintained that literariness was incompatible with brevity, Shiki promoted the haiku as a form whose brevity was one of its desirable traits. The *shintaishi* had been invented to give Japanese poets more expansive lyric possibilities; Shiki riposted that brevity alone was no sufficient ground for rejecting the haiku.

Variation from Sameness: Shiki's Haiku

To conclude this chapter with a poem: in *Kainan shinbun* (a local newspaper in Shiki's native Matsuyama, Ehime Prefecture) on October 22, 1895—the same day as he published the first installment of *Haikai taiyō* in *Nippon*, famously pronouncing the haiku to be literature—Shiki published the following haiku:

how heavy they hang on the mountain of masts
the autumn gusts

hobashira no / yama ni motaruru / nowake kana

帆柱の山にもたるゝ野分かな

(Masaoka 1975–78, 2:305)

The last five *moji* of this haiku match the last five *moji* of the 1892 haiku about the beggar quoted above; the final two *moji* of the poem's midsection, *ruru*, also match. The first five *moji* here, *hobashira no*, invite comparison with the phrase *kotsujiki no* that begins that earlier poem: in both cases, a four-*moji* noun is followed by the possessive particle *no*. All in all, the later poem repeats, in exactly the same positions, eight of the seventeen *moji* of the earlier poem: just under half the poem.

The two haiku have other similarities if we also consider their syntax. In each poem, the first twelve *moji* all modify the word *nowake*, which therefore seems to be the poem's culmination or central focus. If the earlier poem seemed to call on so many noteworthy stylistic devices, what shall a reader think of this later poem, which resembles the earlier one so much? Whatever else one might conclude from juxtaposing the earlier poem involving the beggar with the later poem about the mountain of masts, one would have to acknowledge that the reuse of diction was an element of Shiki's style.

There are also intriguing differences between these poems. One difference is that the later haiku is notably ambiguous. What is meant, precisely, by "mountain of masts," *hobashira no yama*? The first thing to observe, here, is that there are mountains called Hobashira-yama, in Fukuoka Prefecture; perhaps a topographical allusion has been embedded in the poem. But the particle *no* intervenes between the two parts of that toponym, suggesting that the allusion, even if present, is not the primary or only freight of the words *hobashira no yama*.[31]

The particle *no* has multiple possible functions, two of which seem germane in the context of this poem: possession and apposition. If the *no* indicates possession broadly construed, then one interpretation of *hobashira no yama* would be "(the) mountain(s) of (the) mast(s)." The meaning even of this uncomplicated phrase is not immediately clear: it might refer to a gathering of ships, perhaps. Or it might be referring to a forest: wood that will be used for making masts eventually. But if the *no* indicates apposition, then *hobashira no yama* could mean "the mast that the mountain is": a mountain so angular and so high that it appears a mast in comparison to the surrounding landscape; or a chain of such mountains, perhaps. Notice that these renderings of *hobashira no yama* take the poem in quite different directions: Is the prospect one of ships, or one of mountains? At what exactly are we looking? The poem is so brief that additional clues—supplementary words that, in a longer text, might nudge us toward preferring one interpretation to the other—cannot be included, with the result that the phrase *hobashira no yama* leaves a reader in permanent suspense.

Translation theorists have commented on the snares set by short poems. The translation scholar Peter Robinson has written, "'the poetry' [of any poem] in so far as it is translatable . . . is in the relations between the parts"— and brevity can make it difficult for a translator to determine those relations (2010, 149). With a phrase like *hobashira no yama*, it is, I believe, difficult even to determine what the parts are—and that is to say nothing of translating the relation between them into English. "Translators of poetry will have a sense of this," Robinson continues, "if when rendering the lines of a short poem they feel that . . . it is incumbent upon them to try and render the order not of the words but of the sequenced revelation of sense units—implying thus that at least some of the poetry is in the ordering of this information release" (149). I have rendered *hobashira no yama* as "mountain of masts," reordering two crucial words in this brief poem (*hobashira* means "mast," *yama* means "mountain"). I cannot claim that "mountain's mast" would be less preferable—it would entail the same reversal as "mountain of masts." "Mast(s) of the mountain(s)" has the attraction of replicating the sequence of the words in Japanese. It seems that what has led me to prefer "mountain of masts" is its rhythm, which rounds out an anapestic tetrameter with the first syllable omitted:

how héavy they háng on the móuntain of másts

But the second line is iambic dimeter (the áutumn gústs). The translation I have offered here is provisional at best.

Although the two poems that end in *nowake kana* may seem similar on first acquaintance, a closer inspection reveals that the poems, brief as they are, differ considerably. Even the cutting word *kana* is written differently: in one poem, it is written phonetically; in the other, it is written as a single ideograph.[32] The juxtaposition of these two poems, which might seem to make them less interesting ("They're 47.06% identical!"), has had the perhaps surprising effect, in this reader's view, of bringing their differences into the open, widening the disparity between them. Shiki was right not to dwell too much on the potential troubles facing the haiku form, whose finitude, once he discovered it and broadcast it in his published criticism, did not stop him from composing more verses. His own finitude weighed more heavily on him: he had developed symptoms of tuberculosis as early as 1889, and his attempt to serve as a war correspondent in the First Sino-Japanese War in 1894–95 had worsened his health considerably. He died in 1902, shortly before his thirty-fifth birthday, and did not live to see the great changes soon to transform Japanese poetry utterly.

CHAPTER 4

Difficulty in Poetry

Kanbara Ariake and the Experimenters in Prosody

Writing of the Japanese symbolist poet Kanbara Ariake 蒲原有明 (1876–1952) in 1907, the poet and critic Yone Noguchi (1875–1947)—his Japanese name was Noguchi Yonejirō 野口米次郎, but when he wrote in English (as he often did) he shortened his first name and followed English name order—took an ambivalent view of Ariake's poetic accomplishments:

> Some critic said that Mallarmé was obscure, not so much because he wrote differently, as because he thought differently, from other people. Now I should like to say the same thing of Kanbara. He thinks with the Western minds. How many people in Japan could understand Rossetti and Mallarmé? (1907, 60)

There is a pot-and-kettle quality to Noguchi's description of Ariake: Noguchi was already ten years into his career as a bilingual writer in both Japanese and English. The fact that he of all people would characterize Ariake as "think[ing] with the Western minds" is thus deeply ironic. Yet by trading on his familiarity with contemporary writings both in Japanese and in European languages (English and French)—as he did in this article—Noguchi was also signaling the reliability of his assertions about Ariake's work.[1]

In the comment I have cited above, Noguchi did not intend to imply the Japaneseness of the French poet Stéphane Mallarmé (1842–98), a major figure in French symbolism, or of the English painter-poet Dante Gabriel Rossetti (1828–82). Rather, what Noguchi was asserting was the difficulty of Ariake's verse. Like Mallarmé, Ariake "thought differently from other people"—from other *Japanese* people, Noguchi stopped just short of saying. The claim that "[Ariake] thinks with the Western minds" was unambiguous enough on that point, in any case. Noguchi did not entirely approve of the poetry that Ariake created by thinking differently from his contemporaries: Ariake "is a genius," Noguchi wrote, "but his enemy is himself; he has too much restraint, a certain heaviness, unmistakeable [*sic*] difficulty with his lines" (59). Noguchi's essay is a feast of quotable phrases—I will cite him again: "He [*sc.*, Ariake] is not a free bird who sings to a star; he is a caged nightingale who is obliged to sing. . . . His mind is too systematic; he is a mathematician" (58).

Although Noguchi did not specify the identity of "some critic," he was drawing liberally, and sometimes even quoting verbatim, from Arthur Symons's *The Symbolist Movement in Literature* (1899). For example, Noguchi adapted Symons's statement that "Mallarmé was obscure, not so much because he wrote differently, as because he thought differently, from other people" (Symons [1899] 2014, 61), applying it wholesale to Ariake. Symons's text had not yet been translated into Japanese—a translation would be published in 1913, by a poet named Iwano Hōmei (whom we will see again below)—but Noguchi and other Japanese writers were already aware of Symons's work and of European symbolism more generally. (Noguchi's 1914 book *The Spirit of Japanese Poetry* would be dedicated to Symons.) As the allusion to Symons suggests, Noguchi regarded Ariake as a symbolist, and he was not alone in doing so. What is intriguing is that Noguchi suggested both that Ariake was a symbolist and that his very symbolism made him un-Japanese. As we will see below, much of the debate over Japanese symbolism centered on the extent to which that movement should be considered Japanese or un-Japanese.

Symbolism, a transnational literary movement generally said to have begun in France in the second half of the nineteenth century, has inspired many works of analysis and criticism at a degree of detail that cannot be attempted here, but a quick summary may be useful. Symbolism was a cluster of styles and critical tendencies that favored indirectness and obscurity, as opposed to the descriptive overtness of realism and naturalism, against which symbolism was perceived as a reaction. For a symbolist, reality was not empirical; it was rather subjective, and therefore something that language could only suggest, never fully convey.[2] Most accurately regarded as a movement that made inroads into many different literatures and languages over a span of several decades, symbolism left its deepest mark on Japanese literature in the first decade of the twentieth century, especially—as it had done in other languages—on poetry.[3] The Japanese poets whose works form the primary textual archive of this chapter—Ueda Bin 上田敏 (1874–1916), Susukida Kyūkin 薄田泣菫 (1877–1945), and most importantly Kanbara Ariake—were all either regarded as or associated with symbolists. The proximate reasons for that association are matters of critical consensus. Bin introduced the term *symbolism* (in its narrow sense) in Japanese and published important translations of European symbolist poems,[4] while Kyūkin and Ariake wrote about symbolism and were regarded, by contemporary critics and later readers alike, as symbolist poets, largely because their poetry was seen as difficult: difficult in point of vocabulary, challenging in point of poetic form.

The fact that there were Japanese poets who were and are dubbed symbolists—in Japanese, *shōchōha* 象徴派 (the symbolist group)—is not open to question.[5] What is open to question is why symbolism took root in Japanese poetry at all. The same question can be raised about other literatures to which symbolist ideas spread: as Anna Balakian wrote of (what she argued were) the roots of European symbolism, "It is strange that, in the midst of the Age of Enlightenment, such [ideas as we find in symbolism] should have become a popular philosophy" (1977, 14). That sentence is about an eighteenth-century thinker (Emanuel Swedenborg, 1688–1772) and his influence on poets in the early nineteenth century. Extending Balakian's line of thinking, it would therefore be even stranger that in the (one would suppose) even more rationalized final decades of the nineteenth century, a hermetic, inwardly facing literary movement like symbolism should attract the interest and energies of some of the most highly regarded writers of the time. In France and elsewhere in Europe there was the phenomenon of fin-de-siècle decadence, which may have added to the allure of the more skeptical and negative overtones of symbolism; but in Japan the years of peak symbolism occurred during the first decade of the twentieth century. Sakamaki Kōji, a scholar of Japanese symbolism, has observed that symbolism in both France and Japan arose in times of social turmoil: in France, the period of symbolism embraced the Franco-Prussian War (1870–71), the Paris Commune (1871), Boulangisme (1886–89), the Panama corruption scandals (1892), various incidents of Anarchist revolt and terrorism (1893–94), and the *affaire Dreyfus* (1898); while in Japan, the height of symbolism was contemporaneous with the Russo-Japanese War (1904–5) (Sakamaki 2016, 13).[6] However, such broad-brush historical observations cannot account for the symbolist coincidence in both countries: similar tallies of upheavals could be found in periods both earlier and later than French and Japanese symbolisms. Likewise, there were other European poetry movements that were contemporaneous (or nearly) with symbolism—such as Parnassianism or the Pre-Raphaelite Brotherhood—that Japanese poets also knew about but did not embrace as wholeheartedly, or in numbers as great, as they did symbolism. While symbolism was hardly amenable to transplantation, it nevertheless was adopted in many literatures around the world.[7]

With the above observations about symbolism as a point of entry, this chapter takes up the larger topic of difficulty in Japanese poetry of the first decade of the twentieth century, especially as it relates to meter and translation. Difficulty was almost invariably treated as an undesirable attribute in a poem, and describing a poem as hard to read was, in Japanese as in English, never intended as a compliment. Even as Japanese symbolist poets were perceived as testing the limits of poetic diction in Japanese, they invented an unprecedented number of poetic meters and stanza forms. Critics responded variously to these formal and stylistic experiments, suggesting that in some cases the fit between form and style was regarded as a source of readerly delight, in others as a source of readerly displeasure.

The informal protagonist of this chapter will be Kanbara Ariake, whom at least one contemporary critic regarded as being "largely responsible" for the vogue of Japanese symbolist poetry (Sakurai [1905] 1972, 228). Beginning with an analysis of a challenging early poem by Ariake, the chapter goes on to examine the contemporary reception of Japanese symbolism more broadly conceived, focusing on claims that symbolist poetry was difficult. What made some poems difficult but not others? Who decided what counted as a difficulty? The concluding movement of the chapter then traces, step by step, the invention and dissemination of a poetic form—a form that was invented as a vehicle for translation by Ueda Bin, then adapted and repurposed by the symbolist poets Susukida Kyūkin and Kanbara Ariake in their own poems.

Ariake's Proliferating Meters

Ariake was difficult before he was symbolist. In late 1901, when Ariake was twenty-five years old, he had not yet published a book of poems but had been publishing verses—generally, *shintaishi* in the usual five- and seven-*moji* phrases—in literary magazines since as early as 1894. However, in the August 1901 issue of the literary magazine *Myōjō* 明星 (The morning star), Ariake published three poems, under the general heading "Dokugen aika" 独絃哀歌 (Laments on a single string),[8] in a meter of his own invention: each line followed a 4-7-6 *moji* pattern, in fourteen lines arranged as a sonnet in an octave and a sestet. The first of these single-stringed laments was titled "Ada naramashi" あだならまし (How futile it would seem), which I quote in the 1903 version for reasons that will become clear:

In the long shadows of a humble untrodden forest
let your song of wandering now resound;
singing because your heart is on fire,
wandering because you are O! how weary of the world's ways.
Although the stars' light glimmers in the houses of the night sky,
the pillars carved by the ferocious waves of Eternity cannot be seen,
and how, then, does one convey the piercing sadness
of the field of withered souls rising, falling?

You, now: when you would hasten down the road that traverses life
the evening light suddenly moves and the tears go dry,
and even if the fountain of brief life is spent,
in the end what will you have known of triumph?
And without a sacred blessing on which to depend, the fire
in the breast, like the voice of song—how futile it would seem.

Ada naramashi

michi naki / hikuki hayashi no / nagaki kage ni
kimi samayoi no / uta koso / nao hibikame,—
utau wa / mune no hitakaku / moyuru ga tame,
mayou wa / yo no michi umite / yuku ni yoru ka.
hoshikage / yaten no shuku ni / kagayakedomo
jigō no / ōnami kizan / hashira miezu,
mashite ya / shinae okifusu / rei no nonobe
shimiiru / sabishisa ikade / hito tsutaen.

kimi ima / inochi no kayoiji / hase yuku toki
yūkage / tachimachi ugoki / namida karete,
mijikaki / sei no izumi no / tsukisaru tomo,
hatashite / nani o ka hokori / shiriki to nasu.
sei naru / megumi ni tayoru / sore narazuba
mune no hi / utagoe tomo ni / ada naramashi.

あだならまし

道なき低き林のながきかげに
君さまよひの歌こそなほ響かめ、 ─
歌ふは胸の火高く燃ゆるがため、
迷ふは世の途<ruby>途<rt>みち</rt></ruby>倦みて行くによるか。

星影夜天の宿にかがやけども
時劫の激浪刻む柱見えず、
ましてや靡へ起き伏す靈の野のべ
泌み入るさびしさいかで人傳へむ。

君今いのちのかよひ路馳せゆくとき
夕影たちまち動き涙涸れて、
短かき生の泉は盡き去るとも、
はたして何をか誇り知りきとなす。
聖なるめぐみにたよるそれならずば
胸の火歌聲ともにあだならまし。

(Kanbara [1903] 2009, 14–15)

I will say more about the meter of this poem in a moment, but first I want
to consider the poem's rhetoric. The title names *ada*—futility, transience—as
the poem's theme, but Ariake's poetry frequently proceeds by oscillating
between contrary concepts. This poem is no exception: while the title pro-
claims the theme of *ada*, the contrasting concept *jigō* (eternity) is mentioned
in line 6, establishing the two poles—we might term them impermanence
and permanence—between which this poem's contest unfolds. The titular
transience, however, is called into question by the final verb, which ends in
mashi: the phrase *ada naramashi* implies that something *would be* transitory,
would be futile. Taken together, the final two lines suggest that futility is a
problem, in the absence of a *sacred blessing*: what that sacred blessing might
be is not at all clear. Tautologically we might conclude that anything that
offered a stay against futility would constitute such a blessing. Poetry itself,
perhaps.

The points of difficulty in this poem are numerous. For one, the omission
of grammatical particles—a technique common in classical Japanese poet-
ics, too—is a recurrent feature. Just to mention a few examples, *michi umite*
would typically be *michi ni umite*, "wearying of the way"; *ōnami kizamu* could
be either *ōnami no kizamu* or *ōnami ga kizamu*, "[which] the ferocious wave
carves"; and *hito tsutaen* could be either *hito ga tsutaen* or *hito ni tsutaen*, "a per-
son would convey" or "would convey to a person," respectively. While these
omissions make the poem metrically regular by leading to the necessary *moji*
counts, they also make the meaning difficult to piece together. Other matters
of orthography raise questions to which I have only conjectural answers: for
instance, the word *michi* (way, road, path) is written with the ideograph 道

in line 1 but with the ideograph 途 in line 4, for reasons that are not clear to this reader; the verb *yuku* (to go) is written using an ideograph in line 4 but completely phonetically in line 9. With these and still other points of internal dissonance and internal resonance, the poem defies its reader to encounter it with a sufficiency of attentiveness.

Observing comparable points of difficulty in Franz Kafka's German prose style, the French philosophers Gilles Deleuze and Félix Guattari have written of what they call the *tensors* of Kafka's prose fiction. These tensors are stylistic features that establish the difference between Kafka's writing—inflected by Kafka's familiarity with other languages and other dialects of German (in his case, Prague German)—and the style appropriate to writers from the centers of German culture, a difference that, in Deleuze and Guattari's analysis, Kafka then deployed for the purpose of evading the metropole's hermeneutic tools (1986, 23).[9] Kafka wrote a literature that lay athwart the main trunk of German literature: a *minor literature*, as Deleuze and Guattari put it, with each term carrying equal weight (it is *literature*, but *not* of the major sort). As the above paragraph has shown, Ariake's poetry similarly abounds with tensors. But I hesitate to assert that the tensors in Ariake serve the same purpose as in Kafka. My hesitation springs in part from the paucity of Ariake's prose writings from the first decade of the twentieth century: he wrote many essays at the time, it is true, but these tended to be occasional pieces and reviews, not explicit statements of purpose.[10] But we can survey the poems Ariake wrote and his contemporaries' reactions to them and infer that he had an ambition to make a name for himself—to make, as the cultural theorist Rein Raud would put it, a "bid" for recognition in the cultural marketplace (2016, 8). With the *shintaishi* having come in for repeated criticisms almost since its inception, Ariake saw an opening for the creation of something new.

"Ada naramashi" was reprinted as the first poem in Ariake's second collection, *Dokugen aika* (1903); the poem clearly represented a significant new direction in Ariake's work. When Ariake's first *dokugen* poems were serialized in 1901, the founder and lead editor of *Myōjō*, the tanka poet Yosano Hiroshi 与謝野寛 (1873–1935), had noted in his editorial summary that "starting in this issue, this magazine will carry Mr. Kanbara Ariake's new work, *Dokugen aika*; it will be a great work, expected to include more than fifty poems" (1901, 45). If what Yosano and other readers expected was a series of fifty sonnets in the manner of "Ada naramashi," they were disappointed—only sixteen *dokugen aika* sonnets were ultimately published in *Myōjō*, fewer than one-third of the expected number. As the editors of a 1969 anthology of Ariake's poetry commented, these sixteen poems were "considerably fewer than the original plan. Nevertheless," these later editors continued, "from this we may get a glimpse of the extent of Ariake's ambition" (*Nihon no shiika* 1969, 217–18).

What Yosano did not call attention to was the poem's meter: "Ada naramashi" was a sonnet with lines in a 4-7-6 *moji* pattern, a new meter in Japanese. To put it as clearly as possible, Ariake's ambition was to revitalize Japanese poetry by doing two things: first, by creating new meters and stanza forms—meters that frequently avoided fives and sevens; second, by implicitly setting forth a program of prosodic invention for other poets to follow. Ariake was not the first or only poet to deviate from fives and sevens, but he was the most committed: as Wakui Takashi has written, "no other [poet] had strived so hard to avoid the monotony of the regular meter of seven and five syllables as Ariake" (2017, 429).

The launch of the *dokugen* meter did not happen as Ariake would have hoped. The first publication of the poem "Ada naramashi" included a mistaken pronunciation gloss in the first line, which strongly suggests that someone in the production chain—whether editor or compositor we may never know—had failed to grasp Ariake's intentions. In the poem's first published version, the ideograph 林 is glossed as the two-*moji* word *mori* rather than the more usual, three-*moji* word *hayashi*—which is what the meter requires. The reading *mori* is so unusual that I hypothesize the printer or compositor, confused by the prosody, had inferred that actually a two-*moji* word was required. But the line *michi naki hikuki* **mori** *no nagaki kage ni*, too, would be atypical in its scansion. It might be interpreted as beginning with a seven-*moji* phrase: *michi naki hikuki*, but then the remainder of the line—*mori no nagaki kage ni*—would run to an unusual nine *moji*, scannable either as 6-3 or 3-6. When juxtaposed, however, with the other thirteen lines of the poem—each of which contains seventeen *moji*—a reader would have every reason to infer that the first line, too, should contain seventeen *moji*. The mistaken gloss—*mori* instead of *hayashi*—marred the *dokugen* project's very first line.

That is not to say that Ariake's first sustained metrical experiment met with unanimous incomprehension. The September 1903 issue of *Myōjō* published two reviews of Ariake's work, both titled "Reading *Dokugen aika*" (Dokugen aika o yomu 独絃哀歌を読む). The first of these was a short article about Ariake's poetry collection, which concluded with an explicit, laudatory mention of the 4-7-6 meter of the sonnets in that collection (Tatsumi-sei 1903, 83). The second was not a review, in the ordinary sense: it was a poem by Ōi Sōgo 大井蒼梧 (1879–1937) that was, metrically speaking, radically nonrepetitive. It included several lines in 4-7-6, beginning with the following:

In an instant a powerful wind, beating its wings, circles the sky
tsuka no ma / sora o megurite / hayachi ha utsu
束の間虚空を廻りて疾風羽搏つ

(Ōi 1903, 83, *rubi* as in the original)

獨絃哀歌

———あたならまし

蒲原有明

道なき低き林のながきかげに

君さまよひの歌こそなほ響かめ

歌ふは胸の火高く燃ゆるがため

迷ふは世の道階みて行くによるか

星影夜天の宿にかがやけども

時刻の激湍刻む柱見ねず

野にまた鳴く蟲しげき聲あれども

廣野のさびしさつひに傳へがたし

君今いのちのかよひ路馳せゆく時

夕影たちまち動き涙かれて

短かき生の泉の盡きぬると

FIGURE 4. Ariake's "Ada naramashi." The arrow is pointing to the ideograph 林, which is usually read as *hayashi* but has here been given the rather unusual gloss *mori*—making nonsense of the poem's meter. (A comparison between the version of the poem shown here and the slightly later revision that I have cited in the text will reveal the extensive rewriting to which Ariake subjected his works.) Source: Kanbara 1901, 2.

The poem continued in an Ariakean vein, examining stark contrasts—between light and darkness, between what endures and what fades away—while simultaneously eschewing *shintaishi* prosodic expectations.

Even the favorable reviews, however, did not always evince a clear understanding of Ariake's ambitions, where metrical invention was concerned. Among Ariake's early advocates, Tsunashima Ryōsen 綱島梁川 (1873–1907) in a 1903 review praised *Dokugen aika* for its rendering of emotions. The poetry of Ariake, in Ryōsen's opinion, conveys "sublime passions" in poetry that "may be read without difficulty"—a comparatively rare assertion that Ariake's poetry might be regarded as something other than hard to read (Tsunashima [1903] 1922, 300). Ryōsen made glancing allusion to the rhythms of Ariake's verse, but from his review it is unclear whether he recognized the persistence and scope of Ariake's prosodic invention. Near the end of his review, Ryōsen concluded:

> I think it quite mysterious that our many journalists and literary critics have reacted so coldly to this collection. Some have objected to the collection's diffuseness [*mōrō*] of thought. I agree that the collection does perhaps reflect such a tendency in places; but it is not the diffuseness of vacuous flights of fancy. In this collection, even where there is a sort of diffuseness, there is always, I would say, something to compensate for it. (304)

The quality of "diffuseness" (*mōrō*) mentioned here by Ryōsen had been a critical bugbear in the years preceding the publication of Ariake's second collection. As early as 1896, poetry critics had written articles debating the merits of what they had called a *mōrōtai* (obfuscating style) that had crept into the *shintaishi* (Tomasi 2007, 116–18). The same term, *mōrōtai*, would soon be used also in the field of visual arts, as a term of opprobrium against paintings in a new style—a controversy in the art world that peaked in 1900–1901 (Weston 2004, 173–217; Weston 2012, 117–18). Poetry critics came to apply the label *mōrō* to Japanese symbolist poetry, too, and Ryōsen was quick to assert that, in Ariake's poetry at least, "something . . . compensate[d]" for the elusiveness of his style. That something, for Ryōsen, was the profound feeling of Ariake's verse. Ryōsen did not call attention, however, to the metrical novelty of the *dokugen* poems; perhaps it had escaped his notice. Even Ariake's most avid readers sometimes glossed over his work's most salient technical traits.

Another early proponent of Ariake's work did call attention to its metrical inventiveness: Sakurai Tendan 桜井天壇 (1879–1933), a critic best known for his later essays on German literature. Writing in the journal *Teikoku bungaku* 帝国文学 (Imperial literature) in 1904, Tendan praised the 4-7-6 line: "The seventeen-*moji* line [*jūshichi on kaku*] that Ariake has created is kaleidoscopic, overall, and it does not at all become [monotonous like] the rhythm of pattering raindrops" (Sakurai 1904, 103). Examining specific passages in the *dokugen* poems, Tendan demonstrated that, in some lines, it is difficult to decide where to place the caesuras—meaning, as Tendan claimed, that the reader is kept guessing as to the precise metrical pattern, which nevertheless can be scanned neatly as 4-7-6 in retrospect (Sakurai 1904, 102–3).[11] For Tendan, Ariake's willingness to bend a prosodic rule, even one of his own devising, counted as a point in his favor. The attention to detail on display in Tendan's article is formidable—to the point that it received praise decades later from another student of Ariake's poetry, the poet Shibusawa Takasuke 渋沢孝輔 (1930–98). Writing in the last quarter of the twentieth century, Shibusawa claimed that "then [in Ariake's time] or now, one almost never encounters such a lucidity of explication" as one finds in Tendan's favorable 1904 assessment of Ariake's work (1980, 79).

But the readers who, like Tendan, could explain precisely what made Ariake's work distinctive, what made it merit attentive reading, were few. As Shibusawa has noted, Ariake was first fortunate and then unfortunate in his contemporary reception: Ryōsen and Tendan, in particular, were capable and effective advocates—who exited the scene at an inauspicious time for Ariake. Ryōsen, who had been ill for several years, died in September 1907; Tendan, for his part, abandoned poetry criticism and devoted himself to German thought and literature (Shibusawa 1980, 80). Other circumstances worsened Ariake's prospects. *Myōjō*, the periodical in which Ariake had published so much of his work, folded in February 1908. One of the more outspoken boosters of Ariake's more symbolist work, the important critic and translator Ueda Bin (whom we will see again below), was traveling in the United States and Europe in 1907–8 and was therefore not present to advocate for Japanese symbolist poets as he had done in the preceding years (*Nihon no shiika* 1969, 279). When Ariake's fourth collection, *Ariake shū* 有明集 (Ariake anthology), was published in 1908 and it garnered mixed-to-negative reviews, Ariake went into what might best be described as seclusion, and the steady output he had maintained between 1901 and 1908 shrank rapidly thereafter.

The critical reaction to Ariake's work was bound up with the broader reception of Japanese symbolism. That reaction, in turn, pivoted—not solely, but in part—on the perceived degree to which symbolism could be described as Japanese. In the eyes of some critics, Japaneseness in longer lyric poetry was incompatible with difficulty, while other critics held that symbolist difficulty should pose no problem since Japanese poetry had been, as some alleged, symbolist for centuries.

As Old as the Hills? Symbolism in Japanese Poetry

Ueda Bin has been mentioned above as the writer who introduced symbolism to Japanese readers. Bin was a precocious introducer of significant ideas from European literature: at age sixteen, Bin published an article in which the German playwright and poet Johann Wolfgang von Goethe's notion of *Weltliteratur* (world literature) first appeared in Japanese.[12] A polyglot reader with a seemingly infallible eye for the most newsworthy literary trends abroad, Bin also read widely in Japanese classics, bringing to his Japanese translations of contemporary European-language verse a vocabulary culled from centuries' worth of Japanese poetry anthologies.

One striking feature of the introduction of symbolism in Japanese poetry was the extent to which its advocates sought to domesticate symbolist dicta by communicating them in terms of Japanese aesthetic vocabulary, assimilating recent French poetics to Japanese literary techniques of older vintage. In the introduction to his 1905 translation anthology *Kaichōon* 海潮音 (The sound of the tide), Bin famously declared that "the use of symbols in poetry is, of course, not merely a modern invention, but is as old as the hills," evoking an antiquity older than the nations themselves (Ueda B. [1905b] 1972, 2). However, in other of his key writings about symbolism, Bin described the *symbol* as being comparable with *yūgen*, a term meaning something like "mysterious profundity" that had come to prominence as a Japanese poetic (later also as a dramatic) ideal as early as the twelfth century. As a short commentary to his translation of Stéphane Mallarmé's poem "Soupir," Bin appended a translation of a paragraph from one of Mallarmé's critical writings about symbolism, "Enquête sur l'évolution littéraire" (An investigation into literary evolution), rendering the sentence "C'est le parfait usage de ce mystère qui constitue le symbole" (The perfect use of this mysteriousness is the essence of the [poetic] symbol) as "The use of this *yūgen* is called the symbol" (Ueda B. [1905b] 1972, 238; *shahan yūgen no un'yō o shōchō to nazuku* 這般幽玄の運用を象徴と名づく).[13] In another early article about symbolism, Bin asserted that symbolist texts were not *nankai* 難解, "hard to understand," but were rather *yūgen* (Ueda B. 1903, 14). By reminding his readers that Japanese literature, too, had affirmed *yūgen* as an ideal, Bin attempted to defend symbolist works—of which he was the pioneer translator in Japanese—from the imputation of difficulty.

Bin was quite consistent, however, in describing symbolism as having originated in France. Ariake, for his part, also acknowledged the *francité* of symbolism in its then-recent guise, but contended that symbolist practices could be found at earlier periods in Japanese literary and cultural history. In the introduction to his third poetry collection, *Shunchōshū* 春鳥集 (Spring birds), Ariake observed that Japanese haiku poets such as Matsuo Bashō 松尾芭蕉 (1644–94) had used poetic symbols (Kanbara 1905, 7–8). In a 1908 essay, Ariake also called attention to what he saw as the symbolist strain in Buddhism, especially Zen Buddhism: "the central idea of Zen," Ariake wrote, "is the symbol" (Kanbara 1908a, 50; *zen no chūshin shisō wa shinboru de aru* 禅の中心思想は象徴である). In a still later text, Ariake repeated the comparison between symbolism and Zen Buddhism, and mentioned the Chinese poet Du Fu 杜甫 (712–70 CE) as a writer in whose verses symbolist effects could be found (Kanbara [1914b] 1980, 275). A student of Buddhism, Ariake tried to write—perhaps the better word is rewrite—the history of Japanese symbolism in Buddhistic terms. While he acknowledged that Mori Ōgai 森鴎外 (1862–1922) had coined the word *shōchō* in modern Japanese as a translation of the German *Symbole*, Ariake claimed that *shōchō* had actually appeared much earlier in a Buddhist sutra; he further admitted, however, that he had been unable to relocate the passage in which he thought he had seen the word (273). Ariake insisted—even though he lacked textual evidence—that one should consider *shōchō* as a word Ōgai had derived from Buddhist precedent (273).[14]

If Japanese defenders of symbolism sometimes constructed Asian and even Japanese antecedents for a literary movement whose origins, from one angle, were indubitably European, the critics of symbolism might be expected to have insisted on how *un*-Japanese this new movement was. But I have found they generally did not do so: Japanese critics of symbolism tended to criticize it on grounds other than its degree of relative Japaneseness (assuming that Japaneseness would have been deemed a positive trait—which clearly not every writer would have maintained). The reasons for this may not be far to seek. Perhaps there was no need to proclaim the foreignness of a literary movement that made no secret of having its roots in Europe: anybody who knew anything about contemporary poetry would have known that symbolism had come from French-language poet forebears.

Japanese critics of symbolist poetry tended instead to allege the poetry's difficulty—or, to be more precise, its *excessive* difficulty. We will examine that difficulty in a moment. First, though, there was by contrast a desirable kind of difficulty, which usually was called *complexity* in the critical writings of the first decade of the twentieth century. Such difficulty—known most often as *fukuzatsu* 複雑 or *buzatsu* 蕪雑—was treated as a mark of the modernity of the longer Japanese lyric. Modern Japanese people were thinking in complex ways, and they therefore (critics reasoned) wrote complexly, too; the new science of psychology gave credibility to such inferences. The implication was that the simple old ways of writing were unsuitable for expressing modern thoughts: the psychologist Motora Yūjirō's 元良勇次郎 (1858–1912) criticism of the *shintaishi* reflected such an axiom, as did some of the more famous passages in the prose commentaries included in *Shintaishi shō* 新体詩抄 (New-style poetry collection, 1882). A paradigmatic example from the first decade of the twentieth century was Fujioka Sakutarō's 藤岡作太郎 (1870–1910) February 1907 article "On the *shintaishi*" (Shintaishi ron 新体詩論). Fujioka, a historian of Heian-period Japanese literature, wrote that *waka* and haiku were suitable for the "expression of simple and brief feelings," but added that "there is no need to rehearse the arguments for the necessity and value of the *shintaishi* for expressing the feelings and thoughts of the complex [*fukuzatsu*] new era" ([1907] 1972, 205). As a point about the syntax of the claim I have just cited here, the adjective *fukuzatsu* might apply either to the new era or to the feelings and thoughts, and that ambiguity is telling.

Later that year and partly in response to Fujioka's article, the poet and critic Iwano Hōmei 岩野泡鳴 (1873–1920) published a long article "On Naturalist Symbolist Poetry" (Shizen shugi teki hyōshōshi ron 自然主義的表象詩論, April 1907). As the title of Hōmei's article suggests, he was fascinated by the idea that symbolism could be fused with naturalism, a view that Hōmei had earlier explored in *The Mystic Semi-Animalism* (*Shinpiteki hanjūshugi* 神秘的半獣主義, 1906).[15] Later scholars, I should note, have regarded Hōmei's symbolist-naturalist syncretism as an anomaly: Ikuho Amano, for example, has written that Hōmei was "something of a black sheep for his audacious view that Naturalism taken together with Symbolism constituted a unified picture of human reality" (2013, 38). The view that symbolism and naturalism are incompatible relies on assumptions about the European incarnations of those two movements, which are understood to have had differing (when not altogether opposed) relationships to earlier Romanticism. In the Japanese case, though, it makes more sense to say that the various nineteenth-century European trends and movements were received almost simultaneously, in a rush of translation in the late nineteenth and early twentieth centuries. To return to Hōmei's view, the scholar Yōichi Nagashima has commented: "[Hōmei's] highly awkward mixture of two very different movements is due to the fact that the two were introduced almost simultaneously in Japan and that they were both accepted uncritically" (1997, 69n26), adding that Hōmei was therefore "different from all other Japanese naturalistic writers" (70).[16]

This seemingly unusual stance, however, was perfectly consonant with the aim of representing the complexity of human thought in poetic form. Toward the end of "On Naturalist Symbolist Poetry," Hōmei articulated a view of poetic rhythm that was in harmony with his brand of naturalism, according to which the primary nature that a true naturalist should represent was the one contained within human minds: *this* was where naturalism and symbolism would fuse. In pursuit of what he called a "psychological poetry" (Iwano [1907] 1972, 254; *saikorojikaru poetorī*), Hōmei argued in favor of a "new [poetic] rhythm" to suit the "new era" and its "new thinking" (253). One of the distinguishing marks of this new poetic rhythm would be a match between content and form, a conclusion Hōmei reached circuitously, by approaching it through the subject of rhythm in music:

> The other day, a certain friend of mine returned from a sightseeing tour of the world and said that when she listened to the music of other countries, the good feeling lasted until long afterward; but not so with the music of our country, she said. Then I answered that we could see this as meaning that it was the rhythm [*rizumu*] [i.e., of the foreign music] that had remained with her; the rhythm of our country's music, being complex [*fukuzatsu*], does not leave a strong impression. That is not the case with some foreign music, such as Wagner's. Long after listening to it, one's mind feels oppressed as by dismal weather. It is [therefore] necessary [for poets, too,] to develop [distinct] techniques corresponding to rhythms that are light, complex [*fukuzatsu*], or heavy. (253–54)

It is possible to overdo complexity, Hōmei suggested, but complexity remained a necessary part of a poet's toolkit. Hōmei would go on to add that he did not believe poetry need always be beautiful or give pleasure; that in the course of a life, one has many experiences that are neither beautiful nor pleasurable; and that poets must have on hand a variety of styles and forms, to suit the variety of human feelings (254). For Hōmei, simplicity was univocal—it served a purpose, but sometimes it needed to be leavened by more intricate constructions.

In a series of 1905 articles about "The Dark Literary Establishment" (Ankoku naru bundan 暗黒なる文壇), Nakajima Kotō 中島孤島 (1878–1946), one of a number of critics who had begun articulating an opposition to naturalism in literature, also held Japanese symbolism at arm's length. Objecting to what he saw as the excessive complexity of Japanese symbolist poetry, Nakajima took aim at Ariake, quoting the third and fourth stanzas of the latter's poem "It is Morning" (Asa nari 朝なり), which had gained rapid fame and notoriety. Nakajima wrote:

> The diction is unharmonious, the versification is unskilled; it is almost comical. If we say that in this poem there are points that are difficult to explain, it is not because the conception of the poem is indistinct [*mōrō*] but because the rhetoric is stylistically unpolished; and so I cannot even concede that this poem has the beauty of ambiguity [*mōrō*]. ([1905] 1972, 236)

Nakajima went on to acknowledge the novelty of the poem's subject matter—a dirty river. Yet, as Nakajima claimed, the symbolist presumption that the seemingly empirical world outside the poet was determined by the subjective world within the poet undercut the poem's overall effect.

Before I continue with Nakajima's criticisms, I will cite the final two stanzas of Ariake's "It is Morning":

A number of vegetable carts; beside these,
the workers; the beggars with
their empty hands; the water lapping as a boat passes;
and at the stern, using a pole to steer
while drawling his song, the boatman.

It is morning; the reflections take on colors;
and so the muddy river glints in the sunlight.
It is morning; already it is sparkling,
the white wall of the riverside warehouses
at the market: is this my mind?[17]

aomonoguruma, / ikutsu,—hata,[18]	[7-5]
kasegi no hitora,— / monogoi no	[7-5]
munade,—nitari no / tabutabu ya,	[7-5]
tomo ni saooshi, / kaji torite,	[7-5]
he ni uta o hiku / funaotoko.	[7-5]
asa nari, kage wa / iromekite,	[7-5]
kakute hi mo sase / nigorigawa,	[7-5]
asa nari, sude ni / kagayakinu,	[7-5]
ichiba no kashi no / namigura no	[7-5]
shirakabe—kore ya / waga mune ka.	[7-5]

青ものぐるま、いくつ、──はた、
かせぎの人ら、──ものごひの

空手、――荷足のたぶたぶや、
艫に竿おし、舵とりて、
舳に歌を曳く船をとこ。

朝なり、影は色めきて、
かくて日もさせにごり川、――
朝なり、すでにかがやきぬ、
市ばの河岸の並みぐらの
白壁――これやわが胸か。

(Kanbara 1905, 12–13)

This is paratactic profusion with a critical edge. The penultimate stanza is a list of substantives, with commas and dashes marking the places where, perhaps, the connectives—if there were any—would be spelled out in a looser poem. In the last line, the pronoun *kore*, meaning "this," is markedly ambiguous in its reference: it could refer to the whole scene of the poem; it could be limited to the subject matter of the final stanza; or, even more narrowly, it could refer to the nearest preceding noun, the *shirakabe* or white wall, blank but illuminated. Whatever *kore* is, the speaker is led to wonder whether it is his mind. The last line of the poem, in particular, invited Nakajima's disapproval. Nakajima objected that such a turn at the very end of the poem causes "the novelty of the subject matter [to end], we must say, in utter meaninglessness. All we are left with is a skeletal form" ([1905] 1972, 237). His comments on Ariake continued for several more paragraphs, throughout which he used the term *nankai* to impugn the difficulty of symbolism. Nakajima thought Ariake's poetry had taken its complexity too far: it was hard to read.

Invention and Adaptation: Ueda Bin's 7-5-7 / 5-7-5 Meter and Its Progeny

During the first decade of the twentieth century one variety of poetic experimentation in Japan reached its peak: the invention of new meters and stanza shapes. Later years have not seen anything to compare with the sustained creation of new prosodic patterns as alternatives to the prevailing *shintaishi* fives and sevens. As the poet and critic Kawai Suimei 河井酔茗 (1874–1965) observed in his 1908 *How to Write Shintaishi* (*Shintaishi sahō* 新体詩作法),

> While the 7-5 and 5-7 meters are used by many [poets] even today, meters other than the 7-5 and 5-7 have also become common.

> 7-6, 7-7, 7-5-7, 8-5, 8-6, 8-7, 8-8, etc. all have a greater number of
> syllables [*on*] [per line] than the 7-5 [meter]; while 7-4, 6-6, 5-5, 5-4,
> etc. meters are also used, and these have fewer syllables [*on*] than the
> 7-5 meter. (219)

Suimei was only scratching the surface. His description here mentioned variations in the patterns of single lines of poetry, with two clauses per line in nearly every case; he made no mention of stanza forms in which consecutive lines have *different* arrangements of *moji*. If he had wanted examples of alternative prosodies, he would not have had to look far: in the poetry of Kanbara Ariake alone, the range of metrical patterns and stanza contours was vast.[19] (See Appendix A: Ariake's Meters.)

It is possible to misrepresent—to underrepresent—the novelty of what poets like Ariake were attempting in their metrical experiments. Their refusal to continue using the *shintaishi* building blocks of five- and seven-*moji* phrases was seen at first as poetic heterodoxy. With time, however, a manual like Suimei's would treat prosodic variability as being, if not the *shintaishi*'s most common feature, then at least an accepted possibility. Ariake's poetry went far beyond anything Suimei described: it was the most radically different poetry of its time and place. Because Ariake and the other prosodic experimenters among his contemporaries had few professed followers, however, their work has been described as being merely transitional.[20] For an example of this latter view, the Japanese poetry scholar Tsuboi Hideto has written that "Kanbara [Ariake] and the other symbolist poets chose the variable fixed-form poem as a path between the hitherto attested fixed-form poems, on the one hand, and the free-verse poem, on the other" (2015, 188). Tsuboi's claim needs to be qualified: although the most knowledgeable Japanese poets of the first years of the twentieth century would have been aware of free-verse poetries in other languages, there was no recognized free-verse poetry in Japanese at the time. (Kitamura Tōkoku's works from 1889–91 had been largely forgotten, and were not identified as free verse.) As I see the matter, it is not accurate, or it is at best anachronistic, to claim that Ariake's poetry occupied a category somewhere between metrical extremes: in its time, it was the metrical extreme. In the collections he published between 1902 and 1908, he wrote poems in over fifty distinct stanza forms. (See Appendix B: Ariake's Stanza Forms.)

There were readers who opposed such unfamiliar poetry. Consider, for instance, the following comment by the scholar and poet Nakamura Akika 中邨秋香 (1841–1910), written in 1898—just three years before the publication of Ariake's first *dokugen* poem:

> Because it was difficult to express one's thoughts sufficiently in the language of this country if the words of *uta* were not in the 7-5 meter, [that

meter] came to be combined even with the Japanese readings of Chinese texts—as early as the time of the Heian court [794–1185 CE]. (15)[21]

This comment can be read as supporting not only metrical regularity, but also strict adherence to established metrical norms. Nakamura added that the 7-5 meter is "pure" (*junzen taru*), and treated the antiquity of the meter—it could be traced as far back as *Kokin waka shū*, Nakamura claimed—as evidence of that purity (14–15).

But if the 7-5 and 5-7 meters had the imprimatur of tradition, there were other commentators who envisioned the use of unattested, untested meters as well. Ōwada Takeki 大和田健樹 (1857–1910), a poet and songwriter, provided examples as early as 1893 of verse in meters other than those based entirely on fives and sevens. In his 1893 *Study of the shintaishi* (*Shintai shigaku* 新体詩学), he wrote, "The standards [*sc.*, of *shintaishi* composition] must be clearly established beforehand. But I am not saying that once those standards have been established, one may not deviate from them. Furthermore, for the purposes of research, one must produce *new styles*" (40–41). Takeki then listed a number of possible *shintaishi* meters—a list strikingly similar to the one Suimei would offer fifteen years later—and provided short textual examples of verse written in each of the meters in his list. "My aim in giving these examples," Takeki wrote, "is to show how broadly the new style might be applied by anyone among my readers. Please understand, I've submitted my work as a kind of parliamentary motion, as it were [for your approval]" (45). Approval for nontraditional metrical patterns was not always so explicitly sought as this.

Many of the most successful metrical inventions of the fourth decade of the Meiji years were created by the poet and translator Ueda Bin as vehicles for translating lyrics from Western languages. Bin's best-known work, his October 1905 translation anthology *Kaichōon*, introduced Japanese readers to poems from Italian, German, French, Provençal, and English, influencing both the topical range and formal diversity of the Japanese poetry of its time. In regard to its prosody, Bin's 1905 anthology relied almost entirely on fives and sevens. However, Bin deployed these familiar units flexibly, in new and supple stanza forms that frequently allowed his translations to hew quite closely to the meters of their originals.

Closely, but never exactly. Even when one grants that the European-language originals of the poems in Bin's anthology all emanated from prosodic traditions that emphasized stresses (strong-weak) rather than the syllabic prosody characteristic of Japanese, it is nevertheless also true that European-language poetries, when they followed regular meters, tended also to arrive at regular syllable counts. Just to choose one common example from

English-language poetry, an iambic pentameter normatively has ten syllables per line—which would even be quite a favorable meter for transference into Japanese, via a ready combination of two five-*moji* hemistichs to replicate a ten-syllable original. But Bin decided against such a course. What he did instead was to follow an idiosyncratic program of adaptation, keeping one eye on the prosody of the original and the other on that of his translation.

As an example, one of Bin's most famous translations was his version of the French poet Paul Verlaine's (1844–96) "Chanson d'automne" (Song of autumn). In the original, Verlaine's poem begins:

Les sanglots longs   [4 syllables]
Des violons   [4]
        De l'automne   [3]
Blessent mon coeur   [4]
D'une langueur   [4]
        Monotone.   [3]

                    (1986, 39)

[The long sighs of the autumn violins wound my heart with a monotone languorousness.]

In Bin's version, these lines become:

秋の日の   *aki no hi no*   [5]
ギオロンの   *vioron no*   [5]
ためいきの   *tameiki no*   [5]
身にしみて   *mi ni shimite*   [5]
したぶるに   *shitaburu ni*   [5]
うら悲し。   *urakanashi.*   [5]

            (Ueda B. [1905b] 1972, 73–74,
                rubi as in the original)

Each line in Bin's version contains five *moji*, an adaptation that recreates for the eye and ear alike the rapid iteration of syllable clusters observable in the French. The motivation behind just this arrangement of lines and metrical features, surely not accidental, must remain a matter for speculation, since Bin wrote so little about his translation choices. As the modern literature scholar Ikuho Amano has put it, "Ueda does not theorize his translation method in [*Kaichōon*] or elsewhere" (2011, 66). As far as I have been able to determine, Amano's generalization is accurate—and it is, from a metricist's perspective, most unfortunate, because Bin so thoroughly explored the prosodic possibilities of modern Japanese verse.[22]

The translation of poetic form has been a topic of ongoing debate in the twentieth and twenty-first centuries, and not only in Japan. The meters of poetry raise questions and pose problems that translators resolve according to available means, which will depend on variables such as the languages involved and the resources of the translator. If a poem is metrically regular in its home language, does it behoove a translator to produce a metrically regular translation? If so, should the translation recreate the meter of the original exactly? The latter question assumes the possibility of metrical transfer from the source language to the target language; but what if the languages in question rely on altogether different notions of prosody (e.g., accentual versus syllabic)? These questions probably do not have definitive answers, but various writers have sought solutions nonetheless. Burton Raffel, himself a prolific translator, approaches the matter by focusing on the pragmatics of translation, and concludes: "No two languages having the same literary history, it is impossible to re-create the literary forms of one culture in the language and literary culture of another" (1988, 79). Raffel also recognizes, however, that "there are poetic forms which travel well, and poetic forms which do not" (70). As late as the nineteenth century, when free-verse poetry was not yet widely recognized as a viable verse form, poems that were metrically regular in their original language tended to remain metrically regular in their target language—even if, at times, the precise dimensions of meter and rhyme shifted during relocation into another language.

In the twentieth century, however, free-verse translations came to be accepted, even when the originals were metrically regular, and for some translators the use of free verse became the norm regardless of the meter of the source text. There is the famous example of Vladimir Nabokov's 1964 translation of Aleksandr Pushkin's *Eugene Onegin*. Pushkin's poem is a long poem in metrically regular, rhyming stanzas of fourteen lines each; but Nabokov's English version eschewed rhyme and meter altogether. Nabokov's translation privileged the poem's semantic content—despite the fact that, as he demonstrated elsewhere in his writings, he was perfectly capable of recreating Pushkin's metrical frames in English (Robinson 2010, 45). Siding against a translator like Nabokov, the poetry scholar Peter Robinson, an advocate of prosodically faithful poetry translation, has asked rhetorically: "How can it be accurate to translate a poem that rhymes or is in a set metre without producing a translation that also renders, or at least structurally alludes to, this fact about the text being translated?" (44). For Robinson, the answer is: it cannot be accurate. I offer these references to other writers as illustrations of the disagreement that the question of metrical translation has provoked, a question that (in my view) does not admit of a one-size-fits-all solution.

Bin evidently believed that prosodic regularity itself was a feature deserving of translation: if an original was metrically regular, then Bin translated it in a metrically regular way. However, it should be observed that not all regularities are necessarily familiar. In *Kaichōon*, Bin did something striking: the poems in their original languages tended to exemplify common and familiar prosodic forms in their home literatures (e.g., iambic pentameter in English), but rather than hewing to a comparable degree of prosodic familiarity in Japanese, Bin treated the act of translation as an occasion for prosodic invention. The abundant inventiveness of his translations can make the originals seem timid by comparison.

One of Bin's metrical inventions was an alternating 5-7-5 / 7-5-7 meter, in which the line lengths alternated between seventeen *moji* and nineteen. With its lines being longer than those of *shintaishi* in 7-5 or 5-7, this form nevertheless still evoked familiar poetic structures by relying on fives and sevens, while avoiding the pitfall of having an identical syllable distribution in every consecutive line. The new form was attractive to many other poets, Ariake among them, who adapted it to their own ends. While other meters—Ariake's *dokugen* meter, for one—were perceived as "lacking in a generality broad enough to be made into a standard [poetic] form" used widely by other poets (Matsubayashi 1996, 187–88), Bin's alternating meter met with immediate acclaim, and other poets began using it when composing poems of their own. More than just using it, they modulated it.

The details of how Bin's meter was transformed by other Japanese poets are worth close attention, and I beg the reader's patience as I examine, link by link, three poems: a translation by Bin, then a poem by Susukida Kyūkin, then a poem by Ariake. The first of Bin's translations in the alternating meter was a January 1905 version of the Cuban-born French poet José-Maria de Heredia's (1842–1905) sonnet "The Conquerors" (Les conquérants), from the collection *Les trophées*. The original poem is a Petrarchan sonnet—two quatrains and two tercets, in alexandrines (dodecasyllables) throughout—in rhyme scheme *abba, abba, ccd, ede*:

Comme un vol de gerfauts hors du charnier natal,
Fatigués de porter leurs misères hautaines,
De Palos de Moguer, routiers et capitaines
Partaient, ivres d'un rêve héroïque et brutal.

Ils allaient conquérir le fabuleux métal
Que Cipango mûrit dans ses mines lointaines,
Et les vents alizés inclinaient leurs antennes
Aux bords mystérieux du monde Occidental.

Chaque soir, espérant des lendemains épiques,
L'azur phosphorescent de la mer des Tropiques
Enchantait leur sommeil d'un mirage doré;

Ou penchés à l'avant des blanches caravelles,
Ils regardaient monter en un ciel ignoré
Du fond de l'Océan des étoiles nouvelles.

(Heredia 1893, 111)[23]

While Heredia's poem was a competent demonstration of a sonnet form that was altogether familiar in French, Bin's version of the poem introduced a meter new to Japanese:

To the Front Lines of Battle

Like the young hawk that takes flight from its nest high on the mountain,
bone-weary, its thought exhausted with melancholy,
past Moguer, setting sail from the port of Palos,
behold such manliness! How robust the virile dream.

From afar they desire to take possession of the gold
said to be in the mines of Cipango,
the ships' sails do not slacken in the favorable wind,
to the mysterious, distant, rocky shore of the world to the west.

Night after night they dream of magnificent tomorrows:
fire-sprites of the sea: they sail the tropic ocean
while the specter of gold haunts them. Or at times

standing on the bow of the sailboat they look up,
to the ends of the clouds, at a sky unrecognized,
at the new stars rising even today from the ocean depths.

Shussei

takayama no / togura su dachishi / shō no goto,	[5-7-5]
mi koso tayumane, / kanashimi ni / omoi wa unji,	[7-5-7]
Mogeru sugi, / Parosu no minato / fune dashite,	[5-7-5]
otakebu yume zo / takumashiki. / aware masurao.	[7-5-7]
Chipango ni / ari to tsutōru / kanayama no	[5-7-5]
shima ōgon ya / wagamono to / tōku motomuru	[7-5-7]
fune no ho mo / shiwarinikeri na / tokitsukaze,	[5-7-5]
nishi no sekai no / fushigi naru / tōtsuariso ni.	[7-5-7]

yūbe yūbe wa / sōdai no / ashita o yumemi,   [7-5-7]

shiranui ya / nettaikai no / kaji makura,   [5-7-5]

kogane maboroshi / kayōran. / mata aru toki wa   [7-5-7]

shirotae no / hobune no hesaki / tatazumite,   [5-7-5]

furisakemireba / kumo no hate, / mishiranu sora ya, [7-5-7]

wadatsumi no / soko yori idenu, / kyō mo niiboshi.   [5-7-7]

出征

高山 の鳥栖 巣だちし兄鷹 のごと、
身こそたゆまね、憂愁 に思は倦 じ、
モゲル過ぎ、パロスの港 船出して、
雄誥 ぶ夢ぞ逞ましき。あはれ丈夫 。

チパンゴに在りと傳ふる鑛山 の
紫摩黄金やわが物と遠く求むる
船の帆も撓 はりにけりな時津風、
西の世界の不思議なる遠 荒 磯 に。

ゆふべゆふべは壮大の旦 を夢み、
しらぬ火や熱帯海のかぢまくら、
こがね幻 通ふらむ。またある時は

白妙の帆船 の舳 さきたゝずみて、
振放 みれば雲の果、見知らぬ空や、
蒼海 の底よりいでぬ、けふも新星 。

(Ueda B. 1905a, *rubi* as in the original)

While retaining the fourteen-line stanza structure of the original, Bin's version of the poem avoided repetitiveness in point of rhythm (such as might arise if every line were a 5-7-5, for example).

Fittingly for a translation of a poem about an imagined voyage of discovery, Bin's rendering of Heredia's sonnet launched confidently into new prosodic territory. Even as it was formally unprecedented, Bin's poem teemed with diction taken from old tales and poetry anthologies: for example, *togura* (a place where a bird reposes), *tokitsukaze* (a favorable wind), the pillow-word *shirotae no* (white as of cloth), and *furisakemiru* (to look upward into the distance) all appear in *Man'yōshū*, the eighth-century poetry anthology; *shō* (a male bird of prey) appears in *Tale of Genji*, an eleventh-century tale; *shima ōgon* (a kind of ore) appears in *Konjaku monogatari shū*, a medieval tale collection. All of that linguistic material represented the old world, as it were, of Japanese poetry. Bin also mined the new worlds of diction that had been opened up in recent decades: the mentions of a *nishi no sekai* (for *monde Occidental*) and of a *nettaikai* (for *Tropiques*) would have been simply unimaginable in poetry written even thirty years earlier. Heredia's original, too, contained words for diction-hunters in French: *gerfaut* (falcon) is an old word for *faucon*; while *antenne* (part of a lateen rig, which is a kind of triangular sail) and *vents alizés* (trade winds) verge on being specialist maritime language.[24] As the scholar Wakui Takashi has noted, Japanese symbolist poets "mix[ed] Japanese words of different time periods" (1994, 136), but this feature of their work had analogues in the symbolist poetry of other languages, as the example of Heredia's poem suggests. In his translation of Heredia's poem, Bin plucked verbal gems from multiple strata of Japanese poetry history, juxtaposing words of great antiquity with ones from periods nearer the present. It is true that, even centuries before Bin's time, classical Japanese poetry anthologies had frequently juxtaposed *waka* from vastly different periods; what is different about the modern poetry of Bin and others is the sheer variety of vocabulary drawn together in a single poem—an effect made possible by the greater length of modern Japanese verses.

Whether the poem's first readers would have registered the shifting literary-historical depths of the Japanese words in Bin's translation is very much open to doubt, but there is I think no doubt that the unfamiliar toponyms—*Chipango, Parosu, Mogeru*, all written in katakana—would have been nodes of intense interest and puzzlement, slotted into their places in an evidently intentional metrical scheme. The word *Chipango* is of particular note: it derives, in Heredia as in Bin, from *Cipango*, Marco Polo's name for a gold-filled island country about which he learned while in China. Due to the popularity of the published account of Marco Polo's travels, the word *Cipango*, some scholars believe, gave rise to the toponym for Japan in many European languages (Amino 1992, 131n38). When Christopher Columbus set sail in 1492, he departed from Palos—Bin's *Parosu*—in southern Spain, hoping to reach Cathay (China) by way of Cipango, whose abundant gold Marco Polo, never having seen it himself, had described in such excited, exaggerated terms. Even after making landfall on islands in the Caribbean that bore little resemblance to the "Indies," Columbus persisted in believing that Cipango and its riches lay nearby.[25] Like Columbus, though, the *routiers et capitaines* of Heredia's sonnet would never reach Cipango. Nor would their voyage, or their dreams of glory, ever really end: the verbs in

Heredia's poem are in the imperfective tense throughout, indicating recursion or incompleteness of past actions. Bin's version conveys a similar effect by stringing one clause after another without arriving at an end-stopped past-tense verb. Given the technical aspects and the historical frame of the original poem, Bin's version was, in all, a suitably diamantine performance.[26]

Like the explorers to which Heredia's poem alluded, Bin uncovered something he himself might not have appraised at its full value, at least not initially. Bin's alternating meter flourished in the years immediately following its appearance, especially among poets who aspired to be in the vanguard of Japanese poetry. One of those was the noted Japanese symbolist poet Susukida Kyūkin, who gathered many of his prosodic experiments in a collection titled *Hakuyōkyū* 白羊宮 (Aries, 1906). The many favorable notices included one from Ueda Bin, whose June 1906 review of the collection ended with the statement that "for my taste, at least, this poetry is of the highest interest" (quoted in *Nihon no shiika* 1969, 143). The first poem in *Hakuyōkyū*, "The Sea on Which I Sail" (Waga yuku umi わがゆく海), used a variant of Bin's alternating meter. I quote the first published version from *Myōjō*, January 1906:

I

The direction in which I am headed: at the same time as moonlight appears,
the *sawara* cypress lies down, lowering its limbs;
the *akame* oak, making its forbearance audible, lets fall its tears from its leaves;
the rhododendron that is the breathing mountain remoteness—Isolation and Silence of the forest's repose.

II

The direction in which I am headed: the smiling field-walnuts fall;
the mikans like gold hang heavy on the laden branch;
the newly cultivated field; the grasses' and fruits'
wine is fragrant in a little flask—Companionship
and Sweet Feasting's garden.

III

The direction in which I am headed: through the withered reeds
the rays of the setting bloodshot sun gleam giddily
upon the waves at the surface of the detritus-strewn water;

the pond where the crane weeps—Lamentations
and Remembrance's hometown.

IV

The direction in which I am headed: the distant sea where there thunder
eight hundred confluent tides—O the morning sails unfurling; the pilots'
kami himself rises up, the wild divinity, with shoulders
as broad and sunburned as a whaler's, O let Charity
and Striving be the sails.[27]

waga yuku kata wa, / tsuki akari / sashi iru nabe ni,	[7-5-7]
sawaragi wa / kaina daruge ni / fushi shizumi,	[5-7-5]
akamegashiwa wa / shinobine ni / ha zo nakisobochi,	[7-5-7]
shakunagi wa / ikizuku miyama, / hijiri yo to,	[5-7-5]
shijima no agumu / mori naraji.	[7-5]
waga yuku kata wa, / nogurumi no / mi wa emikobore,	[7-5-7]
kogane nasu / kōju wa eda ni / tawawa naru	[5-7-5]
niibari ono no / arakibata, / kusa kudamono no	[7-5-7]
hitoyo sake, / komika ni kaoru, / shitashimi to,	[5-7-5]
umashi utage no / niwa naraji.	[7-5]
waga yuku kata wa, / uragare no / ashi no hagoshi ni,	[7-5-7]
tadarame no / irihi no hizashi / hitahita to,	[5-7-5]
misabi no omo ni / matataku o, / mi zo eishirete,	[7-5-7]
ubasagi wa / sashigumu minuma, / nagekai to,	[5-7-5]
omoide no sumu / sato naraji.	[7-5]
waga yuku kata wa, / yaoai no / shiozai doyomu	[7-5-7]
tōtsu umi ya, / —aa asabiraki, / miobiki no	[6-7-5][28]
kami koso tatere, / aramitama, / isanatoruko ga	[7-5-7]
higuromi no / hiroki kata shite, / iza jihi to,	[5-7-5]
nuriki no ho o to / yobitamō.	[7-5]

—

わがゆくかたは、月明（つきあか）りさし入るなべに、
さはら木（ぎ）は腕（かひな）だるげに伏し沈み、
赤目柏（あかめがしは）はしのび音（ね）に葉ぞ泣きそぼち、
石楠花（しゃくなぎ）は息（いき）づく深山（みやま）、聖（ひじり）り世（よ）と、
沈黙（しじま）のあぐむ森ならじ。

二

わがゆくかたは、野胡桃の實は笑みこぼれ、
黄金なす柑子は枝にたわわなる
新墾小野のあらき畑、草くだ物の
ひと夜酒、小甕にかをる、親みと、
うまし宴會の場ならじ。

三

わがゆくかたは、末枯の葦の葉ごしに、
爛眼の入日の日ざしひたひたと、
水錆の面にまたたくを、見ぞ醉ひしれて、
姥鷺はさしぐむ水沼、なげかひと、
追懐のすむ郷ならじ。

四

わがゆくかたは、八百合の潮ざゐどよむ
遠つ海や、——あゝ朝発き、水脈曳の
神こそ立てれ、荒御魂、勇魚とる子が
日黒みの廣き肩して、いざ慈悲と、
怒力の帆をと呼びたまふ。

(Susukida 1906, *rubi* as in the original)

That the diction of this poem could strike even contemporary readers as difficult is evident in the fact that an essay was published in November 1907 to explain the poem word by word, paraphrasing each stanza in turn and clarifying the obscurer terms ("Kaishaku 'Waga yuku umi'" 1907). As with Bin's version of Heredia's poem, the lines of Kyūkin's "The Sea on Which I Sail" are end-stopped, in the main, with only a few exceptions: for example, the enjambment in the second stanza (*kusa kudamono no / hitoyo sake*) and the other in the fourth (*miobiki no / kami*). The use of punctuation *only* at boundaries between clauses and especially at the end of most lines suggests the poet was attentive to the possibility his poetry would be read aloud: the stanza profile is evident enough to a silent reader, but a listener would have to rely on pauses—pauses such as could be indicated by punctuation marks. Kyūkin could have written the poem as a *shintaishi* in a familiar mode: for example, if the lines were rearranged according to a *shintaishi* prosody in 7-5, the first stanza would become

> waga yuku kata wa, / tsuki akari
> sashi iru nabe ni, / sawaragi wa
> kaina daruge ni / fushi shizumi,
> akamegashiwa wa / shinobine ni
> ha zo nakisobochi, / shakunagi wa
> ikizuku miyama, / hijiri yo to,
> shijima no agumu / mori naraji.

But that is not the arrangement Kyūkin adopted. Each five-line stanza begins with four long lines in three clauses each, only to end with a shorter fifth line in two clauses. Yet this slightly imbalanced stanza profile becomes a source of stability in the poem: the same configuration is repeated in all four stanzas. The poem's diction heightens the sense of recursion: each stanza begins with the refrain-like phrase *waga yuku kata wa*—which an early reviewer (Yosano Hiroshi, mentioned above) praised as being "a beautiful turn of rhetoric . . . never before seen in Japan" (Yosano, Baba, and Chino 1906, 1). Furthermore, at the end of each stanza there is an invocation to two abstractions: although the abstractions invoked are different in each stanza, the act of invocation is repeated. Despite his evident neophilia, Kyūkin did not eschew recursion as a principle of poetic structure; his impulse toward novelty was apparent in his creation of a new kind of stanza to iterate.

This chapter began with citations from a text by Yone Noguchi, "Twenty Four Paragraphs on Mr. Ariake Kanbara." In the very same issue of the same publication in which Noguchi's essay appeared, Ariake published the first version of one of his most highly regarded poems, "Daytime Thoughts" (Hiru no omoi 畫のおもひ), which was later published in Ariake's 1908 collection *Ariake shū*. Where Kyūkin's "The Sea on Which I Sail" diverged somewhat from the pattern set forth by Bin's translation of Heredia,[29] Ariake's sonnet returned to Bin's implicit template of alternating lines of 7-5-7 / 5-7-5, only to inflect it in a different way. The poem can afford us a point of entry into the putative complexity of Ariake's verse:

Daytime Thoughts

The tapestry my daytime thoughts have woven:
pleasure the woof, and anguish the warp;
the colors of the knotted tangle of lines
dazzle—now I cry out, and now I go numb, intoxicated.

When I look again carefully, now, in the lap of night,
at the reversed web under the tentative light of a candle,
the forms seem different from themselves, faintly
menacing: fatigued beasts, curtailed birds.

Shall I sew this cloth to adorn myself
for a banquet? It would not suit. Perhaps for my last day,
to wear in my coffin? This too would be madness.

Over life there lies, alas!, a death-shroud; over death, life's
faint fragrance accumulates; and it is not reality
but a dream that flickers in the waves of mellow firelight.[30]

Hiru no omoi

hiru no omoi no / ori ideshi / aya no hitokire,	[7-5-7]
kanraku no / nuki ni, kumon no / tate no ito,	[5-7-5]
yorete midaruru / suji no iro / sakebinu, sate wa	[7-5-7]
mekurumeki / ei shirete koso / utainure.	[5-7-5]
ima, yoru no hiza, / yasurai no / tomoshi no moto ni	[7-5-7]
makikaeshi, / sono orizama o / tsukuzuku to	[5-7-5]
mireba oboro ni / ayauge ni / nebureru kemono,	[7-5-7]
umeru tori, / mono no katachi no / kotoyō ni.	[5-7-5]
tachite nuwasan ka / kono kire o, / utage no ori no	[8-5-7]
mi no kazari, / fusawaji sore mo, / tsui no hi no	[5-7-5]
kakeginu no ryō, / sore mo hata / monokuruoshi ya.	[7-5-7]
sei ni wa aware / shi no koromo, / shi ni wa yo sei no	[7-5-7]
soradaki no / nioi o tomete, / utsutsu naku	[5-7-5]
yume wa yuraginu, / yawarakaki / hokage no nami ni.	[7-5-7]

畫のおもひ

畫の思の織り出でし紋のひときれ、
歡樂の緯に、苦悶の經の絲、
縒れてみだるる線の色叫びぬ、さては
眩めき醉ひ痴れてこそ歌ひぬれ。

今、夜の膝、やすらひの燈火のもとに
巻き返し、その織りざまをつくづくと[31]
見れば朧に危げに眠れる獸、
倦める鳥、物の象の異樣に。

裁（た）ちて縫（ぬ）はさむかこの巾（きれ）を、宴（うたげ）のをりの
身（み）の飾（かざり）、ふさはじそれも、終（つひ）の日（ひ）の
棺衣（かけぎぬ）の料（れう）、それもはたもの狂（くる）ほしや。
生（せい）にはあはれ死（し）の衣（ころも）、死（し）にはよ生（せい）の
空炷（そらだき）のにほひをとめて、現（うつつ）なく
夢（ゆめ）はゆらぎぬ、柔（やはら）かき火（ほ）影（かげ）の波（なみ）に。

(Kanbara 1907c, *rubi* as in the original)[32]

In this unrhymed sonnet, the tangle of binaries is notable: the orthogonal opposition between woof and warp is homologous with the various oppositions (pleasure and anguish, intoxication and cries, day and night) that structure the poem. It is consistent with the theme of entanglement that the positive term is not always delivered first: the shrieking precedes the intoxication, the night precedes the light. In the first line of the fourth stanza the principle of opposition is brought to a point with a chiasmus: life-death / death-life.

It is at this chiastic line that the poem's prosody wrinkles, in a way that makes the poem stand out from the other sonnets Ariake wrote in the alternating meter. In his sonnets in the alternating meter, the even-numbered lines are usually 5-7-5, the odds 7-5-7. In "Daytime Thoughts," however, the meter is jolted at line 12, an unexpected 7-5-7; after which, line 13 is in 5-7-5, and line 14 in 7-5-7. That prosodic variation adds emphasis to a line that already calls attention to itself rhetorically by opposing and reiterating the ultimate antonyms, life and death. Of these two, death would seem to be more urgently on the speaker's mind: the possessive particle *no* joins "death" and "garb," fusing the poem's overarching textile metaphor with the idea of mortality.

The titular theme of the poem is *thought*, a word that Ariake retained in successive versions of the text. In the revision that appeared in the 1922 *Ariake shishū* 有明詩集 (Poems of Ariake), the title was changed to "Fleeting Thoughts" (Adashi omoi あだしおもひ); this in turn was rewritten in kanji as 異想 (again, *adashi omoi*) for the 1928 *Ariake shishō* 有明詩抄 (Kanbara 1957, 399). The revised title is a perspicacious reformulation of the poem's freight. As the metaphor of weaving suggests, the poem is about a specific kind of thinking: an oscillation between contraries, a meditation upon the presence or absence of pattern. Since the ideograph 異 commonly appears in the verb *kotonaru* (to differ), the later title "Adashi omoi" might also be translated "Different Thoughts," or "Thoughts of Difference": fittingly, what the poem presents is a series of antonyms, terms that are usually understood as occupying opposite ends of a given spectrum of meaning. Yet the theme of antonymy gives the reader a clue to the poem, creating an early expectation that paired opposites will continue to appear—which they do. Although the irregular alternation between positive and negative semantic fields might threaten to disorient the reader, in fact there appears, as early as the second line, a pair of coordinate axes (the warp and woof) by which to map the poem. Binary opposites are woven into a single fabric: no matter how melancholy the poem, one can find reassurance in the idea that cognitive disorder can be described and thus contained. The alternating metrical pattern—the oscillation between 7-5-7 and 5-7-5—offers another kind of twofold map of the text; but that pattern, as already mentioned, is significantly disrupted when life and death are juxtaposed. That disruption causes the form of the poem to appear "different from [itself]": the sonnet draws upon a recognizable prosodic pattern, namely the alternating meter that Bin had invented, yet varies that pattern to great effect. Contemporary reviewers praised this poem as one of the best in *Ariake shū*, and I would suggest that the poem was seen as a success precisely because it exemplified a complexity that was legible: the thoughts are wavering, but in a way that can be charted clearly.[33]

Coda: Ariake's Twilight

Hagiwara Sakutarō 萩原朔太郎 (1886–1942), one of the most important figures in twentieth-century Japanese poetry—his 1917 poetry collection *Howling at the Moon* (*Tsuki ni hoeru* 月に吠える) established his enduring fame—published in 1928 a short essay, "On Learning How Kanbara Ariake is Living Now" (Kanbara Ariake shi no kinkyō o kiite 蒲原有明氏の近況を聞いて). In this essay, Hagiwara described what he had recently heard about Ariake from another poet of note, Kitahara Hakushū 北原白秋 (1885–1942). Passing through the city of Shizuoka, where Ariake was known to have relocated after the destruction of his Tokyo home in the Great Kanto Earthquake of 1923, Hakushū asked around for the address where Ariake was living, hoping to pay the older poet a visit. To his great surprise, Hakushū discovered that no one in Shizuoka knew who Ariake was. Finally Hakushū met a florist who had heard of the name Kanbara: "Yes, yes, you must mean the husband of that woman who teaches ikebana," the florist said (Hagiwara [1928] 1976, 605). In this way Hakushū learned Ariake's whereabouts and paid the poet a visit, seeing firsthand the simplicity and utter solitude of his existence. "If the poetry establishment has forgotten Ariake," Hagiwara wrote, "Ariake has returned the favor": Ariake had cut his ties to poets and poetry almost completely (605).

It is not clear to me what effect Hagiwara imagined his essay might have on readers or on Ariake himself, but evidently he thought the (still relatively young) symbolist poet had retired from poetry too early. Ariake's early retirement, furthermore, had translated into an undeserved neglect. Hagiwara made this latter point by ending his essay with one of the most idiosyncratic comparisons between persons that I have ever read: a comparison between Kanbara Ariake and George Washington. George Washington enjoyed a serene retirement, Hagiwara wrote, as his reward for the great things he had done while president, with a steady stream of visitors paying him their respects, while Kanbara Ariake had been plunged into unremitting isolation, despite his also having done work that should inspire reverent pilgrimages. Washington had founded a country that went on to enjoy some measure of stability and success; Ariake, too, founded something remarkable, albeit in the less public world of poetry, but his contribution was lost in the uproar over other kinds of poetic novelty. Hagiwara closed his essay on a poignant note, stating that Hakushū reported how glad Ariake had been to receive a visitor. Kitahara Hakushū, I might add, was a poet of the first importance: his making a point of visiting Ariake redounded well to the reputation of the latter.

A combination of factors had contributed to Ariake's withdrawal from poetry. In November 1907, he began suffering from a kidney ailment, which caused him to become bedridden for several months. At this time, as he later reported, his outlook became more religious, inclining toward a more Buddhistic view of life. More importantly, there was the reception of his January 1908 collection *Ariake shū*. By Ariake's own account, critics made of his poetry a "blood sacrifice," comparing it unfavorably with the free-verse poetry that was just beginning to be written in Japanese (Kanbara [1929] 1980, 282). By no stretch of the imagination can it be said that the reception of *Ariake shū* was uniformly negative, but evidently Ariake had expected much more favorable notices. Whatever the case, 1908 represents a turning point in his oeuvre. Between 1902 and 1908 inclusive, he published four books of poetry; nearly fifteen years passed before he published his fifth book of poems, in 1922, and it contained, in the main, old poems, most of which he revised, making them simpler and bringing them closer to the new stylistic norms of the more prose-like Japanese lyric of the time. He did continue publishing essays on poetry and Japanese poetry history; he also became a significant figure in modern Japanese prose poetry, writing prose poems of his own and translating prose poems by important French writers (Mehl 2021, 271–75).

I think something else dissuaded Ariake from further pursuing new poetic forms. To return to the *dokugen* meter, Ariake later described his invention of that meter as being merely fortuitous: as he put it, he encountered "by chance" a line in a 4-7-6 *moji* pattern in some text (he could not remember which) and used that line in the *dokugen* sonnet form, as he recalled, to arrive at his first major prosodic innovation (Kanbara 1947, 184). As we have seen, that first prosodic discovery was followed by many others, in an unexampled burst of invention. Ariake's recollections, however, evinced rather a cooler view of that period in his career. He was coming to a view of poetic form that the French narratologist Gérard Genette expresses in the following terms, invoking the finitude of possible combinations of literary elements:

> Personal creation, in the strong sense, does not exist, firstly because literary practice is reduced to a vast "combinatory" play in the interior of a pre-existing system that is nothing else than language. . . . A new creation is ordinarily just the fortuitous encountering of an empty compartment (if any remain) in the table of forms, and consequently the constant desire to innovate in order to set oneself apart from one's predecessors . . . is based upon a naïve illusion. (1999, 480–81)[34]

It is not that Ariake ceased composing poetry altogether, but he wrote few new verses. His poem about the futility of song, so ambitious in itself, came to seem a prediction about the inevitability of the song's end.

CHAPTER 5

Kawaji Ryūkō and the New Poetry

I begin this chapter with two Japanese writers' pronouncements about the state of Japanese poetry. The first is by Ueda Bin 上田敏 (1874–1916), a translator of European-language poetries and a nimble adapter of poetic forms; the second is by Hattori Yoshika 服部嘉香 (1886–1975), a poetry critic, later known as a historian of modern Japanese poetry. What connects these two statements is their shared topic, namely, the viability of free-verse poetry in Japanese in the first decade of the twentieth century; but the attitudes expressed could hardly be more different.

Bin's view, as stated in the preface to his October 1905 translation anthology *Kaichōon* 海潮音 (The sound of the tide), was that the time was not yet propitious for free-verse poetry in Japanese: Japanese poets, as Bin believed, were not ready for such poetry, to say nothing of the reading public.

The poems in *Kaichōon* had originated in various European languages—Italian, German, French, Provençal, and English—but the main attraction was the *poésie*: of the twenty-nine poets presented in the anthology, fourteen were French or Belgian. Most of those were associated with the two movements known as Parnassianism and symbolism (Ueda B. [1905b] 1972, 1–2; Kamiyama et al. 1975, 111). The different French poetry movements are worth mentioning because, as Bin went on to explain in his preface, the transition from Parnassianism to symbolism was what gave rise to the French *vers libre* or (as it is called in English) free verse:

> Modern French poetry reached a height in Parnassianism, the resplendent beauty of which was the result of ultimate refining and polishing. But then, at the very apogee of Parnassianism, a "change of state" was necessitated, and the necessity was realized by Mallarmé and Verlaine. The moment was decisive; they provided the impetus. They began to propagandize for "Symbolisme"; they encouraged and elucidated the phenomenon of the *vers libre* form [*jiyūshi kei* 自由詩形]. (Ueda B. [1905b] 1972, 3; Kamiyama et al. 1975, 111)

In the next sentence, however, Bin explained that Japanese poets might not find *vers libre* amenable: "The translator of this volume is scarcely the one to say that Japanese poetry should imitate them exactly; my particular bent is more in sympathy with the Parnassians" (Ueda B. [1905b] 1972, 3–4; Kamiyama et al. 1975, 111).[1] The Parnassians' poetry, it should be observed, was metrically regular.

As against Bin's gradualism, Hattori, writing in May 1909—not even four years after Bin's anthology—surveyed the scene of Japanese poetry and concluded that free-verse poetry was not gaining popularity quickly enough. "In our poetry establishment," Hattori wrote, "in which there is need of a free, modern, lyric poetry [*jiyūna kindaiteki jojōshi*], it is lamentable that there are those [poets] who still dabble in the old methods" (1909 [1972], 386). This statement came at the end of a long essay on the history of French poetry in the late nineteenth century, in which Hattori described the *vers libre* as a poetic form ideally suited for expressing *jikkan*, the "immediate sensations" of a poetic subject—a subjectivity such as could not, or could not easily, be expressed by more conventional verse forms. By presenting a reasoned history of free verse in French, Hattori was also implicitly justifying free-verse poetry in Japanese—itself a better medium for self-expression, Hattori implied, than the poetic forms on which Japanese poets had hitherto relied (385).

Between late 1905 and early 1909, what had changed was that free-verse poetry had begun to be written in Japanese, starting with four free-verse poems published by a young poet named Kawaji Ryūkō 川路柳虹 (1888–1959) in September 1907. The creation of this new poetic form in Japanese came about as a result of many factors: trends in criticism, trends in poetry composition and translation, frictions between different philosophies of versification, anxieties about the standing of Japanese culture abroad. It is surprising that translations of free-verse poetry played only a minor role in the invention of Japanese free verse: far more important than direct translation were the writings of Japanese poetry critics.

Having just suggested that Japanese critics contributed more to the invention of Japanese free verse than did poetry translators, I should confess I find it hard to gauge how much importance to ascribe to any individual critic. It is not easy to resist what we might call the priority fallacy, according to which the first, chronologically earliest contribution is invariably the most important. The same for poets: I have mentioned Kawaji Ryūkō, who is usually regarded as the first poet to write modern free-verse poetry in Japanese. Readers who have been following this book's argument will be surprised to hear this claim, since Kitamura Tōkoku's 北村透谷 (1868–94) metrically nonregular verse—written in 1889–91—would fit any standard definition of free verse.

There are two significant differences between Tōkoku's work and Ryūkō's: style and reception. In Japanese poetry criticism, Ryūkō's free verse is generally called *kōgo jiyūshi*, meaning "vernacular free-verse poetry," as opposed to Tōkoku's metrically irregular verses, which are styled *bungo jiyūshi*. The difference between *kōgo* and *bungo* will be examined in greater detail below, but suffice it to say that while *kōgo* was understood to be a nearer representation of spoken standard Japanese, *bungo*, by contrast, was the style of elevated written Japanese. Writings in *bungo* tended to retain classicizing conjugations and declensions even as they largely retained the diction of ancient tales and poetry anthologies. *Kōgo*, conversely, was the style used in modern Japanese prose, both narrative and non-narrative. Those who ascribe greatest importance to this difference in written registers will tend to minimize Tōkoku's work, since it is not recognized as having influenced subsequent poets in the same way as Ryūkō's.

The point about the recognition accorded (or not) to each poet's work is, in my view, the more important one: critical reception mattered a great deal. Tōkoku's formally audacious work, for example, was met with incomprehension on the part of contemporary critics. Ryūkō's work, however, appeared in a rather different critical context: Japanese critics had come to know of French *vers libre* and English-language free verse and publicly wondered when such poetry would be written in Japanese. When Ryūkō published his "Four New Poems" (Shinshi yonshō 新詩四章) in the September 1907 issue of the coterie magazine *Shijin* 詩人 (The poet), then, it was only natural that some critic—in fact, the critic Hattori Yoshika (mentioned above)—would hail Ryūkō's poems as a striking and important departure from the status quo in Japanese poetry (Hattori Y. [1907] 1972). I say it was only natural that a critic would do so, but it was also vitally important: Hattori's recognition, followed by that of other critics, conferred legitimacy on the new form. Once it had been suitably baptized in this way,[2] the *jiyūshi* became a vehicle that any Japanese poet could use: transposed into critical discourse, free verse ceased being associated only with Kawaji Ryūkō.

For the purposes of this study, therefore, Ryūkō's contribution to Japanese literary history will be accorded relatively minor importance, while more attention will be given to the literary-critical context within which Ryūkō was writing.[3] As this chapter will argue, the significant factor in the creation of a free-verse Japanese poetry was not the work of Ryūkō or any other single poet, but was rather the existence of a literary-critical environment within which the adaptation of a new verse form, based on a foreign poetics of free verse, was construed as both possible and desirable.

Many theorists of the past century have concentrated on the supraindividual aspects of literary creativity, and in this chapter it is Yuri Lotman who provides the primary theoretical model.[4] According to Lotman, researchers tend to isolate their object of study from the sum total of cultural phenomena for analytic purposes, treating that object as self-enclosed and relatively autonomous. For Lotman, this procedure, while little more than an artificial expedient, is also a practical necessity, which is admissible only so long as the researcher grants that the object under examination is a simplification or a reduction: "such simplification," as Lotman has it, "is a common feature of science" (1977, 195). "This approach is entirely warranted as a heuristic," he adds elsewhere, although the danger is that sometimes such a heuristic "leads us to perceive logical convention as empirical reality" (2013, 355). Now, when Lotman warns against the dangers of simplification in semiotic research, he is most explicitly addressing his fellow researchers; but he sees a similar process of simplification at work in semiotic systems themselves, insofar as these systems create self-descriptions that are simplifications. These self-descriptions can play an important role in bringing about cultural change.

In place of the term *self-description*, Lotman sometimes uses the term *metalanguage*, and Lotman's insight is to draw a connection between the history of any given semiotic system, on the one hand, and the formation of metalanguages that describe that semiotic system, on the other. "A description will always be more organized than its object," Lotman claims (1977, 196). From this it would seem to follow that when a semiotic system begins to describe itself, to codify its own characteristics, it then has the potential to rigidify, that is, to begin following its own rules intentionally: "Since a description involves, as we have already mentioned, a higher degree of organization," Lotman writes, "the self-description of a semiotic system . . . is a powerful means for the self-organization of the system" (197). But one of the effects of a semiotic system's self-description is the creation of a boundary between what belongs to the system and what does not belong—a rule of inclusion that is also a rule of exclusion: "The description of the systematic . . . is at the same time an indication of the nature of the extrasystematic" (198).

Once a semiotic system has achieved this state of self-description, it is then in a position to undertake a program of intentional self-transformation, precisely by incorporating extrasystematic elements and rejecting other elements that have hitherto been regarded as systematic. "One of the chief sources of the dynamism of semiotic structures," Lotman writes, "is the constant process of drawing extrasystematic elements into the realm of the system and of expelling systematic elements into the area of non-system" (196).[5] Rephrasing this hypothesis: when a semiotic system changes, often the change is brought about because the system is in contact with another system that is "outside" it (where "outside" is relative to the system's self-description of what it includes "inside" itself). Something similar happened with Japanese free verse.

To repeat, Lotman grants that such constructions are wholly artificial; yet they have an explanatory capability that is far-reaching. The important point is that the metalanguage about a semiotic system, as Lotman shows, may in some cases effect a change in that system. For example, when a semiotic system is described as having traits that a sufficiently high or influential number of its users deem undesirable, then one possible result is that the users of that semiotic system can construct arguments in favor of changing the system; their aim, one imagines, is to alter the semiotic system in such a way that it may subsequently be described as having acquired desirable traits that it had previously lacked.

Some readers may object that Lotman's argument is actually rather simple.[6] It might seem he is saying only that cultural criticism sometimes works; or, in the case of literature, that literary criticism sometimes alters the literary landscape. To such an objection, the rebuttal might be made that Lotman's work on cultural change actually has a wider scope and arrives at subtler conclusions: one of Lotman's insights is that cultural change can have highly counterintuitive origins. For example, the very simplification that is brought about by a system's self-description has the potential, surprisingly, to contribute to that system's transformation. Systems, merely by describing themselves, have the potential to become something else altogether, thereby rendering their earlier self-descriptions obsolete. Critics are therefore in the business of trying, perhaps unwittingly, to make their own criticisms outdated—which then gives them new and more work to do.

The summary of Lotman's theory sketched above is itself a necessarily reductive piece of metalanguage, but it supports the contention that in the study of the semiotic system of poetry, it is difficult to account for change without considering one of poetry's primary metalanguages: poetry criticism. This chapter will argue that the appearance of Japanese free-verse poetry is inseparable from a confluence of two trends in Japanese poetry criticism in the first decade of the twentieth century: on the one hand, contemporary critics tended to disparage the *shintaishi*, the metrically regular modern form of Japanese lyric that was introduced in chapter 1; on the other hand, critics—often the same ones—tended to praise free-verse poetries in Western languages. The confluence of these two tendencies created a situation in which a particular kind of change was, according to Lotman's model, highly likely, a change of the sort brought about by "drawing extrasystematic elements into the realm of the system and of expelling systematic elements into the area of non-system." Kawaji Ryūkō's free-verse poetry, and the concomitant demotion of the *shintaishi*, represented such a change. And a rapid change, at that: toward the end of this chapter, we will examine one of Ryūkō's early free-verse poems, which will, I predict, strike the reader as a remarkable departure from the poetry that has appeared so far in this study.

Japanese Poets' and Critics' Cases against the Japanese Language in Modern Poetry

In a brief reminiscence on his activity as a young poet, Katō Kaishun 加藤介春 (1885–1946) recounted how the poetry group with which he was affiliated in the first decade of the twentieth century, the Waseda Poetry Society (Waseda shisha 早稲田詩社), had been trying to extricate Japanese poetry from the bonds of the *shintaishi* prosody (1934, 310). An alarm had earlier been sounded by the unofficial doyen of the Waseda group, the editor and translator Shimamura Hōgetsu 島村抱月 (1871–1918), who had called for Japanese poetry to be renovated along lines that had already been sketched in the prose fiction of Japanese naturalism. Hōgetsu had written that the Japanese poetry being published even in the first decade of the twentieth century was still burdened with antiquated elements: an elevated diction of the sort that seldom appeared in conversation, and metrical constraints that forced a poet's language into artificial syntax and rhythms.

In a June 1906 essay, Hōgetsu had distinguished between two kinds of written language: one was *gabun* 雅文 (elegant diction); the other was *genbun itchi* 言文一致 (unified speech-and-print), a term that represented, for Hōgetsu as for others, a modern literary language such as had been used in Japanese literary prose since the 1880s (Shimamura 1906).[7] (The distinction between *gabun* and *genbun itchi*, as Hōgetsu was using it here, was homologous with that between *bungo* 文語 or "written language" and *kōgo* 口語 or "spoken [vernacular] language," mentioned earlier.) In Hōgetsu's view, Japanese poetry was being hampered by its too heavy reliance on *gabun* and needed to start incorporating a more modern *genbun itchi* diction to survive.

Hōgetsu knew he was using the term *genbun itchi* in a somewhat idiosyncratic way. Some writers, as he noted, thought that the difference between the elegant language of *gabun* and the (putatively more modern) *genbun itchi* style could be reduced to differences among verb endings and adjective endings;[8] but Hōgetsu maintained that the distinction between an older verb ending like *nari* and a more recently popularized ending like *de aru* "is a merely rhetorical difference" (Shimamura 1906, 67). For Hōgetsu, the more important characteristic of *genbun itchi* was what he thought of as its expressive immediacy: "With *genbun itchi*, the content [of an utterance] eschews the gaudiness of outward form and expresses the feelings nakedly and unreflectively, in a romantic [*romantikku*] and spirited flow" (68). Hōgetsu invoked the example of William Wordsworth, a British Romantic poet whose oeuvre represented a successful program of renovation in poetry:

> The difference between the *gabun* we have seen hitherto and *genbun itchi* is, in a word, the difference between the classical and the Romantic. That is, *gabun* is classical and *genbun itchi* is Romantic. With time, the Romantic *genbun itchi* will take the place of the classical *gabun*. This [transformation] can be seen in other countries, too—for example, in England—albeit [only] in poetry, not prose. This is what Wordsworth meant when he called for the elimination of what he dubbed "poetic diction" [*poetikku dikushon*] and for the expression of the natural flow of the feelings as they well up.[9] In Japan, however, it is in the realm of prose that these phenomena have been most salient. (67)

Hōgetsu maintained further that Japanese poets had attempted to write *genbun itchi* poetry but failed because their poems were not sufficiently spontaneous and natural-sounding (70–71).

Hōgetsu's essay, as Katō indicated, was seen as exhorting Japanese poets to devise a new kind of poetry. For Katō, though, putting such a modernizing program into practice was not a simple matter: "The poetry establishment was so deeply under the sway of the old forms," Katō wrote in his reminiscence almost twenty years later, "that it was not at all easy to be rid of them. It was like being in a swamp into which one kept sinking deeper and deeper the harder one struggled to get out" (1934, 311). Poets like Katō who opposed the Japanese symbolist movement, represented signally by Kanbara Ariake 蒲原有明 (1876–1952), were compromised by the fact that the symbolists and their opponents alike wrote prosodically regular, stylistically archaic-sounding poems; a more naturalistic content, as Katō recalled, would need to be written in some putatively more naturalistic verse form (310–11). This view was shared by Hōgetsu himself in a later essay: "It is not easy to show precisely how to write poetry in *genbun itchi*"—the style in which, as Hōgetsu presumed, a more naturalist poetry would need to be written (Shimamura [1907] 1972, 332).

By 1907 there was already in place a modern tradition of invective against Japanese poetry—or, in Lotmanian terms, invective against undesired elements in the local semiotic system. The first complaints were directed against the brevity of traditional Japanese forms, such as the *waka* and the haiku. After the longer *shintaishi* became established, complaints were subsequently directed against the perceived monotony and unmusicality of this longer but still metrically regular form.

The meter of the *shintaishi* was repeatedly criticized. While for some observers (like the compilers of *Shintaishi shō* 新体詩抄 [New-style poetry collection, 1882]) the main problem was that the haiku and the *waka* and the other fixed forms were too short, for others the problem was that the *shintaishi* seemed too long. The poet and critic Ōmachi Keigetsu 大町桂月 (1869–1925), writing in the journal *Teikoku bungaku* 帝国文学 (Imperial literature) in 1898, commented that "Japanese poets are doomed to be holed up in a fortress made of chains of five-*moji* and seven-*moji* [*goon shichion*] lines" (quoted in Akatsuka 1991, 249). Long Japanese poems written in meter were derided. An unsigned 1899 article, "The Current *shintaishi* World" (Shintaishi kai 新体詩界), stated that it was becoming clearer with each passing year that "the 7-5 [poetic] form is unsuited to long poems" (quoted in Akatsuka 1991, 261), giving as an example the longest poem— an 883-line *shintaishi* in 7-5 meter—in Shimazaki Tōson's 島崎藤村 (1872– 1943) collection *Summer Herbs* (*Natsukusa* 夏草, 1898).[10] Another writer made a similar complaint about a 347-line poem by Doi Bansui 土井晩翠 (1871–1952): with its endless repetition of five- and seven-*moji* phrases, Bansui's *shintaishi* was, in that writer's view, "almost painfully inadequate" ("Shikei no shinka" 1899, 104).

The phrase *senpen ichiritsu* 千篇一律—"a thousand verses, [but only] one meter"—summed up the position of those who were dissatisfied with the *shintaishi* on metrical grounds.[11] It must be admitted, however, that even in the years before free verse, Japanese poetic meters had become strikingly diversified: the previous chapter has given ample proof of that. But the change that was being called for was more fundamental than what Ariake and the other prosodic experimenters had attempted.

Compounding the attacks on the meter of the *shintaishi* were complaints about what was deemed the intrinsically unmusical nature of the Japanese language. For instance, Hattori Yoshika, the young critic who campaigned tirelessly for the adoption of Western methods in Japanese poetry, preferred Western poetries over Japanese verse precisely because "the linguistic variability of the Western poetries brings with it the ability to be freely musical, with their accentual meters, rhyme schemes [*ōinritsu* 押韻律], and syllabic meters—an ability not to be found in Japanese poetry" (Hattori Y. [1908] 1972, 365).

Some Japanese poets voiced similar grievances, claiming that the Japanese language limited the effects they were able to achieve in their poetry. The case of the poet-turned-novelist Shimazaki Tōson is illustrative. Tōson's career as a poet had the most auspicious of beginnings. His debut 1897 collection *Seedlings* (*Wakanashū* 若菜集), with its well-received love poems in regular meters, has been credited with delaying the appearance of free-verse *genbun itchi* poetry (Keene 1999, 204). But within a matter of years, Tōson gave his congé to poetry and became a noted novelist. In 1901 Tōson published his fourth and final poetry collection, *Fallen Plum Blossoms* (*Rakubaishū* 落梅集), at the end of which he included a long essay on Japanese poetics, "Elegant Diction and Poetry" (Gagen to shiika 雅言と詩歌), outlining the "drawbacks" of composing poetry in Japanese (Shimazaki [1901] 1976, 240).[12] The very first of these drawbacks, Tōson claimed, is the paucity of vowels in Japanese, a disadvantage exacerbated by the fact that the few attested vowels are all of a similar length and stress—with detrimental consequences for the musicality of poetry. To demonstrate the poverty of the Japanese language in comparison with the more musical English and Chinese, Tōson resorted, fittingly, to a simplified musical notation. He gave a short sample of English poetry: four lines of Byron's poem *Childe Harold*, in which the unstressed syllables are marked as dark notes, the stressed syllables as light notes, in pleasing iambic alternation. Tōson's second example was a poem by Li Bai 李白 (701–62 CE): four lines of seven syllables each, in which the important variation in syllabic tone is marked by the notes' lightness or darkness. (Light notes are first or second tones, dark notes are third or fourth tones.) Tōson's notation made clear that consecutive lines in Li Bai's poem are tonally non-repeating, in keeping with one convention of Chinese poetry composition.

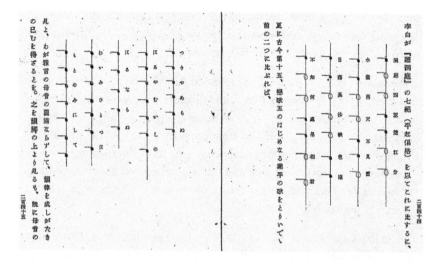

FIGURE 5. Shimazaki Tōson's musical notation of prosodic variety. Tōson contrasted the alleged monotony of Japanese *waka* (left) with Chinese verse (right), in which consecutive lines are tonally nonrepetitive, giving the latter, as Tōson argued, a greater sonic richness. Source: Shimazaki [1901] 1976, 244–45.

The third example was a *waka* from the fifteenth book of *Kokinshū*, with every *moji* marked as a dark note—a graphic representation of what Tōson saw as the monotony of the Japanese language. Having concluded his rapid survey of the musical possibilities of the three languages, Tōson exclaimed, "See how unsatisfactory are the vowels of our elegant language, and how difficult it is [in Japanese] to arrive at an effective meter" (Shimazaki [1901] 1976, 245).

With so many reasons to inveigh against Japanese poetry, Japanese poets and critics sought temporary relief, perhaps not surprisingly, in the poetry of the Western languages. By turning their eyes abroad, they were, as Lotman would put it, seeking an infusion of new material from sources outside the system of Japanese poetry.

Japanese Descriptions of Poetry in European Languages, Including *Vers Libre*

Shimamura Hōgetsu was cited above as an advocate of discarding the allegedly antiquated diction of Japanese poetry in favor of a more modern poetic vocabulary. To cite him again, he criticized the *shintaishi* for its lack of "directness and straightness" (*direkutonesu, sutoreitonesu*) and its failure to use words from "actual life" ([1907] 1972, 331; *akuchuaru raifu* 実際生活).[13] For

Hōgetsu, the diction of the *shintaishi* was incompatible with "directness." As has already been suggested, he was borrowing his ideals from Wordsworth, and from Walt Whitman as well. Hōgetsu wrote:

> Whenever I read English[-language] poetry, in all points the modernity of the language is recognizable; with Whitman and Wordsworth especially, I feel that such is the case. In Japan the [poetic] language is not at all the modern language, and Japanese poets must exert themselves to express modern thoughts and feelings; one immediately senses how much effort our poets expend; and the misshapen and distorted result is inevitable. That said, it is not easy to show precisely how to write poetry in *genbun itchi*. (332)

As Hōgetsu argued here, the language of Japanese poetry was somehow out of sync with the demands of the contemporary age. Western poets had solved the problem of suiting their diction to their expressive goals, but the *shintaishi* still suffered from a mismatch. It is ironic that Hōgetsu should have inveighed against *shintaishi* diction in just this way: the compilers of *Shintaishi shō* had actually believed they were solving the problem of poetic diction. And their solution had been in part inspired by their admiration of Western poetry. The *Shintaishi shō* compilers had anticipated a favorable reception, and insofar as the *shintaishi* became a form in which Japanese poets wrote verses, the *shintaishi* was indeed well received. A later generation of poets, however, found the *shintaishi* to be wanting.

The example of Wordsworth seems to have contributed much to the late-Meiji Japanese poets' dissatisfaction with their so-called antiquated poetic diction, which was so unsuitable (as they believed) for the "modern" matter that they felt compelled to express.[14] As Hattori Yoshika put it, in an October 1907 essay titled "Poetry in *genbun itchi*" (Genbun itchi no shi 言文一致の詩), Wordsworth was an ideal precursor, someone who had achieved in English precisely what Japanese poets wanted to achieve in Japanese ([1907] 1972, 328–29). Phrases from Wordsworth's preface to *Lyrical Ballads* reverberated throughout the Japanese poetry criticism of the first decade of the twentieth century. The article by Hattori Yoshika that I just mentioned included a long block quote that was taken, Hattori said, from the preface to the second edition of *Lyrical Ballads*. Hattori's quote was actually a pastiche of phrases from various sections of Wordsworth's preface. I reproduce them here in the order in which Hattori presented them:

[1] So-called elegant poetic language is "the common inheritance of poets." [2] "The principal object, then, proposed in these poems was

to choose incidents and situations from common life, and to relate or describe them, throughout, as far as was possible in a selection of language really used by men, and, at the same time, to throw over them a certain coloring of imagination, whereby ordinary things should be presented to the mind in an unusual aspect." [3] "There will also be found in these volumes little of what is usually called poetic diction; as much pains has [sic] been taken to avoid it as is ordinarily taken to produce it." [4] "Such a language, arising out of repeated experience and regular feelings, is a more permanent and a far more philosophical language than that which is frequently substituted for it." [5] "Some of the most interesting parts of the best poems will be found to be strictly the language of prose when prose is well written."[15] (Hattori Y. [1907] 1972, 328)

With Wordsworth's authority underwriting his claims, Hattori argued that the Japanese poetry of his time was too reliant on "poetic diction" and therefore should adopt something nearer the vernacular prose style. As another example of Wordsworth-idolatry, consider the following sentence from an unsigned article published in May 1908: ōru guddo, poetori, izu, za suponten'asu, ōbāfurowa [sic], ovu, pawafuru hīringu [sic], derived from the phrase "All good poetry is the spontaneous overflow of powerful feelings" in Wordsworth's preface (quoted in Hitomi 1954, 32).

Frequently associated with Wordsworth in the poetry criticism of the time was the American poet Walt Whitman. To cite Shimamura Hōgetsu again, in a 1908 article he paired Whitman and Wordsworth together as poets who demanded an update of "poetic diction":

The topic of vernacular poetry [kōgoshi] in the West has for quite some time entailed two controversial areas. . . . First is the poetic diction used by poets such as Wordsworth and Whitman, by which is meant a theory of composition [shikuhō no ron]; second, meter, by which is meant a theory of rhythm [rikkaku]. Regarding the former of these [i.e., poetic diction], it is mistaken to claim that poetry must have a vocabulary different from that of ordinary speech (i.e., "choice of words") and a syntax [different from that of ordinary language] (i.e., "order of words"). ([1908] 1972, 369)

For "poetic diction" Hōgetsu wrote poechikku dikushon in katakana, trusting that his readers could make sense of the English of Wordsworth's statements. The phrases "choice of words" and "order of words," likewise, were given in katakana, although these were also rephrased in Japanese. Wordsworth and Whitman had not only solved the problems faced by Japanese poets in 1908, Hōgetsu suggested, but they (the Wordsworths and the Whitmans) had devised a vocabulary—in English, of course—for describing their solutions.[16] Their metalanguage was an integral part of the revolution they had fomented.

The above paragraphs are not intended as an exhaustive account of the early Japanese reception of Wordsworth or Whitman; the citations given above rather serve to show how Wordsworth and Whitman were reduced to a few salient traits. Most importantly, they were described as poets who had faced and overcome the same poetic quandaries that Japanese poets faced in the first decade of the twentieth century.[17] A similar simplification occurred in the early Japanese reception of the French *vers libre*. At the beginning of this chapter I cited Ueda Bin's statement that Japanese readers were not ready for free verse, and here it is fitting to note that Bin's prediction could be either corroborated or not, depending on one's view of the critical reaction to Japanese *jiyūshi*. Some Japanese writers viewed the French *vers libre* with enthusiasm. The poet Iwano Hōmei 岩野泡鳴 (1873–1920), for instance, excitedly explained that *"vers libre"* (in roman letters in the original) had proclaimed "a new law" that entailed "the rule of breaking all the rules" ([1908] 1972, 373).[18] Once free verse began to be written in Japanese, enthusiasm for the free-verse form fed a disparagement of those Japanese poets who still wrote *shintaishi*.

The Japanese free-verse poem also had its early detractors. The critic Oritake Ryōhō 折竹蓼峰 (1884–1950), on encountering Ryūkō's free-verse poems, reacted harshly: "At the beginning [of the recent issue of the poetry magazine *Shijin*] there are four works by a poet who goes by Ryūkō or some such name. The titles make them sound consequential—'Rubbish Heap,' 'Cactus Flower,' 'Love's Return,' 'Lovebird'—but in fact they aren't even bad poetry, they're just poetry-like" (quoted in Fukushima 1997, 57). In an article written a year later, Oritake lumped the *vers libre* together with the vernacular poem (*kōgoshi*) as a variety of poetry that left him more puzzled than indifferent ([1908] 1972, 350). In the view of the scholar Okkotsu Akio, Oritake's repeated criticisms of Ryūkō's work "went beyond textual critique and became insulting attacks on Ryūkō's character" (1991, 337–38). Hattori Yoshika and another writer, Morikawa Kison 森川葵村 (1888–unknown), felt compelled to visit Oritake's home to try to persuade him to desist from his "irresponsible criticisms" of Ryūkō's work ("Musekinin naru hihyō" 1907, 66). Another reviewer wrote that free-verse poetry made him "want to vomit," and he castigated the free-verse poets as "criminals who, by writing such poems . . . make our national language [*kokumin no gengo*] ugly" (quoted in Hitomi 1954, 49). Perhaps Ueda Bin was right to hesitate before offering examples of free verse to the Japanese reading public.

The Japanese symbolist poet Kanbara Ariake, writing in 1914, looked back with bemusement on the first appearance of Japanese free verse less than a decade before. Reviewing Iwano Hōmei's translation of Arthur Symons's *The Symbolist Movement in Literature*, Ariake surveyed the impact of foreign literatures on Japanese poetry and concluded:

> Then the so-called "free-verse" movement arose in our country. It has a rhythm such as you find in "The bell is ringing, a pitch-black funeral procession is passing by, ding dong." Japanese poetry has had to go back and start everything over again from the first page of the elementary school textbook, a fact that has implications both good and bad.
>
> And here I've reached a point where I may end this description and put down my brush. (Kanbara [1914a] 1972, 291)

In another essay from the same year, Ariake recycled his tintinnabular parody of the free-verse poem ("ding dong" and so forth) and concluded that "the free-verse movement begins not from the liberation of poetry but its opposite" (Kanbara [1914b] 1980, 278). One can hear the overtones of despair in Ariake's writings on this subject, and indeed by 1914 Ariake's career as a poet was effectively finished.[19] His *Ariake shū* 有明集 (Ariake anthology) had appeared in 1908 and was received with a storm of negative criticism: the once-new style of poetry was coming to be seen as the old.

Kawaji Ryūkō's Free Verse

Given that many Japanese poets and critics took a jaundiced view of contemporary Japanese poetry and a sanguine view of the possibilities of poetry in European languages, one might expect that the best resolution would be to write poetry in European languages. A few Japanese poets did precisely that. For example, Yone Noguchi (Noguchi Yonejirō 野口米次郎 [1875–1947]) wrote poetry in English, most of it free verse, as in the following lines from his 1903 collection *From the Eastern Sea*:

> Fuji Yama,
> Touched by thy divine breath,
> We return to the shape of God.
> Thy silence is Song.

(7)

Most of Noguchi's poetry in English was unrhymed free verse in the manner of the lines just quoted. The novelist Natsume Sōseki 夏目漱石 (1867–1916), too, wrote verse in English but did not publish it; his English poetry was found in his notebooks at his death (Natsume 1995, 708–9). Sōseki's first English-language poem was written in 1901; it was written in a loose trimeter with rhymes on alternating lines (163–68). In 1903–4, having just returned from England, Sōseki wrote a handful of short English lyrics in free verse, as in the following lines from the beginning of his poem "Dawn of Creation":

> Heaven in her first grief said: "Wilt thou kiss me once more ere we part?"
> "Yes dear," replied Earth. "A thousand kisses, if they cure thee of thy grief."
> They slept a while, souls united in each other's embrace.
>
> (172)

Sōseki's English poems remained uncirculated until the publication of an edition of his collected works in 1918 (709).

For most Japanese poets at the time, however, writing poetry in English or other European languages was not an option. It was a young poet on the verge of his nineteenth birthday, Kawaji Ryūkō, who published the first Japanese poems to be recognized as free verse. In September 1907, as has already been noted, Ryūkō published his "Four New Poems"; in the following month, Hattori Yoshika published his article "Poetry in *genbun itchi*." Hattori's essay on Ryūkō's poems was of crucial importance: it signaled to other poets that here was a kind of Japanese poetry that avoided the faults of monotony and unmusicality, while approximating the traits of Western poetries that some Japanese poetry critics deemed desirable. In Lotman's terms, Hattori's article set in motion an important self-revision in the metalanguage for describing the system of Japanese poetry: Hattori hailed Ryūkō's work as "marking an epoch in the history of Japanese poetry" because it was "pure *genbun itchi* poetry" ([1907] 1972, 327; *junzentaru genbun itchi shi*). Hattori did not yet use the term *free verse*, but by singling out metrical constraint (*mītā no yakusoku*) as a matter of primary importance, he reoriented the critical discourse, emphasizing the aspect of Ryūkō's poetry that was most distinctive: its freedom from such constraint (329).

In a case such as this one, critical reception was decisive. Sōseki's free-verse poems were unknown, and Yone Noguchi's English-language free verse, although recognized as such by the tanka poet Ishikawa Takuboku 石川啄木 (1886–1912), did not achieve wide public notice in Japan.[20] However, an important precursor had already written poetry in Japanese that

must be described as free verse: Kitamura Tōkoku. In a classical poetic regis-
ter (the *bungo* style that I mentioned above), and using a "poetic diction" that
Japanese advocates of Wordsworthian ideals would have found unacceptable,
Tōkoku had written free verse as early as April 1889, with the publication of
his *Soshū no shi*, and again in 1891 with his *Hōraikyoku*. Tōkoku's example,
as far as I have been able to determine, was not recognized as a forerunner
by the Japanese poets who were experimenting with free verse in 1907–8.
On the contrary, Tōkoku was already being forgotten. In a January 1907 arti-
cle, Kanbara Ariake lamented the fact that even *shintaishi* poets ignored the
works of the major poets of the previous decade: he named Yamada Bimyō
山田美妙 (1868–1910) and Kitamura Tōkoku among the principal of the
forgotten precursors. Ariake's article went so far as to provide a pronuncia-
tion gloss for the second ideograph in Tōkoku's given name, suggesting that
he or his editor thought his readers might find the name unfamiliar (Kanbara
1907a, 12). Tōkoku had committed suicide in 1894 at age twenty-five, so the
reception of his works depended entirely on critics and historians, and these
saw no reason to be kind to him.

Following the publication of his free-verse poems, Ryūkō himself wrote
a number of occasional articles on poetics; he shaped the reception of his
poetry and gave a positive vector to the critical discourse about the free-
verse form. One of Ryūkō's early essays, "The Free-Verse Form: Forceful
Impressions" (Jiyūshi kei: Kyōretsu naru inshō 自由詩形：強烈なる印象),
sought to assuage the critical establishment's doubts by claiming (to put it
schematically) that the free-verse poem avoided all the alleged faults of Japa-
nese poetic language and had all the contrasting favorable traits of Western
free-verse poetries—a strategy that would be described decades later in Lot-
man's writings on cultural change. For an example of how Ryūkō distanced
the new Japanese free-verse poetry from prior poetic forms, take his state-
ments on the rhythm of free verse. Critics who had disparaged the metrically
regular *shintaishi*, as has been shown above, tended to object to its repetitive
rhythm. Ryūkō harped on this very string, and he did so by invoking a dis-
tinction between the form of a poem and its content. For Ryūkō, form and
content should contribute in equal measures to the overall musicality of a
poem; or, as he put it, the "tone" of the form and the "tone" of the content
should harmonize:

> In poetry of the old sort, a 7-5 verse is a 7-5 verse no matter how many
> you read; a 5-7 verse is a 5-7 verse no matter how many you read. [In
> the earlier poetry] there were works, of course, that achieved an *unité*
> [統一] between the *tone* of content and the *tone* of that [particular]

form [i.e., the *shintaishi*]. But the content was always dictated by the form and was sung accordingly, creating a clear distinction between content and form. In the new free-verse poetry, [however,] the form *is* the content. (Kawaji 1909, 28)

Form and content in harmony: thus, Ryūkō concluded, free-verse poetry extricates Japanese poets from the morass of the *shintaishi*. The tenability of the distinctions Ryūkō was drawing, between form and content, between tonal unity and disunity, is not at issue here; what most catches my attention is how Ryūkō adapted the complaints that earlier critics made against the *shintaishi* and used them to shed favorable light on the free-verse poem.

In the same essay, Ryūkō claimed that Japanese free-verse poetry resembled poetry written by certain prominent Western poets. At a crucial argumentative turn, Ryūkō invoked the name of Walt Whitman to parry an objection that the critic Ikuta Chōkō 生田長江 (1882–1936), a translator of German literature, had raised against the new Japanese poetry. Ikuta's 1908 article "Laughing at the Vernacular Poem" (Kōgoshi o warau 口語詩を嗤ふ) had faulted the newer kind of poetry because it seemed to erode the difference between prose and poetry. Ikuta wrote:

> It's not that I'm claiming there should be no vernacular poetry. It's that I must believe that there are some poems that should not be written in the vernacular. I'm not opposed to the existence of vernacular poems, but in the end it's difficult for me to understand the reasoning behind the claims that all poems must be in the vernacular. Even if a poem is in the vernacular, it must have some kind of rhythmical constraint [*ritsubunteki yakusoku*]. If it does not, then the boundary between prose and poetry vanishes. The vernacular poetry of today has forgotten the fundamental difference between prose and poetry. (quoted in Hitomi 1954, 48)

Ryūkō replied, in effect, that lineation is what makes a poem rhythmical; moreover, lineation distinguishes poetry from prose. Ryūkō's supporting evidence was the example of Whitman:

> In prose poetry [*sanbunshi*] there are two varieties: prose poems based on prose, and prose poems based on poetry. I prefer to see the vernacular poem [*kōgoshi*] as the latter. For convenience's sake, to give examples of prose-based prose poetry—or to put it differently, poetry written in prose ([in roman letters:] "prose poem," or "poem in prose")—there are the [prose] poems of Turgenev or Baudelaire, which are poems in

terms of their content even though they have borrowed prose for their form. They are prose. But in my view, the prose-style poems [*sanbuntai shi*] of someone like Whitman are utterly different [from the prose poems of Turgenev and Baudelaire] in several points. . . . In Whitman, there are lines. These [lines] have the form [*katachi*] of prose, but it is evident that in places they lose the quality of being mere prose. And what, after all, is the significance of dividing [the text] into lines and shaping them as stanzas? The point, it goes without saying, is the poem's rhythm. (Kawaji 1909, 27–28)

In this essay, Ryūkō staked everything on what he called rhythm as a means to distinguish a poem from a piece of prose; lineation, not meter, was what determined rhythm.[21]

To give some specificity to Ryūkō's analyses of *jiyūshi*, it is fitting to examine one of his poems. "The Moment of Sensation" (Kankaku no shunji 感覚 の瞬時), published in the journal *Bunko* 文庫 (Library) in November 1908, provides a snapshot of Ryūkō's poetics at the time:

The Moment of Sensation

. . . .
. . . .

kichi, kichi, kichi, kichi, kichi,
                    kichiri, kichiri,
riri, ririri, ririri,
ririri, ririri,
        ririri,

                            ri
                            ri,
        ririri,

. . . .
. . . .

dew covers the shingles
the stars are smiling coolly—

        the wind—

the sound of the clock ticking on the table. . . .

. . . .
. . . .

the sound of a whistle is drawn out, becomes thin—sweet—sad. . . .
with a blue color it trembles and fades away. . . . .

——— ——— ———

. . . .

the lamp is making noise. . . .

the silence is like water. . . .
a somber echo. . . .

and then

. . . .

riri, ririri,
       chokitsu, chokitsu,
ri, ri, ri,
      riririri, ri,

a somber sound. . . .!

     ri, ri, riri, ri. . . .

there is something that walks, as it were, through my mind. . . .
a voice. . . .
on the road, doubtless. . . .

ta, ta, ta,
. . . .
there is a sound in my ears.
. . . .
. . . . *kaka.* . . . *ta.* . . .
wooden clogs. . . .
     my heart becomes cold as ice. . . .
. . . . . . there is a flash. . . .—

the sound of an approaching woman's footsteps. . . . [22]

Kankaku no shunji

. . . .
. . . .

kichi, kichi, kichi, kichi, kichi,
               kichiri, kichiri,
riri, ririri, ririri,

ririri, ririri,
    ririri,

                    ri,
                    ri,
        ririri,

. . . .
. . . .

kawara ga tsuyu ni shimiru
hoshi wa suzushiku waratteta—

    kaze—

okidokei no kizamu oto. . . .

. . . .
. . . .

fue no oto ga hosoku nagareru—amai—kanashii. . . .
aoi iro ni furuete kieru. . . . . . .

—— —— ——

. . . .
ranpu ga oto o tateru. . . .

mizu no yō ni shizuka da. . . .
shimeyakana kodama. . . .

mata
. . . .

riri, ririri,
    chokitsu, chokitsu,
ri, ri, ri,
        ririri, ri,

shimeyakana oto. . . .!

        ri, ri, riri, ri. . . .

kokoro o aruiteru yōna mono ga aru. . . .
hanashigoe. . . .
tashika ni michi de. . . .

ta, ta, ta,
. . . .

mimi wa jīto naru

. . . .

. . . . *kaka. . . . ta. . . .*

geta da. . . .

       kokoro wa kōri no yō ni hiekaetta. . . .

. . . .*hikatta. . . .*—

onna no kuru ashioto. . . .。

感覚の瞬時

. . . .

. . . .

キチ、キチ、キチ、キチ、キチ、

       キチリ、キチリ、

リリ、リリリ、リリリ、

リリリ、リリリ、

    リリリ、

             リ

             リ、

      リリリ、

. . . .

. . . .

瓦が露に沁みる

星は涼しく笑つてた— —

     風— —

置時計の刻む音. . . .

. . . .

. . . .

笛の音が細くながれる— —甘い— —悲しい. . . .

青い色にふるへて消える. . . . .

—— —— ——

. . . .

洋灯(ランプ) が音(おと) をたてる. . . .

水のやうに静かだ. . . .

しめやかな反響(こだま). . . .

また
. . . .

リリ、リリリ、
　　チョキツ、チョキツ、
リ、リ、リ、
　　リリリリ、リ、

しめやかな音....!

リ、リ、リリ、リ....
心を歩いてるやうなものがある....
話し声....
たしかに路で....

タ、タ、タ、
. . . .
耳はじーと鳴る
. . . .
.... カカ.... タ....
下駄だ....
　　心は氷りのやうに冷えかへツた....
......光つた....──

女のくる足音....。

(Kawaji 1908)

Perhaps the first thing that will strike first-time readers of this poem today is its use of punctuation. In contrast with the poems appearing earlier in this study, Ryūkō's poem flaunts its use of punctuation marks—ellipses, commas, dashes, exclamation points, and a single conspicuous period at the very end. As the poetry scholar Clive Scott has observed, punctuation— "necessarily an inexact science," as he describes it—is "a language as rich in styles and intertexts as its verbal counterpart" (2018, 191 and 184 respectively). Scott finds the deployment of punctuation a useful means for conveying rhythm in translated poetry, a view echoed by other translators. Anne Carson, rendering the words of Sappho's poems as they have come down to us on fragments of papyri—sometimes no more than a single word per fragment—uses punctuation to communicate something of the experience of handling such manuscripts, so atypical of the material conditions most readers take for granted when encountering poetry: "When translating texts read from papyri, I have used a single square bracket," Carson writes, "to give an impression of missing matter. . . . Brackets imply a free space of imaginal adventure" (2002, xi). With its adventurous arrangement of punctuation marks, white space on the page, and written words, Ryūkō's poem reaches for a similar freedom. In "The Moment of Sensation," the written symbol has been strikingly reimagined, in such a way that the punctuation seems almost to suggest (the suppression of?) speech, even as some of the phonetic katakana are repeated in a way that makes them seem percussive—almost like a variant form of punctuation. The poem opens with a couplet comprised entirely of periods, after which the next cluster of signs is an arrangement of "words" made up of *ki*, *chi*, and *ri* (written in katakana), separated by commas. It is scarcely clear what, if anything, *kichiri* or *kichi* or *ri* represent—whether audible phenomena, visible phenomena, or something else. A bit further into the poem, the *wind* and the ticking *clock* present themselves as plausible candidates for the sources of the sounds—if that is what they are—represented by the mysterious words that appeared earlier in the poem. The syntax of the poem is fragmentary: nouns—"the wind," "the sound of the clock," "the sound of an approaching woman's footsteps"—tend not to be followed by conjugated verbs. The impulsive formatting that characterized Tōkoku's poetry is here intensified in Ryūkō's poem, so that the disposition of empty space, written characters, and punctuation marks anticipates the visual poetry of later decades in the twentieth and twenty-first centuries.

To what does the word "sensation" in the poem's title refer? The word is ambiguous, suggestive of many discourses—psychology, philosophy, aesthetics. We might observe that, in this poem, phrases of affective import are frequently juxtaposed with (or follow immediately upon) phrases of a more neutrally descriptive sort, with the result that terms that designate affects—the inward states of the poem's speaker—are made to combine with terms that designate the speaker's sense perceptions of the external world (for example, "a somber [*feeling*] echo [*sense perception*]"). What might appear to be the insistent interiority of the poem is moderated by the speaker's heightened, exaggerated attention to every external stimulus: his waiting is made to feel even longer by the very density of his perception, pointing in two directions, outward and inward, simultaneously.

The juxtaposition, or perhaps the simultaneity, of the (external) perceptions and (inward) feelings of this speaker calls attention to the theme of temporality, literalized here in the ticking clock. Although clock time is often associated with metronomic regularity, the rhythms of this poem are highly unpredictable. The poem is written with no regard to *moji* counts, to the point that when a line in 7-5 does appear (*hoshi wa suzushiku waratteta*), it seems a mere fluke. When this poem was published again in Ryūkō's 1910 poetry collection *Flowers by the Wayside* (*Robō no hana* 路傍の花), many minor edits and small alterations in punctuation were made, but there was one striking change: after the poem's final line was added the phrase "1908, seven minutes before 9:00 p.m. on the *n*th of September" (133; 一九〇八、九月 X 日　夜九時七分前). This attribution is almost comical in its specificity on every chronometric count except the date. The speaker gives the impression that he could reveal the date, if he wanted. Is the omission a way of protecting the privacy of the woman whose approaching footsteps mark the end of the writing of poetry on that evening? The very fact that the speaker knows that the approaching footsteps are a woman's suggests that the poem is a product of (if only fictional) retrospect, an after-the-fact recreation of a series of sensations rather than a *currente calamo* transcription of moments as they are lived.

The other principal word of the title presents a problem in its own right: Should it be translated as *moment* or *moments*? This poem leaves the matter of duration unspecified. It is all well and good that the later version of the poem includes a timestamp at the end of the poem—but to what does that timestamp refer? Does it suggest that the poem recounts a minute's worth (say) of sensation—the sensations experienced at seven minutes before 9:00 p.m. on such and such a night? Or does it simply mark the terminus at which the composition of the poem ended?

The poem, a confounding text by any criterion, differs in many important formal respects from every other poem that has been examined so far in this study. The *moji* as a prosodic unit seems to have been very far from this poet's mind—witness the entire lines composed of punctuation marks alone. One might observe that the poem's near-total avoidance of regular or traditionally attested *moji* counts is itself impossible to imagine without a prior understanding of the history of Japanese prosody before Ryūkō's time. To which I would reply: yes, I agree. That is the point.

An important objection may be raised against the claim that Ryūkō's poetry represented a new departure in Japanese verse—namely, the objection that Kitamura Tōkoku wrote free-verse poems in 1889–91. But Tōkoku, writing nearly twenty years earlier, did so without critical support. The argument I am making here, with Lotman's ideas forming part of the background, is that the contemporary Japanese critical discourse, cognizant of non-Japanese poetic and critical models, was of central importance for the appearance of Japanese free verse. Because of the example of Tōkoku, I am reluctant to endorse the position of Clive Scott, whose histories of European free-verse poetries have argued for "the multiple sources of free verse's inevitability" (2015, 47). The likelihood of Japanese free verse—as a productive form, rather than as a misunderstood curiosity—never rose to the level of inevitability.

And the Next Revolution?

Other poets soon joined Ryūkō in publishing free verse. After publishing his "Four New Poems" in September 1907, Ryūkō continued publishing free-verse poems: five poems in October 1907, three more in December 1907, and another in March 1908, all in the poetry magazine *Shijin*. In May 1908 two other poets published free-verse poems in the literary journal *Waseda bungaku* 早稲田文学: Sōma Gyofū 相馬御風 (1883–1950) and Miki Rofū 三木露風 (1889–1964). In the same month Ryūkō published another free-verse poem in *Shijin*. In the remaining months of 1908 several other poets would begin publishing poems in the new form, among them Hitomi Tōmei 人見東明 (later Enkichi 円吉) (1883–1974), Fukuda Yūsaku 福田夕咲 (1886–1948), Iwano Hōmei, Katō Kaishun, and Kawai Suimei (Okkotsu 1991, 337–40). Ryūkō's first poetry collection, *Flowers by the Wayside*, was published in September 1910; it contained both free verse and prosodically regular poems. Four months earlier, Kawai Suimei's collection *Mists (Kiri* 霧) had been published (May 1910), and it too contained free-verse poems. Within a few years, the poets Takamura Kōtarō 高村光太郎 (1883–1956) and Hagiwara Sakutarō 萩原朔太郎 (1886–1942) would begin publishing their free-verse poems: Takamura's first poetry collection, *The Road Ahead* (*Dōtei* 道程), was published in 1914; Hagiwara's first collection, *Howling at the Moon* (*Tsuki ni hoeru* 月に吠える), in 1917.

Like William Wordsworth, whose poetry "successfully created the taste by which it is now judged" (Mellor and Matlak 1996, 563),[23] Ryūkō helped bring about a transformation in how Japanese poetry was conceived and composed. He played a crucial role in establishing an important new form of Japanese poetry that is still being written today. But Ryūkō's reputation in Japanese poetry is not nearly as high as Wordsworth's in English. The work of the poets who began publishing poetry a few years later than Ryūkō—Takamura and Hagiwara among them—eclipsed the contributions of Ryūkō and the other early experimenters. Ryūkō continued to publish poetry collections, but with decreasing frequency over the following decades; he had a career as a prolific art critic throughout the 1920s and 1930s (Takizawa 2011, 571–86). In a brief autobiographical sketch written for an anthology of his poetry, he noted with evident pride (Kawaji 1955) that he had contributed the preface to the first anthology of modern Japanese poetry translated into a European language, the *Anthologie des poètes japonais contemporains*, published in Paris in 1939 (K. Matsuo and Steinilber-Oberlin 1939).

Looking back on his first poetry collection forty years later (1950), Ryūkō continued to shape and burnish his legacy, letting it be known which foreign texts had influenced his early poetry:

> My first published vernacular-style new poems [*kōgotai no shinshi*] were in the September 1907 issue of Kawai [Suimei]'s [journal] *Shijin*. I should make a minor clarification here. In Hinatsu [Kōnosuke]'s history of Japanese poetry, he conjectures that [my poems] were influenced by Katayama Koson's prose translation of a poem in [the essay] "Sensitive Literature" in [the journal] *Teikoku bungaku*. But that is just [Hinatsu's] conjecture. (Kawaji [1950] 1974, 5)

Before continuing with Ryūkō's account, it is fitting to mention here what Hinatsu Kōnosuke 日夏耿之介 (1890–1971) had written to elicit Ryūkō's rebuttal. In *History of [Japanese] Poetry in the Meiji and Taishō Eras* (*Meiji Taishō shishi* 明治大正詩史, 1948), a multivolume history of modern Japanese poetry, Hinatsu wrote that "Ryūkō's experiment [the poem 'Rubbish Heap'] was clearly modeled on a translation that [Katayama] Koson had published; and thus it should be realized how important Koson's text is for the history of Japanese poetry, even though Koson hated modernity" ([1948] 1971, 225). The translation by Katayama Koson 片山孤村 (1879–1933) to which Hinatsu alluded was a version of a poem by the German poet Richard Dehmel (1863–1920). In Koson's 1905 essay "Sensitive Literature" (Shinkeishitsu no bungaku 神経質の文学),[24] Dehmel's poem "The Dead Sound" (Der tote Ton) was given first in German and then in Japanese translation. Dehmel's poem was written in metrically regular rhyming couplets, but Koson's translation, a line-for-line rendering of the original, followed no discernible metrical pattern. The first line of Dehmel's poem is rich in inner rhymes that suggest the repetitive gonging of a bell: "Ton von Glocken. Drohn von Glocken. Wo nur? Weh, ich falle!" The first line of Koson's translation was "Kane ga naru gōn, gōn, doko darō, yaa taihen watakushi wa taoreru yo" 鐘が鳴るゴーン、ゴーン、何処だらう、やあ大変私は仆れるよ. (It was surely this line that Ariake had in mind in his 1914 retrospective, mentioned above.) Koson's brief comment on this poem began: "It may seem foolish of me to introduce a poem such as this one, but any inspection of the egregious faults of the *décadents* must go to these lengths." His further explanation of Dehmel's rhyme-heavy "Klangmalerei" (sound-painting) was not written in laudatory terms (Katayama [1905] 1974, 175–76).

Perhaps predictably, Ryūkō denied that he modeled his poetry on Koson's version of Dehmel. Ryūkō alleged he did not see Koson's essay in print until later:

> At the time, I was still living as a student in Kyoto and in fact I'd not read or even heard about that [issue of] *Teikoku bungaku*. Therefore his [i.e., Koson's] experiment with the vernacular style [*kōgotai*] had no bearing whatsoever. It wasn't until half a year after I had published my poems that I came to Tokyo, which is when Hattori Yoshika showed me [Koson's translation]. And even then, I only thought it was just a bit of translated prose [*sanbun yaku*]. (Kawaji [1950] 1974, 4–5)

Having cleared up Hinatsu's misunderstanding, Ryūkō was quick to assert that his poetry did have models, just not the ones that Hinatsu imagined. The relevant intertext, in Ryūkō's retrospective account, was the French *vers libre*. Ryūkō also named Hattori Yoshika as an important interlocutor during the crucial early period of his career:

> The term *kōgoshi* was taken from common parlance; my [preferred] term [at the time] was *kōgotai no shi* . . . because the idea was that it had done away with the old rhythms, breaking the old forms and creating a new one; in any case it was not a term that I liked. Then the poetry critic Hattori Yoshika told me about the French *vers libre*, which he had found in Vance Thompson's *French Portraits*, a book that I too was reading at the time. We took that as our term and translated it just as we found it, coining the term *jiyūshi*.[25] I later learned more about the *jiyūshi* form from . . . *Poètes d'aujourd'hui*, an anthology of modern French poetry. (5)

In a manner that should remind us of Ryūkō's earlier critical essays, here he stressed the affinities between his work and that of European poets. But in this retrospective essay the *shintaishi* against which Ryūkō's early free-verse poetry had originally reacted was no longer worth so much as a mention. From this, one should not conclude that the *shintaishi* had stopped being written altogether; but one may surmise that, in 1950, Japanese poets no longer felt it necessary to distinguish their verses from the *shintaishi*—the distinction had come to be taken for granted.

Let us return, by way of conclusion, to Yuri Lotman's model of cultural change. This chapter's first section delineated how Japanese poetry critics cast certain features of Japanese *shintaishi* poetry in a negative light, focusing their criticism on the monotony of the *shintaishi* meter and the unmusicality of the Japanese language. As Lotman would have it, the critics' description of Japanese poetry was a purposive simplification: they excluded the full range of poetic phenomena from their account so that their negative criticisms loomed larger. The following section of the chapter then showed Japanese poetry critics looking abroad (outside the semiotic system of Japanese poetry, as Lotman would put it) to poetries in Western languages, to see whether Western poets might have developed techniques that would, if adapted, ameliorate the perceived drawbacks of Japanese poetry. Here again, the critics' description of Western poetries was selective, and intentionally so: their primary aim was to highlight the alleged successes of the *vers libre* in particular. The third section then showed how a poet, Kawaji Ryūkō, wrote a form of Japanese poetry designed to avoid the drawbacks that critics had located in *shintaishi* poetry and to approximate the more desirable features of the Western poetries that critics had singled out for praise. Ryūkō's own poetry criticism tends to corroborate this model.

It should be granted here, though, that as a piece of selective criticism in its own right, this chapter falls short of the full complexity of the material it takes as evidence. The choice of free verse as a topical focus has entailed, in this chapter at least, the consideration primarily of the *shintaishi* and free-verse poetry, to the exclusion of the contemporary haiku and tanka. It need not have done so, as is shown by, for example, Leith Morton's meticulous accounts of the revolution in modern Japanese tanka (2004, 11–33; 2009, 43–72). Furthermore, there is a limitation in Lotman's model of cultural change: as Lotman would have it, a semiotic system that formulates its own rules will then rigidify under some circumstances or change under other circumstances, but it remains difficult to predict whether the result will be the one or the other. Take the difference between the creation of the *shintaishi* and the later creation of Japanese free verse. Both events, in my view, can be described using Lotman's model, but they had very different sequels. The *shintaishi*, like the later free verse, was created in response to criticisms of other, earlier poetic forms; but the *shintaishi* gave rise to other criticisms in turn, and another major change—the creation of free verse—followed twenty-five years later. But the creation of free verse, one could argue, has not been followed (yet) by any other comparably major change. The free-verse poem continues to be written on a wide scale, while the *shintaishi* has come to be seen as a throwback. This difference remains to be explained.

The explanation might have something to do with the fact that free-verse poetry is still a prominent form in many other literary languages with which Japanese poets are familiar. As the Russian philologist Mikhail Gasparov wrote:

> *Vers libre* is international: it has integrated *all* [emphasis added] the traditions developed by different languages and cultures. Earlier *vers libre*

was perceived against the background of the traditional, more rigorous forms, through its contrast with the latter; now, having become widespread, *vers libre* itself constitutes a background against which *all other* [emphasis added] verse forms are perceived. (1996, 286)

Gasparov's comment referred to the poetries of all European languages, but he might also have mentioned poetry in Chinese, Korean, Persian, Arabic, Hebrew, and Japanese, for starters. And it seems that there does not exist any comparably widespread verse form to challenge free verse's eminence.

Epilogue
A Form to Express Anything Whatsoever

Of the three compilers of *Shintaishi shō*, only one of them, Inoue Tetsujirō, lived to see the twentieth century. Toyama Masakazu died in 1900; Yatabe Ryōkichi, in 1899. Inoue died in 1944, aged eighty-eight. His views on the career of the *shintaishi* in the twentieth century are therefore of particular interest.

In an article published in *Teikoku bungaku* in 1918, Inoue reminisced on the events that led to the publication of *Shintaishi shō*. His article begins: "We can very well say that the *shintaishi* arose almost completely by chance" (1918, 87). He described how Yatabe, a botany professor, showed him a draft of a translation of the "To be or not to be" soliloquy from *Hamlet*; a fortuitous encounter it was, Inoue wrote, because Inoue himself had been writing poetry in Chinese for the previous two or three years but, finding such poetry "somehow not right for the times," had been imagining a different, more timely kind of poetry (87). Yatabe's translation seemed to answer Inoue's hopes, and the two men agreed it would be interesting to devise a new form of poetry. They were joined by Toyama, a literature professor (Inoue had studied under him) who was Yatabe's friend. Toyama, too, attempted a translation of the same soliloquy from *Hamlet*, and thenceforth the three spent several days looking over drafts of translations and of original poems that they had written in the new form (87–88). With time, they had enough poems to publish.

As Inoue recalled, they devised the name *shintaishi* when they were choosing the title of their anthology. "I said we should call it *Shintaishi shō*," Inoue wrote, "because if we just called the poems *shi* that would have been taken to mean *kanshi*," or poetry in literary Chinese (91). Toyama and Yatabe did not object to Inoue's proposed title, and after the publication of their anthology the designation *shintaishi* became the common term for the new lyric.

The great success of *Shintaishi shō* gave the compilers much satisfaction, as Inoue recalled, and they had many imitators within months of publishing the anthology. More collections of *shintaishi* were published throughout the 1880s and 1890s—a success that Inoue had to enjoy at second hand for several years, since he was studying in Germany from 1884 until 1890.

In time, however, something happened that Inoue found incomprehensible:

> The *shintaishi* went into a gradual decline, and today the number of *shintaishi* poets is extremely small. One hardly ever hears the word *shintaishi* anymore. This is just a matter of course. Today if you want to refer to a *shintaishi* you just call it a *shi*. It is no longer necessary to distinguish between the *kanshi* and the *waka* as we used to do in the early years of Meiji. When people use the word *shi* their interlocutors understand that they are referring to Japanese poetry—it is unnecessary to specify even whether the poem is long or short. It is just *shi*. Of course, it is fine if you say the poem is long or short, but just saying the word *shi* is sufficient. (92)

The shift in nomenclature reflected a shift in the kind of poetry being written: a shift away from the composition of *shintaishi*.

Inoue cautioned his readers against abandoning the *shintaishi* altogether, however, and he linked the well-being of the *shintaishi* to the well-being of Japan. The following quote is long, but it resonates with statements made in every chapter of the history we have been tracing up until this point:

> The *shintaishi*'s decline is only a temporary phenomenon. There is absolutely no reason why the *shintaishi* should decline. The Meiji *shintaishi* was an experiment, and it is necessary to refine it by honing it in various ways. And in any case, a civilized country must have poetry [*shi*]. If poetry goes into a decline, that is no reason to conclude that poetry should die out altogether. Nor should we want it to. Poetry must be made to rise again. To the extent that we want progress in culture, we must have poets. The cultural progress of a country that has no poets is indeed a sorry thing. And if poets reappear [in Japan], the form

of the poetry they write must be in a form like that of the *shintaishi*. It must assume a form capable of conveying complex thoughts and feelings with perfect freedom. One volume long, two volumes long, even ten volumes long, it must be a form of poetry without constraints. Reviving the *shintaishi*, naturally, need not entail the eradication of the *waka* as we have known it, nor of the haiku. They are ineradicable. The *waka* and the haiku each have their strengths, and if they continue following their traditions, they will be fine. But *waka* and haiku alone are not enough. *Waka* and haiku as they have hitherto been written are too simple, and they are altogether incapable of conveying continuous, complex thoughts and feelings. Even great epics are incapable of that. The Japanese people have a tendency to revere simple things. They find interest and distinctiveness in tanka [*mijikai uta*] and even in haiku. Those forms are advanced enough for the Japanese. In the haiku there can be found a strength sufficient for turning the worst trials and tribulations of a life into affirmations. But more than that, a poetic form is needed that can express anything whatsoever. That poetic form is the *shintaishi*. (93)

Inoue concluded that the trail he and the other *Shintaishi shō* compilers had blazed was the only way forward for Japanese poetry (94).

What kind of poetry was Inoue hoping to see? His claim that even epics would fall short catches the eye, because he was deprecating works such as Milton's *Paradise Lost*, which had held a place of honor in many admiring Japanese studies of the poetries of Europe. In a telling comment, Inoue observed also that there had been a number of outstanding Japanese novelists since the beginning of Meiji, "but no great poets" (93). Was he hoping, then, for the composition of a novel in verse? His article gave no specific examples of the kind of writing he admired, whether in Meiji-period Japanese prose or in the poetry of other languages.

In this article Inoue made no direct mention of the free-verse poetry that, by 1918, had put down firm roots among other forms of Japanese verse. The nearest he came to alluding to it was in his demand for "a form capable of conveying complex thoughts and feelings with perfect freedom." Yet he evidently found the free-verse poem lacking. If he was proclaiming, however, that a return to pattern would constitute an improvement in the situation of modern Japanese lyric poetry, then he was issuing a most unusual sort of proclamation. Over the next hundred years there would be few voices— not none, but exceptionally few—calling for a longer Japanese lyric poetry founded on recurring patterns to take the place of free verse. There was, for example, the metrically flexible but elaborately rhyming poetry of the philosopher Kuki Shūzō 九鬼周造 (1888–1941), which appeared in the early 1930s but had little immediate impact on other poets (Marra 2004, 10–14). There was also a short-lived movement in 1947–48 called *Matinée poétique*, a small group of poets who promoted the exploration of rhyme and meter in Japanese poetry, with emphasis on the composition of sonnets (Morton 2011, 171–75). Not even the *Matinée poétique* poets imagined, however, that the free-verse form would ever stop being viable. While their highly visible adoption of pattern in verse had clear pro-meter implications, they justified their experiments in rhyme and metrical regularity by claiming that such experimentation would in fact teach poets how to write better Japanese free-verse poems (Narita Takaaki 1966, 123).

But here we are coming up against the beginnings of a much larger subject matter—the history of Japanese poetic forms in the twentieth and twenty-first centuries—and we can go no further. As I have already said, pattern has never been absent from the scene. The five- and seven-*moji* phrases of the old Japanese prosody are still thriving in the haiku and the tanka (Mostow 2003, 103). But after the creation of the free-verse poem in Japanese, pattern has come to have a new, a different meaning. I would observe that, with the decline of the *shintaishi*—a longer lyric form based on metrical regularity—poets have experimented with patterns of different sorts altogether. Some poets, for instance, have blended the prosody of earlier centuries with the more recent meter-free poetry: a paradigmatic example is Hoshino Tōru 星野徹 (1925–2009), whose so-called Bashō poems begin with several lines of free verse, only to culminate in a single haiku by Bashō (Klopfenstein 1981). Many poets in the past few generations have created new patterns rooted in graphical or typographical considerations, not prosodic ones. Nishiwaki Junzaburō 西脇順三郎 (1894–1982), for example, wrote a poem that was a perfect rectangle, with ideographs and phonetic kana arranged in an unpunctuated text eight lines long, each line having sixteen written characters.[1] In a similar vein, Mure Keiko 牟礼慶子 (1929–2012) wrote verse in couplets composed of sixteen-character lines.[2] Niikuni Seiichi 新国誠一 (1925–77) wrote visual poems that elaborated on the pattern-ready aspects of the Japanese ideographic writing system. Contemporary Japanese visual poetry relies on modern conventions of reception (the presumption that poems will be read silently, not aloud) and typography (kana and kanji alike will typically occupy equal areas on an invisible grid on the page). Prosody, once a focus of critical attention, is no longer a main concern.

With prosodic regularity now regarded merely as an optional (when not an altogether undesirable) element of longer Japanese lyric, it is as though

Kanbara Ariake and the other prosodic experimenters have finally gotten their wish: poets are free to define pattern for themselves, on a poem-by-poem basis if they so choose. What Ariake and the others did not anticipate, though, was that being at liberty to determine their own patterns would also entail the freedom to eschew pattern altogether—a freedom that many poets eagerly embraced. When readers today encounter longer lyric poetry in Japanese and wonder when and how metrically regular verse became such a rarity, the present study will, I hope, be seen as offering part of an answer.

APPENDIX A

Ariake's Meters

In this appendix and the next, important features of the poetic forms used by Kanbara Ariake in his first four poetry collections are presented tabularly.

Even so narrow a description as the one I am offering in these tables can only be described as an approximation: the ostensibly metrically regular poems of Ariake—or any poet—frequently depart from their own metrical rules.

There still does not exist a full picture of the metrical variety attempted by Japanese poets in the first decade of the twentieth century. For that, one might construct prosody-recognition software and use it to analyze all the poems written in Japanese in that decade.

Until such software is invented, one must use analog means, as I have done here for Ariake's four collections.

METER	NUMBER OF POEMS
Kusawakaba (1902)	24 poems total
8-6	1
7-5	20
5-7	1
other meters	2
Dokugen aika (1903)	34 poems total
7-5-6	1
4-7-6	18
7-5	7
5-7	1
other meters	7
Shunchōshū (1905)	37 poems total
4-7-6	9
7-5	8
6-6	1
5-7	7
4-7	1
5-4	1
4-5	1
other meters	9
Ariake shū (1908)	55 poems total
7-5-7-5	3
5-7-5-7	1
alternant 7-5-7 / 5-7-5	9
alternant 5-7-5 / 7-5-7	3
5-5-7	3
5-4-7	1
7-5	6
5-7	8
5-4	1
4-5	2
5-3	1
other meters	17

Notes:

A hyphen indicates a caesura: for example, 8-6 means a fourteen-*moji* line with the caesura after the eighth *moji*.

A slash indicates a line break: for example, 5-7-5 / 7-5-7 represents two lines, the first of which is a 5-7-5 line, the second a 7-5-7 line.

APPENDIX B

Ariake's Stanza Forms

METER	(LINES PER STANZA) × (# OF STANZAS)	NUMBER OF POEMS
Kusawakaba (1902)		
8-6	2×6	1
7-5	6×7*	1
	(4//2)×5	1
	4×8	3
	4×7*	1
	4×6*	1
	4×6	2
	4×5*	2
	4×5	2
	4×4	1
	4×3	4
	3×9*	1
	2×15	1

(continued)

METER	(LINES PER STANZA) × (# OF STANZAS)	NUMBER OF POEMS
Kusawakaba (1902)		
5-7	4×8	1
other meters:		
16 stanzas: (7-5×4 // 7-5×4 // 7-5/7-5/4-6/4-6) ×4 // 7-5×4 // 7-5×6 // 7-5×14 // 7-5×8* (80 lines)		1
4/7-4/7-6/6-3/8-6	5×6	1
Dokugen aika (1903)		
7-5-6	4×1	1
4-7-6	sonnet (1 octave, 1 sestet)	18
7-5	5×2*	1
	4×11*	1
	4×10	1
	4×7*	1
	4×6	1
	4×3	1
	4×2*	1
5-7	4×5	1
other meters:		
7-5-7/7-7/7/7-5	4×8	1
(9-6×5)/9/5-5/7-5	8×9	1
7-6/7-5/7-5/7	4×7	1
7-5/7-5/7-5/7/6	5×9	1
7-5/7/7/7-5-7	4×9	1
7-5/7/6/8-6	4×16	1
4-4-4/7-7/7-6/5-3/7-5-7	5×3	1
Shunchōshū (1905)		
4-7-6	sonnet (1 octave, 1 sestet)	9
7-5	6×5*	1
	5×8	1
	4×7*	1
	4×7	2
	4×6*	1
	4×5	1
	2×33*	1
6-6	4×8	1

METER	(LINES PER STANZA) × (# OF STANZAS)	NUMBER OF POEMS
Shunchōshū (1905)		
5-7	128 lines, variable stanza length	1
	44 lines, variable stanza length	1
	double sonnet (8×1 // 8×1 // 12×1)	1
	4×56	1
	4×6	1
	4×5	1
	4×3	1
4-7	4×3	1
5-4	4×6	1
4-5	9×3	1
other meters:		
7-5/7-6	2×6	1
(7-5×5)/7	6×7	1
(7-5×4)/7/5-5	6×36	1
7-4/7/7-4/7-4/7	5×5	1
5 stanzas: 9/9/6/7/7 // 9×6 // 4-6 // 5/4/4-6/4-5/5-5 // 5-8 (18 lines)		1
4-5/4-7/4-5/4-7	4×8	1
4-5/4-5/4-5/4-7-5	4×7	1
5/8/5/8	4×6	1
5/7/7-5/7/7/5-5	6×5	1
Ariake shū (1908)		
7-5-7-5	4×9	1
	4×7	1
	3×6	1
5-7-5-7	4×6	1
alternant 7-5-7/5-7-5	4×10	1
	sonnet (2 quatrains, 2 tercets, last line usually in 5-7-7)	8
alternant 5-7-5/7-5-7	28 lines	1
	18 lines	1
	12 lines	1
5-5-7	9 lines	1
	4×6	2
5-4-7	4×6	1
7-5	8×6	1
	8×5	1

(*continued*)

continued

METER	(LINES PER STANZA) × (# OF STANZAS)	NUMBER OF POEMS
Ariake shū (1908)		
	4×5	1
	4×4	2
	3×70	1
5-7	39 lines	1
	4×8	1
	4×6	2
	4×4	1
	4×2 // 2×1 // 4×3 // 2×1	1
	3×10	1
	3×8	1
5-4	4×6	1
4-5	4×7	1
	4×5	1
5-3	2×3	1
other meters:		
7-5-7 / 5-7 / 7-5-7-5 / 7-5-7	4×3	1
5-7-5 / 7-5 / 4-4 / 5-7	4×7	1
5-5-7 / 7 / 5-5 / 5-7	4×4	1
7-5 / 7-5 / 7-5 / 7-5 / 7	5×10	1
5-7 / 5-7-5 / 7-5 / 7-5-7	4×5	1
5-7 / 5-7-5 / 7 / 7-5	5×9	1
5-7 / 5-7 / 5 / 5-7	4×6	1
5-5 / 5-7	2×4	1
7 / 7-5 / 7-5 / 7-5	4×5	1
7 / 5-7 / 5-5 / 7 / 5-7	5×11	1
3-3 / 7	2×7	1
5 / 5-4 / 5 / 5-4	4×9	1
4 / 4-5 / 4 / 4-5	4×10	1
Rossetti 1: *abba* // *abba* // *aba* // *aba* in which *a* = 7-5-7, *b* = 5-7-5	sonnet	1
Rossetti 2: *abba* // *bba* // *abba* // *bba*	modified sonnet	1
Rubaiyat 1: 7-5-7-5 / 7-5-5-5 / 7-7-5-7 / 7-5-7 // 5-7-5 / 7-7-5 / 7-5-7-5 / 7-6-6-5 // 5-5-7-5 / 7-5-5 / 5-8-7 / 5-7-5 // 7-5-7 / 5-7-5 / 7-5 / 5-7-5 // 7-5 / 5-7-5 // 7-5 / 7-5-7 / 7-5-7 / 7-7		1
Rubaiyat 2: 7-5-7 / 7-5-5 / 7-5-7 / 5-5-5-5		1

Notes:

The hyphen represents a caesura; the slash, a line break; the double slash, a stanza break.

* Indicates a concluding line in 7-7.

APPENDIX C

A Word about Terminology:
syllable vs. *mora* vs. *moji*

Historically, many scholars described Japanese poetry as having a syllabic prosody, one based on the counting of syllables. In recent years, English-language scholarship has shown a preference for the term *mora* instead of *syllable*. However, throughout the present text, with the exception of the introduction, I have preferred the Japanese term *moji*. Since this text is among the first in English to adopt this convention, I think it advisable to explain my reasons.

An important consideration in discussions of prosody is: When poets are composing metrically regular poetry, what units are they counting?

In Japanese poetics, the unit being counted is the *moji* 文字. This term is of ancient provenance, attested in the earliest Japanese writings about poetry. *Moji* is difficult to translate: in many contexts it is rendered simply as "writing," although it can also mean "written character." In the earliest Japanese poetic treatises, *waka* were said to be verses of thirty-one *moji*, made up of five- and seven-*moji* phrases. In place of *moji*, a shorter term, *ji* 字, is sometimes used, as in the common phrases *goji* 五字 and *shichiji* 七字, meaning "five *moji*" and "seven *moji*," respectively.

When the *waka* is defined as a verse having thirty-one *moji*, what does that mean? It certainly does not mean that each *waka* must contain thirty-one written characters, because many ideographic kanji (Chinese characters) are polysyllabic (i.e., poly-*moji*) in Japanese. Rather, it means simply that if the *waka* is rewritten and expanded in phonetic kana then there should in principle be thirty-one written characters. Hence any ideographs that are present in the poem need to be imagined as being rewritten in the syllabary.

It is useful to think of the basic prosodic unit in Japanese poetry as being graphical, not auditory.

In this respect, Japanese prosody is different from all European prosodic systems with which I am familiar. The *moji* is not a unit of sound or time; rather, it is something seen (or imagined) on a page. There is a relation, it is true, between the number of graphical units in a poem and how the poem would be pronounced aloud, of course, but the latter is not of primary importance.

A few examples are in order, to clarify how *moji* are counted. Take the following tanka by Saitō Mokichi 斎藤茂吉 (1882–1953), from his collection *Shakkō* 赤光 (*Red Lights*):

はるの日のながらふ光に青き色ふるへる麦の嫉くてならぬ

(Saitō [1913] 2000, 201)

For clarity, I reformat the poem to show each *ku*:

はるの日の
ながらふ光に
青き色
ふるへる麦の
嫉くてならぬ

The number of written characters in this poem would appear to be only twenty-six; but when we write out the kanji in kana (underlined below), the tanka reads as follows:

はるのひの	*ha.ru. no. hi. no*
ながらふ<u>ひかり</u>に	*na.ga.ra.u. hi.ka.ri. ni*
<u>あおき</u>いろ	*a.o.ki. i.ro*
ふるへる<u>むぎ</u>の	*fu.ru.e.ru. mu.gi. no*
<u>ねた</u>くてならぬ	*ne.ta.ku.te. na.ra.nu*

From such a transcription we may simply read off the number of *moji* in the poem as 5-8-5-7-7, for a total of thirty-two *moji*. (There is a *jiamari* or "extra *ji*," then, in the second *ku*.)

In classical Japanese poetry, it is virtually always the case that the number of *moji* may be correctly tallied from the kana transcription. An ambiguity may arise when a kanji has more than one reading; however, considerations of prosody can render one reading of the kanji more likely than another.

In modern Japanese, there is only one case when a *moji* is not counted: the *yōon* or so-called "contracted sound," when a syllable that begins with *y* (i.e., either *ya* or *yu* or *yo*) is written in smaller font to indicate that it has been assimilated with the previous syllable ending in *i* (i.e., *shi* + small *ya* = *sha*, *bi* + small *yo* = *byo*, and so on). Another tanka by Mokichi:

赤光のなかに浮びて棺ひとつ行き遥けかり野は涯ならん

$$(116)^1$$

The phonetic kana expansion:

しゃっこうの	*sha.k.ko.u. no*
なかにうかびて	*na.ka. ni. u.ka.bi.te*
かんひとつ	*ka.n. hi.to.tsu*
ゆきはるけかり	*yu.ki. ha.ru.ke.ka.ri*
のははてならん	*no. wa. ha.te. na.ra.n*

A tally of the *moji* seems to indicate that the poem is in 6-7-5-7-7. However, the first two *moji*, しゃ, are pronounced "sha" and count as one *moji*. Thus the tanka has thirty-one *moji*.[2]

In my opinion the English-language convention should be simply to follow Japanese convention and speak of *moji* when discussing Japanese poetry.

I should note, however, that I have no objection to the use of the English word *syllable* when discussing Japanese poetry, as long as one recognizes that the word is being applied in a restricted sense. This is just what happens in discussions of poetry in many languages. What is usually meant by *syllable* in European-language poetics is whatever the poet is counting when composing a metrically regular poem.[3] Moreover, we should observe that a syllable in poetry means something slightly different from a syllable in prose. In general, the nature of (what is called) the syllable depends on the language, first, and subsequently on other important factors (the era, the genre or poetic form, and so on).

Just an example or two will clarify what I am taking to be the difference between syllables in poetry and syllables in prose. Let us consider an example from the French. When considered as poetry, the line "La nuit est la muraille immense de la tombe" has twelve syllables—an alexandrine from a poem by Victor Hugo (1995, 334).[4] Using periods to separate the syllables, and using a slash to mark the caesura, the line may be rendered:

La. nuit. est. la. mu.raille / im.**men.se**. de. la. tombe

This line, taken as poetry, is counted as having twelve syllables. The word *immense* is treated as a three-syllable word since the final *e* of that word is appearing somewhere other than the end of the hemistich. (Conversely, the syllables *raille* and *tombe* are counted as one syllable each, because they come at the end of their respective hemistichs; at any other location in the line, they would by disyllables, *rail.le* and *tom.be*, by poetic convention.) The same line considered as prose, however, would have only eleven syllables:

La. nuit. est. la. mu.raille. im.**mense**. de. la. tombe

This detour into another language is intended as an illustration of the fact that *syllable* is regularly given a specialized meaning in prosodic analysis.[5] We should not be surprised if the same happens in analyses of Japanese poetry.

In recent English-language discussions of Japanese prosody there has arisen a tendency to favor the term *mora* instead of *syllable*. Stephen Collington defines mora as follows in an appendix to the translation of Kawamoto Kōji's *Poetics of Japanese Verse*, a study of Japanese poetic diction and prosody:

> Originally a term from classical (i.e., Latin and Greek) metrics, *mora* denotes a unit of metrical time equal to one short vowel (marked as [a breve] in traditional scansion), as opposed to an extended, or long vowel (marked as [a macron]), which counts for two. Thus, for example, while the word *Rōma* ("Rome") is comprised of two syllables (*Rō* and *ma*), it takes up fully *three* morae when used in a metrical context (*Ro·o·ma*). (Collington 2000, 293)

Regarding the use of *mora* for describing Japanese prosodic phenomena, the first thing I would observe is that Japanese prosody differs from Greek and Latin prosodies in important ways.[6] Given my contention that the fundamental unit of Japanese prosody is the *moji*, a graphical unit, then "a unit of metrical time" such as the mora would be no more suitable in the context of Japanese poetics than the syllable would be. Furthermore, Japanese poets managed to discourse about Japanese prosody for centuries before they ever heard of or used the term *mora*, to say nothing of *syllable*. To mention Kawamoto Kōji again, it is interesting to observe that it is the English translators of his *Poetics of Japanese Verse* who introduce the term *mora* into their translation of the text; Kawamoto himself generally uses terms other than *mora*.[7]

An example drawn from an early work of Japanese fiction corroborates my view that the *moji* is the fundamental counting unit of Japanese prosody. Ki no Tsurayuki's 紀貫之 (866?–945?) *Tosa Diary* (*Tosa nikki* 土佐日記, 934), a fictional travel diary, includes the following episode. In the diary entry under the fifth day of the second month, a minor character spontaneously makes an utterance that happens to fit the meter of the *waka*, to the delight

of the other travelers. But the others write down his words in order to verify
that what he said was a poem:

"Orders from his Excellency!" the captain said to the crew. "Hurry
up and get the towrope going before the morning northerly begins"
[みふねよりおふせたぶなり。あさきたのいでこぬさきに、つ
なではやひけ]. His speech sounded like a poem but was quite spon-
taneous and uncalculated. "That's odd. He seems to have recited a
poem," said someone who had been listening. The speaker wrote down
the words; there were indeed thirty-one syllables [*moji*]. (McCullough
1985, 284; Ki 1957, 50)

I have been insisting on the writtenness of *moji*, but perhaps it would be more
accurate to view the *moji* as sharing elements of both spoken and written lan-
guage. In the above episode—drawn, we should remember, from a fictional
account—the travelers suspect, on first hearing, that the captain's utterance
follows the *waka* prosodic outline. Writing the words confirms what hearing
had already suggested.

As I have stated, in my view the best terminology for discussing Japanese
prosody is the Japanese terminology. Hence my preference for the term *moji*.
But, as a final proviso, I should observe that there is more than one Japanese
term for the prosodic unit of Japanese poetry. Above, I have already men-
tioned that *ji* may be taken as an equivalent of *moji*. Another commonly
used term in modern Japanese is *onsetsu* 音節 (sound-unit). This is related
to a slightly older term, *on* 音 (sound). It is not uncommon to see five- and
seven-*moji* phrases referred to as *goon* 五音 and *shichion* 七音, respectively.
A once-common term that is now less frequently used is *gon* 言, derived
from Chinese poetry terminology; *gon* is typically preceded by a number,
as in *gogon* 五言 (five *gon*) and *shichigon* 七言 (seven *gon*). (In the field of
linguistics there is also a set of related but different terms for syllables, which
I will not examine here.)[8] Now, despite the variability in terminology, there
is a marked absence of ambiguity in (Japanese) studies of Japanese prosody:
poets and critics generally have no difficulty understanding what is being
counted when they are discussing meter in Japanese poetry. A reader who
tallies the number of *moji* in any given haiku or tanka will arrive at the same
sum as a reader who tallies that poem's *on* or *onsetsu* or *ji*: these terms name
the same unity, even as they evoke different aspects of that unity.[9]

For all of these reasons, I use the term *moji* in this study. For accuracy's
sake, however, I specify, via a bracketed interpolation, every instance when
the Japanese originals of the various works I cite use a term other than *moji*.
It is an unusual occurrence.

GLOSSARY

The definitions provided here are brief by design. Readers who are coming to Japanese poetry for the first time will find enough here to make sense of the terms in the text, while readers who are familiar with the debates that have swirled around various matters of nomenclature will recognize where I have chosen to minimize the complications.

For fuller discussion of the Japanese terms, see Carter 2019; Miner, Odagiri, and Morrell 1985.

Poetry Terms

alexandrine A twelve-syllable line, typically with a caesura (*q.v.*) splitting the line after the sixth syllable; notable in metrically regular French verse.

bungaku 文学 "Literature." The study of humane letters.

bungo 文語 "The language of letters." A formal, literary register marked by classicizing conjugations and inflections (contrast *kōgo*).

bungo jiyūshi 文語自由詩 "Free verse in *bungo*."

caesura In a line of poetry, a pause or implied break between phrases.

chōka 長歌 "Long song," "long *uta*." A poem of alternating five- and seven-*moji* clauses, longer than a *waka*, sometimes with a concluding doublet of 7-7. An ancient form that peaked in the *Man'yōshū* but had revivals as late as the eighteenth century CE.

dodoitsu 都々逸 Poem in 7-7-7-5.

free verse Surprisingly hard to define. Generally, free-verse poetry avoids predictability; but how we define predictability depends on the language and the era. In English, free verse avoids rhyme and metrical regularity; in Japanese, free verse avoids predictable *moji* counts.

genbun itchi 言文一致 "Unification of speech and print." A written style pioneered in Japan in the late 1880s to write prose in a manner similar to ordinary speech.

haikai 俳諧 "Comic [verse]." Poem in 5-7-5. *Haikai* was a common designation for this form of poetry until the turn of the twentieth century; now *haiku* has become the more common designator. Cf. *hokku*.

haiku 俳句 Poem in 5-7-5. This term comes to prominence in the late 1800s.

hemistich "Half-line." A subdivision of a line of metrically regular verse.

hiragana 平仮名 One of the two syllabaries of the Japanese writing system (cf. *katakana*).

hokku 発句 First stanza, in 5-7-5, of a sequence of *renga* (*q.v.*).

imayō 今様 "Contemporary style." A four-line poem with lines in 7-5.

inbun 韻文 "Verse" as opposed to prose.

ji 字 Written character. In Japanese prosody, equivalent to the *moji* (*q.v.*).

jiamari 字余り Having an extra *ji* in a line of verse.

jitarazu 字足らず Lacking a *ji* in a line of verse.

jiyūshi 自由詩 "Free *shi*." Free-verse poetry in Japanese.

jōruri 浄瑠璃 The musical performance that accompanies Japanese puppet plays (called *bunraku* 文楽).

kami no ku 上の句 "The upper ku." The first three *ku* (5-7-5) of a *waka*; or, the first *ku* (5) of a haiku.

kana 仮名 The nonideographic written characters in the Japanese writing system; the two syllabaries (hiragana and katakana) can be collectively referred to as kana.

kanji 漢字 "The *ji* of the Han (Chinese)." The ideographs in the Japanese writing system.

kanshi 漢詩 "The *shi* of the Han (Chinese)." Poems written in Chinese by Japanese poets.

katakana 片仮名 One of the two syllabaries in the Japanese writing system (cf. *hiragana*). In modern orthography, katakana function in Japanese somewhat like italic type does in English: they give emphasis; they indicate words borrowed from other languages.

kigo 季語 "Seasonal word." In a haiku, a word that indicates which season is the topic of the poem.

kireji 切れ字 "Cutting word." In a haiku, a word (such as *kana* or *ya*) whose function is primarily to indicate a cessation, either of a phrase or of a whole poem.

kōgo 口語 "The language of speech." In writing, a vernacular style (contrast *bungo*). Cf. *genbun itchi* (*q.v.*).

kōgo jiyūshi 口語自由詩 "Free verse in *kōgo*."

ku 句 A subdivision of a metrically regular Japanese poem; usually in five or seven *moji*, but see *kami no ku* and *shimo no ku*.

moji 文字 "Written character." See Appendix C.

mora A unit for measuring syllable durations in (for example) Latin and classical Greek prosody.

pillow-word In traditional Japanese poetry, a fixed epithet (usually five *moji* in length) that modifies another word. In Japanese, "pillow-word" = *makura kotoba* 枕詞.

prosody Study of poetic meter.

renga 連歌 "Linked *uta*." Collaborative composition of a sequence of *waka*, according to various rules.

rubi The small-font kana that appear next to a kanji to indicate its pronunciation.

saibara 催馬楽 A kind of court music that accompanied rhythmical texts.

sanbun 散文 "Prose" as opposed to verse.

sedōka 旋頭歌 Poem in 5-7-7-5-7-7.

senryū 川柳 Comic haiku in 5-7-5. *Kigo* and *kireji* are optional (often absent) in a *senryū*.

shi 詩 Before the contemporary era, this word referred to *kanshi* (q.v.), but in the modern period *shi* refers to poetry in general.

shiika 詩歌 "*Shi* and *uta*." Historically, a word that encompasses poetry in Chinese and Japanese. In the modern period *shiika* often means poetry in general.

shimo no ku 下の句 "The lower *ku*." The final two *ku* (7-7) of a *waka*; or, the final two *ku* (7-5) of a haiku.

shintaishi 新体詩 "New-style poetry."

shōsetsu 小説 Narrative fiction.

tanka 短歌 "Short *uta*." Poem in 5-7-5-7-7; now the more common term for *waka* (q.v.).

uta 歌 "Song." Can be synonymous with *waka* (q.v.). Usually, a Japanese poem in 5-7-5-7-7.

vers libre French phrase from which English derives "free verse."

waka 和歌 "Japanese *uta*." Historically, referred to poetry of any form written in Japanese; at present, *waka* is usually taken to refer to a poem in 5-7-5-7-7.

Titles of Classical Texts and Poetry Anthologies

Hyakunin isshu 百人一首 "One Hundred Poets, One *waka* Each"; collection of previously anthologized poems, compiled in the early thirteenth century CE by Fujiwara no Teika; later formed the basis of various elegant entertainments centered on poetry.

Kojiki 古事記 "Record of Ancient Matters"; a chronicle of Japanese myth and history tracing the Yamato imperial line back to ancient divinities, compiled by ca. 712 CE.

Kokin (waka) shū 古今（和歌）集 "Collection of Ancient and Contemporary *waka*"; first of the imperially ordered poetry anthologies, completed by ca. 920 CE. The preface by the poet and courtier Ki no Tsurayuki is an important and influential early statement of poetic principles in Japan.

Man'yōshū 万葉集 "Collection of Myriad Leaves"; oldest anthology of Japanese poetry, in which the latest datable poem is from ca. 759 CE; includes primarily *waka*, but also many *chōka* by poets of distinction.

Shinkokin (waka) shū 新古今（和歌）集 "New *Kokinshū*"; the eighth imperially ordered poetry collection, ordered in 1201 CE.

Shūishū 拾遺集 "Collection of Gleanings"; the third imperially ordered poetry collection, ordered as early as 1005 CE.

Notes

Introduction

1. As with all poetic texts in this book, I will provide an English translation, a transliteration into roman letters, and a representation of the Japanese original (in modern typographic characters, although I have chosen to leave many of the ideographs in their older forms rather than using postwar orthography). I present the poems in triplicate because I imagine many possible audiences: readers with no Japanese; readers who are learning Japanese or who would appreciate a crib; and readers of Japanese. I am mindful of the scholar and translator Clive Scott's project of "wresting translation from the monopoly of the monoglot reader (with its narrow constraints of fidelity and reliability) and retrieving it for a polyglot reader, able to read the ST [source text]" (2018, 2).

2. Another English translation of this stanza is available at Tomasi 2007, 124.

3. In the introduction, I will be using the word *syllable* to name the fundamental unit of Japanese prosody. Throughout the remainder of the text, however, I use the term *moji* for reasons that I explain in Appendix C. Summarizing those reasons here very briefly, I prefer the term *moji* because it is the term typically used in Japanese.

4. The question of terminology is elaborate. When Japanese literary critics began writing about free verse, they used dozens of different terms to name the new form, until finally a consensus coalesced around the term *kōgo jiyūshi*, "vernacular free poetry" (Mehl 2015, 94–101). The vernacular style is a topic broached in chapter 5.

5. Not to complicate matters unduly in an introductory setting, I will acknowledge that some commentators would object strenuously to the equation between tanka and *waka*, with the latter being ostensibly a much broader designation. Earl Miner generalizes about definitions of *waka* present in Japanese dictionaries and concludes that "any definition of waka based solely on tanka is untenable" (1990, 670). The specifics do not concern us here.

6. Before the Japanese adopted European typographic practices, it was customary in Japan to write poems as a single unbroken text: the divisions between "lines" were in general discoverable only by counting syllables. In cases when considerations of space forced a poem to be "lineated"—when handwritten on, say, a small folding fan—line breaks would bear no necessary relation to phrase boundaries.

7. J. M. Blaut's critique of cultural diffusionism (1993, 11–30) is influential. Where Blaut's critique assumes that imitations are inferior to so-called original works, Linda Hutcheon questions the special authority accorded to mere chronological priority in literary invention (Hutcheon 2013, xv and passim).

8. I state that Moretti's diffusionist model can describe poetic forms, too, in full awareness that some scholars, writing against Moretti's "Conjectures" essay, argued precisely that Moretti's model did *not* adequately map onto "poetry" broadly conceived. Efraín Kristal's essay "'Considering Coldly . . .': A Response to Franco Moretti" (2002) characterizes twentieth-century Latin American poetry as an important exception—and not the only one of its kind, Kristal suggests—to Moretti's generalizations. The discussion sparked by Moretti's essay shows no sign of subsiding; as the authors of a recent study of world literature have observed, "The 'Conjectures' essay has of course given rise to a small library of rejoinders" (WReC 2015, 56). Based on my nonexhaustive reading, I would add that only a small minority of those rejoinders to Moretti have centered on poetry.

9. Moretti himself would later take a critical view of his earlier published opinions on this topic (Moretti 2003).

10. How many times was free verse invented in Japanese? The answer will depend on one's sources and on one's definition of free verse. An 1895 poem by Toyama Masakazu 外山正一 (1848–1900)—one of the original anthologists of *Shintaishi shō*—has been identified as an early instance of pattern-free poetry (Amagasaki 2011, 278), as have the works of Nakanishi Baika 中西梅花 (1866–98), whose 1891 collection *New-Style Poems by Baika* (*Shintai Baika shishū* 新体梅花詩集) has been seen as containing the germ of a form of poetry at variance with metrical expectations (Habu 1989, 10–19). An even earlier instance has been found in certain poetry by the painter and poet Yosa Buson 与謝蕪村 (1716–84) that is seen as fitting no attested form (Shimaoka 1998, 19). I hope the present study will make clear that my interest does not lie in identifying chronological firsts in matters of poetic form.

11. To assert the relative unimportance of content as a determinant of poetic form is to adopt a particular view of verse categorization. In classical Japanese poetry anthologies, poems would be categorized according to topic—suggesting that, for the anthologists in question, subject matter had priority. For my purposes here, form is a more central concern.

12. Many writers decry the Eurocentrism of contemporary (Anglophone, North American, American, academic) critical discourse; I include the descriptors in parentheses because they are, in many cases, implicit in the essays I have encountered. For a brief sample, see Allen 2019, 117; Apter 2013, 5; Chen 2010, 211–55.

The allegation of widespread Eurocentrism must be put in context: there are entire disciplines—East Asian studies, South Asian studies, Asian studies, Australian studies, and so on—that take as their centrism something other than Eurocentrism. What Allen, Apter, Chen, and others are concerned about primarily, I believe, is the origins of their methodologies. While I want to state my agreement with the claim that "the idea of a 'global literary theory' that reflects nothing more than the rest of the world's ability to mimic the language of 'Western' theory is disturbing and worthy of counterdiscourse" (Beebee 2017, 67), I also insist—and I hope I am not alone in believing—that the European origins of a methodology do not necessitate its susceptibility to co-optation for Eurocentric purposes.

13. These quotes—the first from Ian Mortimer, the second from G. M. Trevelyan—appear in Leo Damrosch's *The Club*, an example of the historical recreation I am describing here.

1. New Styles of Criticism for a New Style of Poetry

1. In context, Pound was describing English literature, but there is no reason to suppose he believed only English literature benefited from the existence of translations from other languages. In its brevity, Pound's soundbite simplifies the issues, omitting the various reasons why translations might conduce to a literature's alleged greatness: he is alluding, I think, to periods of history during which translations are published in relatively high numbers, under conditions of relatively amicable intercultural exchange. But other reasons, too, might obtain. Consider, for instance, Doris Lessing's observation about the flourishing of translation in the middle years of the Soviet Union: "writers unable to write what they wanted, because of the persecutions of serious literature, chose to do translating work: this is why the standard of Russian translation was so high" (1997, 161).

2. I agree with the scholar Naoki Sakai's view that the putatively unitary coherence of languages is a limited construct. Sakai poses the following questions: "Is language countable, just like an apple and an orange and unlike water? Is it not possible to think of language, for example, in terms of those grammars in which the distinction of the singular and the plural is irrelevant? . . . My question is: how do we allow ourselves to tell one language from others? What allows us to represent language as a unity?" (2009, 73). Although the UNESCO site, as far as I can determine, does not define language and therefore does not explain how it arrives at that (significantly round) lower bound of 1,100 languages, I surmise that the site is using what we might call the demographer's shorthand, downplaying small differences—the site explicitly does "not count[] dialects"—so that the bigger differences come into clearer focus. Which suggests that 1,100 could be a markedly low estimate of the "number" of languages implicated in translation.

3. One can look in the index of Lawrence Venuti's *Translation Studies Reader* under the heading "impossibility of translation" and quickly find assertions of translation's impossibility in writings from the nineteenth century and earlier, too: in works by Friedrich Schleiermacher (1813), by John Dryden (1680), and by Nicolas Perrot d'Ablancourt (1640) (Venuti 2012, 44, 39, 35, respectively). Even so, in Venuti's anthology the number of references to translation's impossibility increases significantly in twentieth- and twenty-first-century writings. I see no reason to believe that Venuti, a translation studies scholar, would pad his anthology with essays on translation's impossibility.

4. Peter Robinson notes that Frost's famous statement about translation and poetry-loss was never published in print, at least not by Frost, but was pronounced by him in various speeches. Robinson provides a footnote: "Mark Richardson, editor of *The Collected Prose of Robert Frost*, reported by email on 13 March 2008: 'the oft-quoted quip ("Poetry is what is lost in translation") does not appear in the published prose, though RF did occasionally utter it (or forms of it) in public performances. He didn't say this in any essay he published, but he did say it'" (2010, 23n2).

5. I am tempted to conclude that Bolaño could not have intended his prescriptions literally: it is possible to imagine a translation so "bad" that nothing of the original survives, to the point that one cannot detect even a trace of the original. Bolaño is assuming that the translation meets a few basic criteria of fidelity and competence—and that is already assuming a lot.

6. Inada's bibliography is avowedly incomplete, for it excludes "translations of contemporary laws and regulations" and other texts of merely local import (1971, v–vi). But the sheer rarity of translations into European languages during these centuries goes far toward conferring "importance" on any extant document.

7. Scholarly debates on the subject of *sakoku* are ongoing and tend to center on the precise extent to which the Japanese were or were not closed off from news from Europe, often with an aim to explain the perceived successes and failures of the programs of modernization and Westernization that were undertaken in Japan during the Meiji era (1868–1912). Conclusions about the *sakoku* question—which is not, in the end, our concern here—will partly depend on the axioms of whatever scholarly field is involved. For the purposes of the present study, the relevant field is literary history, especially poetry history, which I address later in this chapter.

8. Just how little information about Japanese literature was available in European languages by the early 1800s can be seen in the following studies: for Portuguese, see Rodrigues (1608) 1969 and Cooper 1971; for Spanish, see Collado (1632) 1975 and Oyanguren (1738) 2009; for French, see Titsingh 1820 and Landresse 1826; for Dutch, see the overview at Screech 2006, 69–72; for English, see [Shoberl] 1820 and Titsingh 2006. This list does not represent all the then-available information about Japanese literature broadly conceived, but for information about Japanese *poetry* it comes very close to being exhaustive.

As for information about European poetry that was available in Japanese in the early 1800s, see the indispensable Okamura 1953, Chiba Sen'ichi 1966, and Kasahara 2003. Based on these sources, I would estimate that all Japanese translations of European-language verse available by 1853 would fit on five or six pages, with ample margins. What is more, these translations had virtually no circulation within Japan.

9. The Christian missions of Japan's "Christian century" (late 1500s to early 1600s) did not lead to any wide dissemination of knowledge either in Japan about European literatures or in Europe about Japanese literary culture, and so I omit any consideration of them here.

10. There was no *sustained* attempt at *kanshi* translation of European-language poems, but—as always—there are exceptions. In an essay on early Meiji-period poetry translation, Kamei Hideo (2014, 153–55) mentions Suematsu Kenchō's 末松 謙澄 (1855–1920) *kanshi* translation in 1881 of Thomas Gray's "Elegy Written in a Country Church-yard"; and Nakamura Masanao's 中村正直 (1832–91) *kanshi* translation, also in 1881, of Henry Wadsworth Longfellow's poem "The Village Blacksmith." Keiko Kockum (2006, 107) has written of an 1879 Japanese translation of a forty-four-line poem, "The Last Days of Pompeii," into a *kanshi* fifty-six *characters* long. In the 1889 translation anthology *Omokage* 於母影 (Vestiges), there were fifteen translations of European-language poems, five of which were *kanshi*. On the lamentably neglected field of Meiji-period *kanshi*, see Rabinovitch and Bradstock 2009, 40–48, and Tuck 2018, 34–81.

11. For more about *moji*, see Appendix C.

12. A professor of German at Imperial University in Tokyo, Karl Florenz, translated the beginning lines of Toyama's translation of Hamlet's soliloquy in an essay published in German in 1892, only ten years later than *Shintaishi shō* itself (Florenz 1892, 320). His translation was a useful point of comparison as I revised my own.

13. I have added slashes to show the caesuras between the seven- and five-*moji* phrases.

14. I claim most Japanese readers at the time would not have known the context or background to the partially translated soliloquy despite the fact that Toyama's version of the *Hamlet* soliloquy was not the first introduction of *Hamlet* in Japan. Eight years earlier than *Shintaishi shō*, in 1874, fourteen lines of the "to be or not to be" soliloquy appeared in *Japan Punch* in a translation by that magazine's publisher, Charles Wirgman. The translation was printed in roman letters, rendering the famous first line as "Arimasu, arimasen, are, wa, nan, desuka" (Akiyama 2005, 140–41)— in English: "It exists. It doesn't exist. What is that?" In the following year (1875), in the same publication, the versatile writer Kanagaki Robun 仮名垣魯文 (1829–94) began serializing a kabuki version of *Hamlet*. However, as Akiyama Yūzō has written, "it seems the serialization [by Robun] was not well received," and serialization ceased after three installments (2005, 144). These early renderings of Shakespeare surely would not have been widely known. For more on early Shakespeare reception in Meiji-era Japan, see Katō S. 1991.

15. For other data about Shakespeare reception in Japan in the years 1870–89, including information about the early translation of short quotations or soliloquies (before whole plays were translated), see Yanagida 1961, 281–85.

16. When quoting from *Shintaishi shō*, I will give the page reference to the 1882 original first, followed by the page reference to Morrell 1975. My references to the English translation silently change *syllable* to *moji* to reflect the anthologists' original usage.

17. When Sato described short Japanese verse forms as mono-linear, we must interpret him as asserting something about how the poems look when presented— either typed or handwritten—on a page. When Earl Miner insisted that *waka* are "lineated," he referred specifically to the audibility of the *ku* in aural recitation (1990, 677–78). Sato and Miner's different understandings of the *line* make the tension between their views of the highest interest. To those two, add Mark Morris's seminal essay "Waka and Form, Waka and History" (1986), which attended not to the typography or recitation of the *waka* but to its *syntax* (or "structure"). The exchange of ideas between these three scholars was a mild-mannered but substantive gigantomachia.

18. In descriptions of longer Japanese lyric, the word *ku* was soon eclipsed by the word *gyō* 行 as the term—still used today—for designating a typeset line of poetry. (*Ku* continues to designate the parts of the haiku and the tanka.)

19. As Aoyama Hidemasa (2011, 41) has noted, the handful of *shintaishi* that the anthologists had individually published in various periodicals, *before* gathering them in *Shintaishi shō*, had been printed with the ends of the lines unjustified. In those earlier publications, therefore, the apparent line lengths had varied in direct proportion to the number of characters per line.

20. In a seminal essay about lineation in the *shintaishi*, Ibi Takashi comments that the presentation of the *shintaishi* poems as two rectangles represents a modified continuity with the earlier publication practices of Tokugawa-period books of *waka* and *chōka*. As Ibi points out, those earlier poetry collections were not lineated; by printing the poems in page-filling columns, the earlier publishers were economizing on paper

(2002, 112). Sakaki Yūichi (2005, 157n3) finds precursors to lineated poetry in various kinds of songs: Meiji-era Christian hymns and school songs, and *wasan* or Buddhist hymns by poets such as Shinran 親鸞 (1173–1263). Higuchi Megumi intriguingly speculates that the *shintaishi* and its precursors were lineated with justified margins for pedagogical reasons: the poems were presented in equal-length columns as an aid, Higuchi surmises, to memorization (2000, 26).

21. For a brief biography of Kageki, see Bentley 2017, 19.

22. I will not here unravel the reception history of Wordsworth's *Lyrical Ballads*; suffice it to note that, in the words of the scholar Stephen Gill, Wordsworth's "achievement of 1797–8 [in *Lyrical Ballads*] . . . [is] great and, when all the scholarly footnotes have been written, still a new beginning in English poetry" (Wordsworth 1984, xviii).

23. Inoue's experiences in Europe proved decisive for his later career. He became an ardent advocate of a combination of European secularism (but emphatically not Christianity) with various strands of Asian philosophy, a blend that Winston Davis has called a Japanese "civil theology" (1976, 8–9).

24. For more on statements about differential language change in Japanese poetics beginning in the early nineteenth century, see Árokay 2011. Árokay summarizes: "After around 1800 . . . some poets, writers, and proto-linguists presented the argument that contemporary spoken language was the only effective means of transmitting emotions authentically" (90).

25. The compilers of *Shintaishi shō* were not the first to gloss the ideograph 詩 *shi* as "poetry": just for one example, almost a year before the publication of *Shintaishi shō* as a stand-alone collection, and half a year before the earliest serialized publication of individual poem translations by the compilers, there was a brief article—unsigned, but reputed to have been written by Uemura Masahisa 植村正久 (1858–1925)—in which *shi* is glossed as *poetori* (1881, 294). The compilers of *Shintaishi shō* were the pioneers of perhaps surprisingly few elements of their program. The area in which they had incontrovertible chronological priority was in the translation-cum-theorization of English-language verse in Japanese.

26. For more about Kenchō, first translator of *Tale of Genji* into English, see the analysis at Emmerich 2013, 259–71, and Kamei 2014, 152–57.

27. In my view, Hattori mischaracterized Hagino and Konakamura's use of the term *waka*; their text did draw distinctions between, for example, tanka and *chōka* (e.g., at Konakamura and Hagino 1887, 40).

28. Kamei Hideo speculates that perhaps Yatabe would have prepared his translation while using for reference Suematsu Kenchō's 1881 translation of Gray's poem into a *kanshi*. Kamei gives no in-text evidence for this claim, making only the general observation that "for the literati of the time, translating between Japanese [*wabun*] and Chinese [*kanbun*] was altogether natural—not that it was intralingual translation, but it was translation from one related culture to another related culture" (2014, 155).

29. Another English version of the first stanza is available at Morrell 1975, 17.

30. The poetry scholar Seki Ryōichi has commented (1976, 152) that sheep are extremely rare in Japanese poetry. Seki supposes that the first time the word *hitsuji* had appeared in a Japanese verse was in an 1823 translation into Japanese of a German poem that mentioned sheep. But Seki did not have access to the Internet: an

online search for *hitsuji* (or *hitsushi*, in the old orthography) discovers that a sheep did appear in *Shinkokinshū* poem 20:1934, for instance.

31. Kawamoto Kōji has written an essay on the long tradition of autumn evenings in classical Japanese *waka* (Japanese at 1991, 3–61; English at 2000, 1–44).

32. By removing the space between the stanzas, Kiyokaze, almost certainly unwittingly, was honoring Gray's original intention for the poem. On the poem's first publication, Gray wrote to Horace Walpole, who would be involved in seeing the poem into print: "print it without any Interval between the Stanza's, because the Sense is in some Places continued beyond them" (Tillotson, Fussell, and Waingrow 1969, 943). (Gray's wish regarding the unspaced presentation of his stanzas was honored only intermittently, with some early editions freely introducing spaces.) Whether continuity of sense links the first two stanzas is open to doubt, but the irony stands.

33. It should be acknowledged that Kiyokaze did address the divergent connotations of images in different literary traditions—a matter of content, not form. He observed that in Japanese and Chinese literature, there was an absence of conventional images about the sounds of living things *in autumn*. He mentioned too that it was conceivable that the sound of insects *in the grass* at evening might be mournful; but to treat the sound of insects *in flight* as mournful, as Gray's poem had done, was a bridge too far (Ikebukuro 1889, 15). Since images could not be transferred from one verse tradition to another without confusion, Kiyokaze chose to oppose such transfer.

34. For context about Kageki and the Keien-ha, see Tuck 2018, 180–83.

35. Tani Masatoshi is excellent on the idiosyncrasies of Kiyokaze's views of poetry, which did not simply toe the Keien-ha line (2014, 53). We might also note that whatever Kiyokaze may have thought of *translating* Western poetry into *shintaishi*, he seemed to look favorably upon at least some *original* poems in that form: for example, a long *shintaishi* by Kiyokaze's disciple Yuasa Hangetsu 湯浅半月 (1858–1943), *The Twelve Stone Tablets* (*Jūni no ishizuka* 十二の石塚, 1885), came in for Kiyokaze's praise (Tani 2014, 63–64).

36. For a summary of Motora's career and influence in English, see McVeigh 2017, 71–88. The phrase *seishin butsurigaku*—"mental physics," literally—was a translation of a term used by Gustav Fechner (1801–87), a German psychologist whose *Elemente der Psychophysik* theorized, on an experimental basis, the relation between the intensity of a given external stimulus and the intensity of a subject's corresponding perception.

37. Motora's work represents an early instance, in Meiji Japan, of quantitative reasoning applied to questions of literary interpretation. See Long 2021 for a study of quantitative reasoning in twentieth-century Japanese literary criticism.

38. On the significance of "sustained [or continuous] thought" in *Shintaishi shō*, see Brink 2003, 152–221.

39. On the broader significance of Ebbinghaus's experiment in a European (rather, a German-language) context, see Kittler 1990, 206–15. See also Saussy 2016, 160.

40. Motora seems also to have treated certain verbal endings as being separate units of sense and therefore as being word-like. For example, he analyzes the word *kururan* 来るらん as being two *moji* + two *moji*, *kuru* + *ran*, rather than as being a single four-*moji* word ([1890b] 1975, 441).

41. I have used the word *moji* here, but Yoneyama refers simply to fives and sevens without naming what is being counted—he does not use the words *moji* or *on*, for example.

42. To my knowledge, none of Motora's readers did object to his assumptions about verse taxonomy.

2. "This Dead Form, Begone"

1. Some of these responses are available in Freind 2012. Freind offers a nuanced introductory survey of the drawbacks and successes of what he calls "the Yasusada project" (7–14).

2. Cf. Irokawa 2007, 311–12. On Tōkoku's early years, see also Schamoni 1981, 196–97.

3. Catherine Addison has described *The Prisoner of Chillon* as a kind of "Byronic free verse," but what she seems to mean is that the verse ictus occasionally falls on an unexpected syllable. Despite the poem's flexibility in this regard, Addison notes that *"The Prisoner of Chillon*, perhaps for obvious reasons, since it is a poem about enclosure, favours enclosed rhyme structures" (2012, 91). By contrast, Tōkoku's poem, being about a similar theme of imprisonment, is notably loose in its use of rhythm (*moji* count) even as it, too, incorporates rhyme frequently.

4. I have a specific magazine in mind here: *Kokumin no tomo*, which I have mentioned in chapter 1. In 1887, when *Kokumin no tomo* was launched, it was priced at eight *sen*. Starting in January 1888—just over a year before the publication of *Soshū no shi*—the price of *Kokumin no tomo* was lowered to six *sen*, an amount "less than a weekly newspaper subscription" (Pierson 1980, 168). The fact that Tōkoku made his poem available through the postal service ("plus postage") is itself an artifact of the Meiji years: on the use of the mails for distributing books in early Meiji, see Mack 2010, 36–39.

5. An anonymous reader of an earlier version of this chapter suggested, and I agree, that the term *shi* may mean two different things in these two sentences from Tōkoku's preface. In the first case, *shi* is probably a hyponym (i.e., *kanshi*, which Tōkoku is claiming *Soshū no shi* does not resemble); in the second case, *shi* would be functioning as a hypernym (i.e., like the more general term *poetry*).

6. As with Japanese free-verse poetry, with French *vers libre* I will not dwell on questions of chronological priority, although many other commentators do so. I thank one of the anonymous readers for encouraging me to amplify my treatment of early *vers libre*.

7. It is not clear to me who first discovered the links between Tōkoku and Byron. As will be seen later in this chapter, Tōkoku wrote about his admiration for Byron, but never about the close affinities between their poems.

8. In all, Masuda 1954 indicates six moments where Tōkoku's poem hews closely to Byron's: these six passages amount to a total of twelve lines. (The whole of *Soshū no shi* is 342 lines, by my count.) Cf. Masuda 1956.

9. On Meiji-period adaptations, see also Wakabayashi 1998, 60–62.

10. Suzuki Kazumasa (2001, 286) attributes the unsigned review to Iwamoto Yoshiharu 巌本善治 (1863–1942).

11. As an example of the metrical flexibility of Goethe's *Faust*, the section "Dom" (Cathedral) begins:

Wie anders, Gretchen, war dirs,	[7 syllables]
Als du noch voll Unschuld	[6]
Hier zum Altar tratst,	[5]
Aus dem vergriffnen Büchelchen	[8]
Gebete lalltest,	[5]
Halb Kinderspiele,	[5]
Halb Gott im Herzen!	[5]

(Goethe [1808] 1997, 112)

The fifty-nine-line scene is, with the exception of eight lines of rhymed Latin, unrhymed and metrically unpredictable.

12. Martin is of course writing about English prosody not Japanese; my bracketed interpolation shifts the nationality.

13. Massimiliano Tomasi has mentioned Bimyō's essay (Tomasi 2007, 112). There is a brief treatment of Bimyō's work on rhythm at Maeda A. 1989, 139; in the English translation of Maeda's essay, Bimyō's "Nihon inbun ron" is mistakenly attributed to Uchida Roan (Maeda A. 2004, 238). A mention of Bimyō's "Nihon inbun ron" appears also in Karatani 1993, 58. See also, in English, Kawamoto 2000, 188–93 (based on Kawamoto 1991, 234–41).

14. *Nihon kokugo daijiten*'s entry for *inbun* provides sample sentences dating no earlier than the Meiji period—but later than Bimyō's work. The entry for *sanbun*, however, lists an instance from as early as the eighteenth century, suggesting that the *inbun-sanbun* pairing is an artifact of the Meiji period.

15. Two starting points for English-language scholarship on "civilization and enlightenment" are Howell 2005 and Craig 2009.

16. At the end of the second chapter of *Shōsetsu shinzui*, Tsubouchi Shōyō also quoted the same statement by Macaulay. Shōyō, however, cited Macaulay with approval, hypothesizing that poetry's decline, brought about by the advancement of civilization, would make room for the rise of the novel as the premier genre of an enlightened Japanese literature (Tsubouchi 1885, 19r; Tsubouchi 1981, 23).

17. *Nihon kokugo daijiten* traces the term *sessō* back to as early as the ca. 1777 kabuki play *Meiboku sendai hagi* 加羅先代萩. *Sessō* denotes rhythm: the first definition states that *sessō* is "the rhythm [*shirabe*] of a song"; the second definition is simply the calque *rizumu*, "rhythm" (*Nihon kokugo daijiten* 1972–76, s.v. "sessō").

Whether Bimyō would have been aware of the reference to the kabuki play I just mentioned is unclear. It is possible that Bimyō knew of the term *sessō* as it had appeared in the brief discussion in Tsubouchi Shōyō's *Shōsetsu shinzui*, where *sessō* was described negatively as a rhythmical constraint on verse language—leading Shōyō to favor the greater freedom of prose. For a brief analysis of *sessō* in Shōyō's text, see Suzuki S. 2006, 160.

18. The term *bibun* came to be used as a loose translation of *belles-lettres* in some cases; at times it meant, as the word's components suggest, "beautiful writing." See Levy 2006, 152–53, for an account of the term *bibun*.

19. The poem was published on April 9, 1889. In his diary three days later, April 12, 1889, Tōkoku wrote that he went to the publisher—a family friend—and had

the remaining copies of the text destroyed. Despite these efforts, at least two brief reviews of the text were published. Until the 1902 publication of Tōkoku's collected works, it was believed that no copies of *Soshū no shi* were extant; that 1902 version of *Soshū no shi* bore the marks of much editorial intervention. A copy of the 1889 original was found in an antiquarian bookshop in 1930; two additional copies were found before World War II, one of these coming into the possession of Katsumoto Seiichirō, who edited the three-volume 1950–55 *Tōkoku zenshū* that became the standard edition of Tōkoku's works (Kitamura 1950–55, 1:414–15). These data are often reprised in commentaries on *Soshū no shi* (for example, Schamoni 1983, 92–93).

20. Another translation is available at Mathy 1963, 36. (A quite differently lineated rendering of the passage by Marius Jansen is available at Irokawa 1985, 210.) This speech utters a commonplace view of the divided self: compare Goethe's *Faust*, especially the speech that begins "Zwei Seelen wohnen, ach! in meiner Brust" (Goethe [1808] 1997, 37, ll. 1112–17)—"Two souls, alas, are dwelling in my breast" (1976, 27, ll. 1112–17).

21. For aficionados of Meiji punctuation customs, I should note that Tōkoku's original used both solid commas and hollow commas (*shirogomaten*); I have changed all the hollow commas to solid.

22. Cf. Byron, *Manfred*, 3.1.160–68 (1817, 54–55). The passage begins "This should have been a noble creature" but takes a turn: "as it is, / It is an awful chaos—light and darkness— / And mind and dust."

23. Tōkoku explored ideographic puns and alternative ideographic spellings throughout his writings. See Hashizume 2006, 250, for an ambitious list of Tōkoku's more heterodox spellings.

3. A Disaster Averted

1. Using periods to mark the syllable boundaries: Las. llu.vias. de. ma.yo / no. tea.ta.can. ya(+1) / Tem.plo. deo.ro. Other scansions are also possible. If the second line's direct object pronoun *te* is treated (unnaturally) as a separate syllable, then the line has seven syllables: no. te. a.ta.can. ya(+1). Similarly, it is possible to stretch the third line, if one chooses to stress (quite unnaturally) the preposition *de*.

2. Again using periods to mark syllable boundaries: Ter.coes.plen.dor(+1) / fren.tea. la. llu.viaer.gui.do / tem.plo. de. luz(+1). A Japanese reader—or any reader unfamiliar with Spanish-language counting rules, for that matter—would be highly unlikely to scan "templo de luz" as anything but four syllables: Paz is here localizing the prosody in a most inventive way.

3. Annmarie Drury (2015, 38–43) is excellent on a Victorian-era debate in England over the retention of original prosody in translation.

4. As Nabokov wrote: "Can a rhymed poem like *Eugene Onegin* be truly translated with the retention of its rhymes? The answer, of course, is no. To reproduce the rhymes and yet translate the entire poem literally is mathematically impossible" ([1964] 1981, ix).

5. In this chapter I take up the problem of brevity relative to the haiku but not the *waka*. This is a strategic choice, but it is also historically motivated. On the side of strategy, the haiku's greater brevity is what leads me to concentrate on it:

arguments that apply to the brevity of a brief form will necessarily also apply to an only slightly longer but still brief form. On the side of history, haiku poets felt the pressure of brevity much more than did *waka* poets. A caricature of the historical situation would simplify matters as follows: *waka* poets might have worried about the brevity of their form, but surely (they must have reasoned) as long as the haiku survived, the *waka*, being longer, would also stand a chance of survival. As a point about the history of literary criticism, haiku poets and critics gave sustained attention to brevity mainly in the 1890s and the first decade of the 1900s. In the case of the *waka* or tanka, it was a 1910 essay by Onoe Saishū 尾上柴舟 (1876–1957), "A Personal View of Tanka Extinction" (Tanka metsubō shiron 短歌滅亡私論), that triggered the principal—and still ongoing (as of 2020)—debates about the viability of the tanka as a poetic form. Those debates about tanka, fascinating though they be, fall outside the scope of the present study.

6. Recall that the favorable attitude adopted by some European-language poets—those who regarded brevity as an advantageous trait in a poem, inasmuch as it encouraged condensation and refinement—arose only later, after the first wave of translations brought the haiku (and to a lesser extent the tanka) to the knowledge of a broader readership. Some of the principal figures I have in mind here are Ezra Pound (1885–1972) and Amy Lowell (1874–1925) in English and José Juan Tablada (1871–1945) in Spanish; there were many others. See Johnson 2011 for background.

7. Shiki was aware of certain currents in European thought, but almost always at a remove. For example, his notion of the sketch (*shasei* 写生) is famously said to have stemmed from his acquaintance with Nakamura Fusetsu 中村不折 (1866–1943), an artist who had trained under a Western-style painter, Asai Chū 浅井 忠 (1856–1907), who himself had studied under the Italian landscape artist Antonio Fontanesi (1818–82) (Beichman 1982, 54–55; Tuck 2018, 108). For much of his life, Shiki was not healthy enough to travel outside Japan, and when he did the effect on him was grave.

8. My chronology throughout this chapter relies on the timeline provided in volume 22 of the *Shiki zenshū*.

9. The text of this poem in *Shiki zenshū* gives *tatasumu*. I have interpreted this as *tatazumu* in my translation.

10. The *waka* about the mountain bird to which Shiki refers here was written by Kakinomoto Hitomaro 柿本人麻呂 (660–710 CE): poem 3 in *Hyakunin isshu*. The haiku by Bashō—one of the most famous verses in world poetry—is, on the surface of it, about the sound of a frog jumping into a pond. Shiki is here conveying, perhaps exaggeratedly, a sense of the gulf that divided haiku from *waka* in the minds of at least some poets.

11. G. Clinton Godart, however, casts a critical eye on "the notion of a 'Spencer boom'" in Japan (2017, 243n3).

12. Readers might object to the assertion that there are forty-seven *moji* in Japanese, and I acknowledge that the statement—ambiguously formulated as it is—invites many qualifications, but let us start with the number forty-seven. In Shiki's time, before the various twentieth-century orthography reforms, there were forty-eight kana in the standard syllabary (not counting variant forms), and I am here

implicitly equating *moji* with kana for the purposes of my calculations. Now, one of those kana—the *n ん*—may not appear at the beginning of a word, and therefore I have excluded it. Still, it appears in other positions within words, and for that reason perhaps should not be excluded: its inclusion would bring the base to forty-eight kana. Moreover, there are twenty-five kana derived by the use of diacritical marks (the *dakuten* ゛ and the *handakuten* ゜), which would bring the base total to seventy-three. The calculations based on forty-seven kana, however, already prove my point.

13. Nicholas Albertson gave advice that led to the phrase "meadow-splitter" as a translation of *nowake*.

14. Another translation of this passage is available in Tuck 2018, 119.

15. On the transformations of the concept of *bungaku* or "literature" in Meiji-era Japan, see the works of Suzuki Sadami: e.g., Suzuki S. 1998 (available in English at Suzuki S. 2002 for a summary and Suzuki S. 2006 for the complete text) and Suzuki S. 2009. In recent years, Wiebke Denecke has usefully integrated Suzuki's ideas with German-language scholarship on *Begriffsgeschichte* (Denecke 2015).

16. For further analyses of Mikami and Takatsu's *Nihon bungakushi*, see Brownstein 1987, 444–60; T. Suzuki 2000, 74–77; Lindberg-Wada 2006, 117–30.

17. As Akio Bin has pointed out, Shiki's 1895 pronouncement was not his first assertion of the literariness of haiku: Shiki's 1892 essay "Baseo [i.e., Bashō] as a Poet," written in English, "assumed from the start that Bashō was a *shijin* [i.e., poet], thereby proposing that the haiku was literature" (1999, 83). I thank J. Keith Vincent for directing me to Akio's scholarship on Shiki. For other writers prior to Shiki who asserted the literariness of haiku, see Tuck 2018, 237–38n3.

18. For an examination of the founding of *Teikoku bungaku*, see Shinada 2000, 42–47. On the disciplinary territories demarcated by the various departments at the new university, see Shirane 2000, 6–7; T. Suzuki 2000, 75–76.

19. For a survey in English of Ueda's career and linguistic theories, see Lee 2010, 73–113. For a brief biography of Florenz—including notes on his acquaintance with Inoue Tetsujirō while the latter was studying in Germany—see Wachutka 2001, 51–67.

20. Ueda's review includes the German, lineated, in roman letters. Arthur Lloyd titled the poem "An Ocular Delusion" and translated it as "I watched a petal fall from the tree / It fell—but flew back again: / What could it be? I rushed to see: / There did I spy / A hovering butterfly!" (Florenz 1896, 43).

21. Florenz would have found these views of translation expressed in the essay section of Goethe's *West-östlicher Divan* (1819, expanded 1827), a collection of adaptations of Persian-language poems: see Goethe 2010, 279–81, in English; Goethe (1819) 1994, 280–83, in German.

22. Florenz went on to add that any literary text, poetry included, should be comprehensible to any educated reader without footnotes. The fact that Lange included explanatory material proved, for Florenz, that Lange's translations were not suitable conveyances for poetic sentiments. Then Florenz qualified his own claim by acknowledging that some masterpieces, such as Goethe's *Faust*, contain sections that can be understood only with footnotes; but we must make exceptions for masterpieces, Florenz suggested.

23. An overview of the Ueda-Florenz debate is available at Chiba Sen'ichi 1978, 307–14. In English, see Árokay 2017, 14–18.

24. Earl Miner (1990, 679) raises a fascinating question: When the phrases *kami no ku* and *shimo no ku* refer to *waka* structure, is the word *ku* singular or plural? The answer will depend, Miner suggests, on how one interprets the *ku* as a unit, with Miner's own view strongly favoring treating each five- or seven-*moji* segment as integral. Hiroaki Sato's observations on this problem, also valuable, are more oriented toward the question of formatting translations of Japanese poetry in European-language translation (1987, 350 and passim). In my view, the matter of lineation in Japanese verse is complicated by terminological variety, a rich history of competing schools of thought, and an equally rich history of multiple successive engagements with prosodies in other languages, Chinese foremost among them. A monograph-length historical and orismological investigation of the matter has yet to be undertaken.

25. The paucity of then-available translations of haiku into Western languages was acknowledged in another, more favorable review of Florenz's anthology—an unsigned April 1895 review that thanked Florenz for including any haiku at all ("Nihon shiika no shinsō" 1895, 92).

26. For a list of translations of Japanese poetry into English, French, and German published between 1849 and 1911, see Maeshima 2018, 69–70. Maeshima's list indicates whether the items included translations of haiku; the first such text appeared in 1877.

27. An introduction to Dickins's life and work is available at Kornicki 1999. Early Japanologists working in English were indebted to Dickins for nudging the transliteration of Japanese words toward a more phonetic representation, one that was not rigidly reflective of kana conventions: e.g., ō instead of *oho* (Kornicki 1999, xxiii).

28. Kaneko Mitsuko (2015, 25–37) gives a thorough, compact account of Rosny's work as a translator of Japanese *waka*. According to Kaneko, Rosny's silence on the subject of haiku did much to limit French readers' exposure to those even shorter poems.

29. I should add that Shiki did not assert the literariness of every variety of Japanese verse: he maintained that the *renpai* (i.e., *haikai no renga*), a form of linked poetry, was not literature (Keene 2013, 141). (Keene refers to Shiki's 1893 essay "Miscellaneous Discussions about Bashō" [Bashō zōdan (or zatsudan) 芭蕉雑談], which see in Masaoka 1975–78, 4:224–72.)

30. In English, just as one recent example, see Keene 2013, 93.

31. An article by Mori Shingo transcribes the poem differently, giving the first word as 帆はしら *hohashira*, mixing kanji and hiragana (2017, 10). That transcription, I believe, decreases the likelihood of a reference to the Hobashira Mountains.

Students of Shiki's work are indebted to J. Keith Vincent for making available online a collection of *Shiki kaishi*, the official publication of the Matsuyama Shiki Society.

32. Returning, just for a moment, to the number of possible haiku: if variant spellings—hiragana spellings, katakana spellings, use of kanji—are included, as well, then once again that number is expanded, by probably an enormous amount.

4. Difficulty in Poetry

1. Yoshinobu Hakutani, the editor of a two-volume selection of Yone Noguchi's writings in English, wrote in 1990: "No other Japanese writer in history has ever

written so much and so well in English as Yone Noguchi" (9). However we measure the quantities—number of pages, number of volumes—it is true that Noguchi's bilingual oeuvre, taken in all, was a remarkable achievement.

2. This exceedingly brief treatment of symbolism is based on Cyrena Pondrom's classic account (1974, 1–49), a historical essay that situates symbolism among the French literary movements that influenced poetry written in English in the early twentieth century; and on Anna Balakian's influential (and in my view still unsurpassed) account of how symbolism, so apparently international in its scope, came to favor a paradoxically "esoteric communication" among poets, rather than communication between poets and a wider reading public (1977, 101–22). Wellek (1970, 250–51 and 267–68) is useful on antecedents of symbolism.

3. Earl Jackson Jr.'s essay on symbolism in Japanese poetry (1991) offers many salutary observations about the dangers of treating symbolism as a homogeneous international style: his essay characterizes Japanese symbolism as a synthesis of Buddhism and modernity. My aim here is not minutely to distinguish Japanese symbolism from other varieties, but to isolate aspects of Japanese symbolist poetry that pertain to questions of translation and form.

4. Ueda Bin's (1896, 101) first use of "symbolist"—in the narrow sense, referring to the European literary movement—was written in roman letters.

5. Ueda Bin (1903, 14) appears to have been the first to use the term *shōchōha* 象徴派 to mean "symbolist group." See also Jackson 1991, 563–64; Won 1971, 255.

6. The Russo-Japanese War is the only incident Sakamaki mentions relative to Japan, but other incidents from the beginning of the century could be adduced, such as the suppression of political dissidents in the so-called High Treason Case of 1911; the turmoil attendant on the expansion of the Japanese empire, including the assassination of the Japanese resident-general of Korea, Itō Hirobumi 伊藤博文, in 1909; and unrest in Tokyo over economic conditions, as seen in several riots in 1905–8.

7. The prestige of Paris as a cultural center probably contributed to the attraction of symbolism, but here again that explanation does not clarify why other Paris-centered movements were less successful abroad. The fascination of what's difficult probably played a role in symbolism's spread, even as it played a role in the resistance to symbolism everywhere. For a Europe-centered examination of the decisive attraction exercised by centers such as Paris—albeit, unfortunately, without extensive consideration of Japan or China—see Casanova 2004.

8. The phrase *dokugen aika* 独絃哀歌, translated here as "laments on a single string," would have been derived from *Zhuangzi*. In Burton Watson's translation of that text, the phrase becomes "plucking the strings and singing sad songs all by yourself" (Zhuangzi 1968, 135). Among Ariake's writings, I have not found an explanation for this phrase—which is, incidentally, a signally prescient summary of the poet's later career.

9. The specific tensors to which Deleuze and Guattari refer are "incorrect use of prepositions; the abuse of the pronominal; the employment of malleable verbs . . . ; the multiplication and succession of adverbs; the use of pain-filled connotations; the importance of accent as a tension internal to the word; and the distribution of consonants and vowels as part of an internal discordance" (1986, 23). Cf. Apter 2006, 156.

10. A somewhat similar situation with Kafka did not prevent Deleuze and Guattari from making their claims about how and why he used tensors.

11. Tendan notes that the second line of "Ada naramashi" scans as 7-4-6, *not* 4-7-6, a judgment with which I concur (as suggested by where I place the slashes).

12. It was more than just a mention; in his article, Bin exhorted Japanese writers to meld Japanese and European literatures in order to pursue the ends Goethe described (Satō N. 2005, 43; Ueda B. [1890] 1985, 548).

13. On Bin's interpretation of the symbol, see Hori 2016, 55; Satō N. 2005, 55–58.

14. Other precedents are possible. Writing of the word meaning *symbol* in modern Chinese, Lydia Liu has characterized *xiangzheng* 象徵 as a "Sino-Japanese-European loanword" (Liu 1995, 296, 284)—in other words, a borrowing from Japanese of a word, written in kanji, that had been coined as a translation of a word in a European language. Liu thus suggests that the Japanese term is a modern coinage. *Nihon kokugo daijiten* (1972–76, s.v. *shōchō*) corroborates that assessment: according to that dictionary, *shōchō* appeared first in the journalist and philosopher Nakae Chōmin's 中江兆民 (1847–1901) translation in 1883–84 of Eugène Véron's (1825–89) *L'esthétique* (1878), titled *Ishi bigaku* 維氏美学 (The aesthetics of Mr. V). Ming Dong Gu has stated (Gu 2005, 137), however, that *xiangzheng* arose from a fusion of two words, *xiang* and *zheng*, that had earlier appeared (separately, if I understand correctly) in a commentary by the philosopher Wang Bi (226–49 CE) on the *Yijing* (*Classic of Changes*). Gu's claim, I grant, may also apply to *shōchō*. I thank one of the anonymous readers for pointing me to Wang Bi.

15. I take the deft translation of Hōmei's rather unwieldy title from the scholar Yōichi Nagashima (1997, 57–58).

16. I would question Nagashima's description of the Japanese literary establishment as "uncritically" accepting symbolism and naturalism. For a counterexample, one need look no further than Hōmei himself, whose attempt to fuse the two movements must be seen as nothing if not a stark assertion of each movement's one-sidedness and tendentiousness.

17. Others have attempted to translate this poem, in part or in whole. Donald Keene (1999, 234) translates only the last stanza. Earl Jackson Jr. (1991, 576–77) translates the entire poem, changing the original's eight quintains into seven stanzas of varying lengths. Michaela Manke's lavish study of the poem (1997) includes the original text, a transliteration, three German translations (one a word-for-word translation, one a version recreating the 7-5 meter, and one dwelling on the "bildliche Element" or figurative meaning of the poem), and thirty-nine explanatory notes. Surveying these and other critical responses to the text, I would say that this famous poem's readers, myself among them, are still doing their best to grapple with it.

18. Ariake, a word-spotter of Audenian stature, would have known that *hata* has many possible meanings: "twenty" (二十); "or" (将); "to the side" (傍); and others. The proximity of the implied interrogative *ikutsu* ("so many," "how many?") leads me to wonder whether *hata* should be interpreted here as 二十 (twenty). What dissuades me from that interpretation is the intrusion of the dash, a punctuation mark important in this particular stanza. Manke, too, interprets *hata* as "to the side," while Jackson seems to omit it from his English version. Ariake's decision to spell the word in hiragana instead of using a disambiguating ideograph surely qualifies as a tensor in its own right.

19. The comprehensive examination of Ariake's meters began with the scholarship of Matsumura Midori (1965).

20. Aside from the poem by Ōi Sōgo already mentioned, a few *shintaishi* by Ishikawa Takuboku 石川啄木 (1886–1912) dating to 1903 also showed the influence of Ariake (*Nihon no shiika* 1969, 226). But Takuboku was (and is) known mainly for his tanka, not his *shintaishi*.

21. This, incidentally, constitutes a rare assertion that Japanese pronunciations of Chinese poems were supposed to be metrically regular. Most commentators agree that meter plays no part in the Japanese readings of Chinese verse: Japanese particles and declensional endings are added to each line of Chinese in a completely ad hoc way.

22. One may infer Bin's ideas about translation from comments he made about the translations of others, as the scholar Satō Nobuhiro has observed. For example, in a review of the poetry translations in Ariake's 1905 collection *Shunchōshū*, Bin pointed out that Ariake's reliance on recurring five- and seven-*moji* phrases intro-duced too great a distance from the prosodic contours of the originals—a criticism that applied as well to Bin's own translations, as the latter would surely have been aware (Satō N. 2005, 24).

23. An English translation of Heredia's poem preceded Bin's by less than a decade:

As falcons from their native eyry soar,
So, tired with weight of their disdainful woes,
Rovers and captains out of Palos rose,
To daring, brutish dreams mad to the core.

They longed to seize the fabled metal ore
Which in Cipango's mines to ripeness grows,
And trade-winds willingly inclined their prows
Toward the mysterious occidental shore.

Each eve, athirst for morrow's epic scene,
The tropic sea with phosphorescent sheen
Bound all their visions in mirage of gold;

Or from the fore-deck of their white carvels,
They watched amazed on alien skies enscrolled
Strange stars new risen from ocean's glowing wells.
(Heredia 1897, 113)

24. Forms of the word *alizé* date to at least 1643 (Dauzat, Dubois, and Mitterand 1987, s.v. "alizé"). As for *gerfaut*, it is attested in French as early as 1130, slightly later than *faucon* (ca. 1080) (Dauzat, Dubois, and Mitterand 1987, s.vv. "gerfaut" and "fau-con"). I hesitate to make a positive assertion about word frequencies, but I would wager *faucon* is now more common than *gerfaut*, as is suggested by the absence of the latter from some modern French dictionaries.

25. In the digest made by Bartolomé de las Casas of the logbook of Colum-bus's first voyage, "Chipangu" is mentioned at various moments. See, for example, the entries for Saturday, October 6; Sunday, October 21; and Friday, October 26 (Columbus 1969, 50, 71, 74).

26. I thank the anonymous readers for encouraging me to dig deeper in my read-ing of Bin's translation.

27. For notes about the poem's difficult vocabulary I am indebted to the annotations of Matsumura Midori in Kubo, Awazu, and Hisamatsu 1972, 206–7.

28. In some *shintaishi*, as in the seventeenth line of Kyūkin's "The Sea on Which I Sail" (and again below in the ninth line of Ariake's poem "Daytime Thoughts"), the number of *moji* in a phrase deviates from the number the prosody would lead us to expect.

With regard to the Meiji-era *shintaishi*, I have not seen commentary on this phenomenon of (what we might call) metrical drift. Contemporary readers do not seem to have deemed it worthy of notice: they neither criticized it as a failing nor praised it as a welcome disruption of metrical monotony. Nor did the poets themselves mount a defense of occasionally adding or subtracting a *moji* from a line of verse. (This distinguishes the *shintaishi* from the *waka*, for example: historically, the phenomenon of *jiamari* in *waka* was seen as a significant formal perturbation and inspired vigorous debate.)

29. The annotator of the Chūō Kōron edition believes that Ariake derived the alternating 5-7-5 / 7-5-7 meter from Kyūkin's "The Sea on Which I Sail," who in turn would have derived it from Bin (*Nihon no shiika* 1969, 266). Why Ariake would not have gotten it from Bin directly is not explained.

30. Another English translation is available in Wakui 2017, 434.

31. The original has つくつぐと here. I take the likelier reading つくづくと.

32. Ariake was an obsessive self-reviser of his poetry: variorum notes about "Hiru no omoi" are available at Kanbara 1957, 399.

33. My comment has to remain at the level of a suggestion, however, because contemporary reviewers wrote little by way of analysis of the poems in *Ariake shū*. The reviews listed best and worst poems by title: for example, in a 1908 review of the collection, the poet Katō Kaishun 加藤介春 (1885–1946) listed "The Frame-Saw" (Oga 大鋸), "The Hermit" (Yamōdo やまうど), and "Daytime Thoughts" as the three best poems of the collection, in that order, but offered only minimal explanation—he described "The Frame-Saw" as "representative" of Ariake's poetry and singled out the first two stanzas of "Daytime Thoughts" as "impressive" (Matsubara et al. [1908] 1972, 266). Other contemporary reviewers offered similar lists and similarly thin reasons.

34. Original French at Genette 1966, 262–63. For further discussion of this passage, see Wesling 1980, 112. I hardly need point out the resonance with the concerns raised by Masaoka Shiki about the haiku.

5. Kawaji Ryūkō and the New Poetry

1. Based on the reception of *Kaichōon*, critics have concluded that many of Bin's contemporary readers found the symbolists, rather than the Parnassians, more interesting and ultimately more influential (Keene 1999, 228; Kawamoto 2015, 619).

2. I am adapting the philosopher Saul Kripke's notion of the "baptism" of a new term (1980, 90–97).

3. Such an approach—minimizing the pioneer's contribution—flies in the face of most criticism written on this subject. Postwar poets and critics who have recognized Ryūkō as the author of the first free-verse poetry in Japanese include Miki R. (1950) 1974, 1; Yano (1950) 1974, 450; Nomura 1954, 109; Hattori Y. 1963, 125–30;

Murano 1968, 6; Ōoka 1969, 17; Okkotsu 1972, 729; Miki S. 1986, 316; Okkotsu 1991, 18 and 333; Suga 1995, 244; Fukushima 1997, 15 and 56; Ikegawa 1998, 62; Noguchi N. 2007, 165; Satō N. 2011, 37; and Takizawa 2011, 533. These studies could explain Ryūkō's achievement by mentioning his storied forebears, but typically do not do so. His great-grandfather, Toshiakira 聖謨 (1801–68), was a major figure in negotiations between the Tokugawa bakufu and Russia; his grandfather, Toshiakira's firstborn son, Akitsune 彰常 (d. 1847), died at an early age, but Ryūkō's father, Kandō 寛堂 (1845–1927), was one of a select group of students—a group that included the young Kikuchi Dairoku 菊池大麓 (1855–1917)—sent by the Tokugawa bakufu to study in England in 1866. Ryūkō recounts this background engagingly in his *Chronicle of the Black Ships* (*Kurofuneki* 黒船記, 1953). His mother, Hanako, studied art with Antonio Fontanesi. If anyone could claim hereditary openness to ideas from abroad, it would be Ryūkō.

There are at least two writers who have minimized Ryūkō's place in the history of modern Japanese poetry. First, Hitomi Enkichi analyzes Ryūkō's first free-verse poem ("Rubbish Heap" [Hakidame 塵溜]) and claims that, since many of the lines can be scanned as combinations of five- and seven-*moji* phrases, the poem is therefore not a good example of free verse at all (1975, 608). This objection does not refer to Ryūkō's other early free-verse poems, just the first one. Second, in his dissertation on modern Japanese poetry, Wakui Takashi acknowledges Ryūkō's status as a pioneer *in Japanese* but asserts that for Japanese free-verse poetry, "the future was already laid out by the West, and thus every step of evolution was more or less anticipated" and therefore trivial (1994, 98).

4. The inspiration for applying Lotman to the appearance of free-verse poetry in Japanese came from Ahmad Karimi-Hakkak's work on similar developments in the history of modern Persian poetry (1995, 6–22).

5. Cf. Lotman 2013, 367: "Only in a heuristic can one isolate the history of literature, painting, or some other type of semiotics from its surroundings. In reality, movement is realized as a continuous exchange—the perception of alien systems, accompanied by their translation into a familiar language."

6. The theory I am summarizing here is, in any case, not Lotman's only stated position on the matter of cultural change: see also his *Culture and Explosion*, especially the chapters "Internal Structures and External Influences" and "Two Forms of Dynamic" (2009, 133–41).

7. Much has been written about the creation of *genbun itchi*: on the use of the vernacular in literature, especially prose fiction, see Twine 1991; Tomasi 2004; and Jacobowitz 2015, 192–93 and passim. On *gabun* and the history of *ga* as a term (whose opposite was *zoku* 俗, "vulgar"), see for example Thomas 1994 and Shirane 2014, 142–43.

8. Examples of this view can be found in Hattori Y. (1907) 1972, 327–28; Kanbara (1908b) 1972, 334; Hitomi 1954, 23.

9. "The expression of the natural flow of the feelings as they well up" is Hōgetsu's paraphrase of Wordsworth's famous dictum that poetry is the "spontaneous overflow of powerful feelings." I have more to say on Wordsworth's impact on late-Meiji poetry criticism below.

10. The number 883 is taken from Morita 1970, 350.

11. The phrase *senpen ichiritsu* was used by various commentators, although not always to belittle the *shintaishi*. The literary critic Sasagawa Rinpū 笹川臨風 (1870–1949), for example, questioned whether the *shintaishi* was actually as monotonous as its detractors would have us believe (Iwaya et al. [1907] 1972, 197).

12. For another appreciation of Tōson's essay, see Naff 2011, 215–16.

13. For an extended treatment of Hōgetsu's poetry criticism, see Tomasi 2007.

14. On the Japanese reception of Wordsworth, see Ogawa 1982, 7–66; Mori H. 1988, 4–57.

15. [1] = 600–601; [2] = 596–97; [3] = 600; [4] = 597; [5] = 601, in Wordsworth 1984.

16. For more on Whitman's reception in Japan, see for example Sadoya 1969, 1–32.

17. For a less uncritical approach to Wordsworth, consider Sōma Gyofū 相馬御風 (1883–1950), who questioned the meaning of the famous dictum about the "spontaneous overflow of powerful feelings." Gyofū suggested that not just any feeling would meet Wordsworth's standards, and that what Wordsworth really called for was "a *complex* thought or the kind of feeling that would accompany it" (emphasis added, Sōma 1908, 41).

18. Hōmei added that the term *jiyūshi* was based on the French term *vers libre* (Iwano [1908] 1972, 373).

19. For an unsparing assessment of Ariake's later attempts at writing free verse, see Satō N. 2011, 17–28.

20. I thank one of the anonymous reviewers for directing me to the work of Hori Madoka on Yone Noguchi. Hori (2012, 86–96) surveys the responses to Noguchi's *From the Eastern Sea* in Japanese and English; the English response appears to have been more enthusiastic. Takuboku was probably the most discerning Japanese reader of Noguchi's 1903 collection: Takuboku's 1904 review described Noguchi's poetry as *muinshi* 無韻詩, "poetry without *in*"—which could mean either rhyme or meter (Ishikawa [1904] 1967, 28). Takuboku also compared Noguchi's poetry to Whitman's (28) and would go on to add that Noguchi's poetry has "the rhythm [*in*] that comes naturally from being without rhythm [*in*]" (29). Takuboku's review originally appeared in a regional newspaper in northern Japan, the *Iwate nippō* 岩手日報.

21. Compare Ryūkō's view with that of the poetry scholar Marjorie Perloff: "What *is* free verse anyway? However varied its definitions, there is general agreement [that] the *sine qua non* of free verse is *lineation*. When the lines run all the way to the right margin, the result is prose, however 'poetic.' The basic unit of free verse is thus the line" (1998, 87).

22. Shō Sugita has published a translation of the slightly revised 1910 version of this poem (Kawaji 2014).

23. Note also this comment that Wordsworth made in a letter to Lady Beaumont (May 21, 1807): "Never forget what I believe was observed to you by [Samuel Taylor] Coleridge, that every great and original writer, in proportion as he is great or original, must himself create the taste by which he is to be relished; he must teach the art by which he is to be seen" (Wordsworth 1969, 150).

24. For further discussion of Katayama Koson's essay, see Exley 2016, 49–50.

25. If Ryūkō believed that he and Hattori coined the term *jiyūshi*, then they had overlooked or forgotten Ueda Bin's use of the term in his 1905 preface to *Kaichōon*.

Epilogue

1. The poem: "Tabi no ichinichi" (Nishiwaki 1971, 29–30).
2. One such poem: "Aru hi watashi wa" (Mure 1995, 48–49).

Appendix C.

1. The transcription of this poem raises various interesting problems relating to the so-called Chinese pronunciation of characters: the reading of 棺, for example, would be written く ゎん (*ku* + small *wa* + *n*) in accordance with pre–World War II orthography, but it is typically counted as a two-*moji* word, かん *kan*. To the small *wa* applies the same rule as to the small *ya*, *yu*, or *yo*.

2. Because of the paucity of these *yōon* 拗音 (contracted sounds) in the range of permitted vocabulary in the older *waka* anthologies, classical Japanese usually avoided this issue. In modern Japanese the name Bashō, for example, would be transliterated using four kana: ばしょう. By convention, however, in the Japanese of Bashō's time his name was written with three kana: ばせを or ばせう. It is, indeed, a three-*moji* name.

3. This generalization does not apply to varieties of poetic regularity that are not metrical in the conventional sense but are based on other forms of measure. Jennifer Moxley, for example, has composed poems in which each line has ten *words*. Nishiwaki Junzaburō and Mure Keiko have written poems in the shape of rectangles. Visual poetry often entails typographical varieties of prosody.

4. The poem is number XVIII in the sixth book of *Les contemplations*.

5. In poetry in Spanish and Italian (among others), the phenomenon of vowel elision (Sp. *sinalefa*, It. *sinalefe*) plays a role in determining the number of syllables. For example, take the first line of the first poem of Petrarch's *Rime sparse*—"Voi ch'ascoltate in rime sparse il suono" (Petrarca 1976, 37). When a word or syllable boundary is both preceded and followed by vowel sounds, then the vowels are elided, and the two syllables—before and after the boundary—are treated as one. Hence the line is hendecasyllabic (has eleven syllables):

Voi. ch'as.col.ta.**tein**. ri.me. spar.**seil**. suo.no

But as prose the same line would count two extra syllables, or three extra if we expand the conjunction "che":

Voi. **che**. as.col.ta.**te**. **in**. ri.me. spar.**se**. **il**. suo.no

How to count prosodic units depends on many factors, as I have already suggested. The language in which the verse is written or spoken is one of them.

6. Japanese prosodic rules differ from those of Latin and classical Greek in part because vowel length was not the only determining factor in distinguishing long from short syllables in Latin and classical Greek prosodies: in Latin and Greek, a

syllable that ends with a consonant, for example, is generally scanned as long even if the vowel is short. (I use the phrase "ends with a consonant" as shorthand for a number of rules and considerations that do not concern us here.)

7. Generally, Kawamoto's English translators use the term *syllable* surprisingly frequently—given their penchant for seeming to insist on the greater aptness of the term *mora*. Kawamoto himself writes of *moji, ji, on* (sounds), and *onsetsu* ("syllables," for lack of a better term) indiscriminately. (Below, I will say more about the terms *on* and *onsetsu*.) Kawamoto uses the term *mōra* as a corrective gloss on *onsetsu* in one place: 音節（正しくはモーラ）(Kawamoto 1991, 66), which Kevin Collins translates as "syllables (strictly speaking, these are 'morae')" (Kawamoto 2000, 45). At other places in the English translation, the term *mora* is not underwritten by comparable usage in the Japanese: for just one example, the translator's English phrase "five verses, or *ku*, of five, seven, five, seven, and seven syllables (or *morae*)" (2000, 173) is based on Kawamoto's 五・七・五・七・七の五句 (1991, 215), in which no mention is made either of syllables or morae. In that passage and others, Kawamoto does not use the term *mora*, but his translators do. That explains why the translators of Kawamoto's book include an appendix about the mora, where no such appendix appears in Kawamoto's Japanese original: there is no need.

8. See, for example, Ren 2007 for a view from the field of linguistics.

9. This latter claim, especially, is open to debate, as I am well aware. Because of the exception for *yōon* that I mentioned above, some Japanese prosodists will insist that the *on*, not the *moji*, is the fundamental unit of Japanese prosody. As I have already stated, any of several factors could cause an analyst to favor one term over another: the period, the poet's idiosyncrasies, and so on. Also relevant is the presumption that Japanese is a unitary and invariant language—a presumption that relies, often, on a politically contentious definition of Japanese as a language. For example, as scholars observed as early as the *inbun ronsō* (Ōnishi [1890] 2001, 447), poetry in the Ryukyuan languages in the southern islands of modern-day geopolitical Japan appears to follow prosodic norms that differ somewhat from those of "official" or "standard Japanese." Adjudicating the question in all of its most obvious facets would require, in my estimation, a study of its own, and—if my own reading in the field is any indication—that study has not yet been written.

REFERENCES

Abbreviations

MBZ   *Meiji bungaku zenshū*. 1965–89. 100 vols. Tokyo: Chikuma Shobō.

MTSS   Koizumi Tōzō, ed. 1975. *Meiji tanka shiryō shūsei*. Vol. 1 of *Meiji Taishō tanka shiryō taisei*. Tokyo: Ōtori Shuppan. Reprint of 1940–42 ed., Kyoto: Ritsumeikan Shuppanbu.

NGST   *Nihon gendaishi taikei*. 1974–76. 13 vols. Reprint of 1950–51 ed. (vols. 1–10), Tokyo: Kawade Shobō.

NKBT   *Nihon koten bungaku taikei*. 1957–67. 102 vols. Tokyo: Iwanami Shoten.

NKSK   Hitomi Enkichi, ed. 1972. *Nihon kindai shiron no kenkyū: Sono shiryō to kaisetsu*. Tokyo: Kadokawa Shoten.

Ancient Poetry Anthologies

Hyakunin isshu. 1987. In vol. 5, pt. 1 of *Shinpen kokka taikan*, edited by Shinpen Kokka Taikan Henshū Iinkai, 933–34. Tokyo: Kadokawa Shoten.

Kokin waka shū. 1958. Edited by Saeki Umetomo. Vol. 8 of *NKBT*.

Man'yōshū. 1957–62. Edited by Takagi Ichinosuke, Gomi Tomohide, and Ōno Susumu. Vols. 4–7 of *NKBT*.

Shinkokin waka shū. 1958. Edited by Hisamatsu Sen'ichi, Yamazaki Toshio, and Gotō Shigeo. Vol. 28 of *NKBT*.

Shūi waka shū. 1990. Edited by Komachiya Teruhiko. In *Shin nihon bungaku taikei*, vol. 7. Tokyo: Iwanami Shoten.

Addison, Catherine. 2012. "Byronic Free Verse: The Tetrameter Romances." In *Byron's Poetry*, edited by Peter Cochran, 82–96. Newcastle upon Tyne: Cambridge Scholars Publishing.

Akatsuka Yukio. 1991. *"Shintaishi shō" zengo: Meiji no shiika*. Tokyo: Gakugei Shorin.

Akio Bin. 1999. *Shiki no kindai: Kokkei, media, nihongo*. Tokyo: Shin'yōsha.

Akiyama Yūzō. 2005. *Atarashii nihon no katachi: Meiji kaimei no shosō*. Tokyo: Ochanomizu Shobō.

Allen, Joseph R. 2019. "The Babel Fallacy: When Translation Does Not Matter." *Cultural Critique* 102 (winter): 117–50.

Amagasaki Akira. 2011. *Kindaishi no tanjō: Gunka to koiuta*. Tokyo: Taishūkan Shoten.

Amano, Ikuho. 2011. "A Modernist Adventure in Translation: Ueda Bin's Rhythmic Poetry as Kinetics of Mind." *Japan Studies Association Journal* 9:57–74.

Amano, Ikuho. 2013. *Decadent Literature in Twentieth-Century Japan: Spectacles of Idle Labor*. New York: Palgrave Macmillan.

Amino Yoshihiko. 1992. "Deconstructing 'Japan.'" Translated by Gavan McCormack. *East Asian History* 3 (June): 121–42.

Angles, Jeffrey. 2011. *Writing the Love of Boys: Origins of Bishōnen Culture in Modernist Japanese Literature*. Minneapolis: University of Minnesota Press.

Aoyama Hidemasa. 2011. "Kinsei inbun toshite no shintaishi: 'Shintaishi shō' to 'Shintai shiika' o megutte." *Nihon bungaku* 60 (10): 40–51.

Apter, Emily. 2006. *The Translation Zone: A New Comparative Literature*. Princeton, NJ: Princeton University Press.

Apter, Emily. 2013. *Against World Literature: On the Politics of Untranslatability*. London: Verso.

Árokay, Judit. 2011. "Discourse on Poetic Language in Early Modern Japan and the Awareness of Linguistic Change." In *Divided Languages: Diglossia, Translation and the Rise of Modernity in Japan, China, and the Slavic World*, edited by Judit Árokay, Jadranka Gvozdanovic, and Darja Miyajima, 89–103. Cham: Springer.

Árokay, Judit. 2017. "Japanese Poetry for Western Readers: Contested Strategies of Translation." *Ōtemae daigaku tokubetsu kyōiku kenkyūhi kenkyū seika hōkokusho* 2016-nendo: 13–20.

Balakian, Anna. 1977. *The Symbolist Movement: A Critical Appraisal*. New York: New York University Press.

Beebee, Thomas. 2016. "Translation." In *Literature Now: Key Terms and Methods for Literary History*, edited by Sascha Bru, Ben de Bruyn, and Michel Delville, 59–72. Edinburgh: Edinburgh University Press.

Beebee, Thomas. 2017. "What the World Thinks about Literature." In *Futures of Comparative Literature: ACLA State of the Discipline Report*, edited by Ursula K. Heise with Dudley Andrew, Alexander Beecroft, Jessica Berman, David Damrosch, Guillermina De Ferrari, César Domínguez, Barbara Harlow, and Eric Hayot, 61–70. London: Routledge.

Beichman, Janine, 1982. *Masaoka Shiki*. Tokyo: Kodansha.

Bellos, David. 2011. *Is That a Fish in Your Ear? Translation and the Meaning of Everything*. New York: Faber and Faber.

Benjamin, Walter. 1968. *Illuminations*. Edited and with an introduction by Hannah Arendt. Translated by Harry Zohn. New York: Schocken Books.

Bentley, John R., trans. 2017. *An Anthology of Kokugaku Scholars, 1690–1868*. Ithaca, NY: Cornell East Asia Program.

Beyers, Chris. 2001. *A History of Free Verse*. Fayetteville: University of Arkansas Press.

Blaut, J. M. 1993. *The Colonizer's Model of the World: Geographical Diffusionism and Eurocentric History*. New York: Guilford Press.

Bolaño, Roberto. 2011. *Between Parentheses: Essays, Articles, and Speeches, 1998–2003*. Edited by Ignacio Echevarría. Translated by Natasha Wimmer. New York: New Directions.

Brink, Dean. 2003. "Intertexts for a National Poetry: The Ideological Origins of *shintaishi*." PhD diss., University of Chicago.

Brownstein, Michael Clifford. 1981. "Prophet of the Inner Life: Kitamura Tōkoku and the Beginnings of Romanticism in Modern Japanese Literature." PhD diss., Columbia University.

Brownstein, Michael. 1987. "From *Kokugaku* to *Kokubungaku*: Canon-Formation in the Meiji Period." *Harvard Journal of Asiatic Studies* 47 (2): 435–60.

Byron, George Gordon. 1816. *Prisoner of Chillon and Other Poems*. London: John Murray.

Byron, George Gordon. 1817. *Manfred: A Dramatic Poem*. New York: D. Longworth. From the 1st ed. London.

Carson, Anne. 2002. *If Not, Winter: Fragments of Sappho*. New York: Alfred A. Knopf.

Carson, Anne. 2016. "Variations on the Right to Remain Silent." Unpaginated chapbook. In *Float*. New York: Alfred A. Knopf.

Carter, Steven D. 2019. *How to Read a Japanese Poem*. New York: Columbia University Press.

Casanova, Pascale. 2004. *The World Republic of Letters*. Translated by M. B. DeBevoise. Cambridge, MA: Harvard University Press.

Cassin, Barbara, ed. 2004. *Vocabulaire européen des philosophies: Dictionnaire des intraduisibles*. Paris: Éditions du Seuil.

Cassin, Barbara, ed. 2014. *Dictionary of Untranslatables: A Philosophical Lexicon*. Translated by Steven Rendall, Christian Hubert, Jeffrey Mehlman, Nathaniel Stein, and Michael Syrotinski; translation edited by Emily Apter, Jacques Lezra, and Michael Wood. Princeton, NJ: Princeton University Press.

Chamberlain, Basil Hall. 1880. *The Classical Poetry of the Japanese*. London: Trubner.

Chen, Kuan-Hsing. 2010. *Asia as Method: Toward Deimperialization*. Durham, NC: Duke University Press.

Chiba Sen'ichi. 1966. "Edo jidai ni okeru seiyōshi no juyō jōkyō." *Kokugo kokubun kenkyū* 34:54–84.

Chiba Sen'ichi. 1978. *Gendai bungaku no hikaku bungakuteki kenkyū*. Tokyo: Yagi Shoten.

Chiba Shinrō. 2006. *Ishibashi Ningetsu kenkyū: Hyōden to kōshō*. Tokyo: Yagi Shoten.

Clements, Rebekah. 2015. *A Cultural History of Translation in Early Modern Japan*. Cambridge: Cambridge University Press.

Collado, Diego. (1632) 1975. *Diego Collado's Grammar of the Japanese Language*. Edited and translated by Richard L. Spear. [Lawrence:] Center for East Asian Studies, University of Kansas.

Collington, Stephen. 2000. "The Japanese Mora." In Kawamoto Kōji, *The Poetics of Japanese Verse: Imagery, Structure, Meter*, translated by Stephen Collington, Kevin Collins, and Gustav Heldt, 293–97. Tokyo: University of Tokyo Press.

Columbus, Christopher. 1969. *The Four Voyages*. Edited and translated by J. M. Cohen. London: Penguin.

Cooper, Michael. 1971. "The Muse Described: João Rodrigues' Account of Japanese Poetry." *Monumenta Nipponica* 26 (1/2): 55–75.

Craig, Albert M. 2009. *Civilization and Enlightenment: The Early Thought of Fukuzawa Yukichi*. Cambridge, MA: Harvard University Press.

Crevel, Maghiel van. 2008. *Chinese Poetry in Times of Mind, Mayhem and Money*. Leiden: Brill.

Damrosch, Leo. 2019. *The Club: Johnson, Boswell, and the Friends Who Shaped an Age*. New Haven: Yale University Press.

Dauzat, Albert, Jean Dubois, and Henri Mitterand, eds. 1987. *Nouveau dictionnaire étymologique et historique*. 4th ed., rev. and corr. Paris: Larousse.

Davis, Winston. 1976. "The Civil Theology of Inoue Tetsujirō." *Japanese Journal of Religious Studies* 3 (1): 5–40.

Deleuze, Gilles, and Félix Guattari. 1986. *Kafka: Toward a Minor Literature*. Translated by Dana Polan. Foreword by Réda Bensmaïa. Minneapolis: University of Minnesota Press.

Denecke, Wiebke. 2015. "'Bun' no gainen o tōshite nihon 'bun' gakushi o hiraku." In *"Bun" no kankyō: "Bungaku" izen*, edited by Kōno Kimiko, Wiebke Denecke, Shinkawa Tokio, and Jinno Hidenori, Nihon "bun" gakushi 1, 1–40. Tokyo: Bensei Shuppan.

Derrida, Jacques. 1985. "Des Tours de Babel." Translated by Joseph F. Graham. In *Difference in Translation*, edited by Joseph F. Graham, 165–207. Ithaca, NY: Cornell University Press.

Dickins, Frederick Victor. 1866. *Hyak Nin Is'shiu; or, Stanzas by a Century of Poets, being Japanese Lyrical Odes. Translated into English, with Explanatory Notes, the Text in Japanese and Roman Characters, and a Full Index*. London: Smith, Elder.

Drury, Annmarie. 2015. *Translation as Transformation in Victorian Poetry*. Cambridge: Cambridge University Press.

Dujardin, Édouard. 1922. *Les premiers poètes du vers libre*. Paris: Mercure de France.

Emmerich, Michael. 2013. *The Tale of Genji: Translation, Canonization, and World Literature*. New York: Columbia University Press.

Exley, Charles. 2016. *Satō Haruo and Modern Japanese Literature*. Leiden: Brill.

Finch, Annie. 2000. *The Ghost of Meter: Culture and Prosody in American Free Verse*. Ann Arbor: University of Michigan Press.

Florenz, Karl. 1892. "Zur japanischen Literatur der Gegenwart." *Mitteilungen der Deutschen Gesellschaft für Natur- und Völkerkunde Ostasiens in Tokio* 5:314–41.

Florenz, Karl. (1894) 1896. *Dichtergrüsse aus dem Osten: Japanische Dichtungen*, 8th ed. Leipzig: C. F. Amelangs Verlag; Tokyo: T. Hasegawa.

Florenz, Karl. 1895a. "Nihon shiika no seishin to ōshū shiika no seishin to no hikaku kō." *Teikoku bungaku* 1 (3): 1–17.

Florenz, Karl. 1895b. "Ueda bungakushi ni kotau." *Teikoku bungaku* 1 (7): 69–76.

Florenz, Karl. 1896. *Poetical Greetings from the Far East: Japanese Poems*. Translated by A[rthur] Lloyd. Tokyo: T. Hasegawa.

Freind, Bill, ed. 2012. *Scubadivers and Chrysanthemums: Essays on the Poetry of Araki Yasusada*. Bristol: Shearsman Books.

Fujioka Sakutarō [Fujioka Tōho]. (1907) 1972. "Shintaishi ron." In *NKSK*, 204–10.

Fukushima Tomoharu. 1997. *Kindaishi no shisō*. Tokyo: Kyōiku Shuppan Sentā.

Gaonkar, Dilip Parameshwar, and Elizabeth A. Povinelli. 2003. "Technologies of Public Forms: Circulation, Transfiguration, Recognition." *Public Culture* 15 (3): 385–97.

Gasparov, Mikhail. 1996. *A History of European Versification*. Oxford: Oxford University Press.

Genette, Gérard. 1966. *Figures: Essais*. Paris: Éditions du Seuil.

Genette, Gérard. 1999. "Paul Valéry: Literature as Such." Translated by David Gorman. *Style* 33 (3): 475–84.

Godart, G. Clinton. 2017. *Darwin, Dharma, and the Divine: Evolutionary Theory and Religion in Modern Japan*. Honolulu: University of Hawai'i Press.

Goethe, Johann Wolfgang. (1808) 1997. *Faust, eine Tragödie: Erster und zweiter Teil*. Munich: Deutscher Taschenbuch Verlag.

Goethe, Johann Wolfgang. (1819) 1994. *West-östlicher Divan*. Vol. 1. Edited by Hendrik Birus. Frankfurt am Main: Deutscher Klassiker Verlag.

Goethe, Johann Wolfgang. 1976. *Faust: A Tragedy*. Edited by Cyrus Hamlin. Translated by Walter Arndt. New York: Norton.

Goethe, Johann Wolfgang. 2010. *West-East Divan: The Poems, with "Notes and Essays": Goethe's Intercultural Dialogues*. Translated by Martin Bidney. "Notes and Essays" translation assisted by Peter Anton von Arnim. Albany: State University of New York Press.

Gu, Ming Dong. 2005. *Chinese Theories of Reading and Writing: A Route to Hermeneutics and Open Poetics*. Albany: State University of New York Press.

Habu Kōji. 1989. *Kōgo jiyūshi no keisei*. Tokyo: Yūzankaku.

Haga Yaichi. (1892) 1975. "Nihon inbun no keitai ni tsukite." In *MTSS*, 485–91.

Hagino Yoshiyuki. (1887) 1975. "Kogoto." In *MTSS*, 81–87.

Hagiwara Sakutarō. (1928) 1976. "Kanbara Ariake shi no kinkyō o kiite." In *Hagiwara Sakutarō zenshū*, 8:604–7. Tokyo: Chikuma Shobō.

Hakutani, Yoshinobu. 1990. Preface to *Selected English Writings of Yone Noguchi: An East-West Literary Assimilation*, edited by Yoshinobu Hakutani, 1:9–10. Rutherford, NJ: Fairleigh Dickinson University Press.

Hashizume Shizuko. 2006. "Kitamura Tōkoku no gengo ishiki: Sezokunai shussekan / shūji / rubi no bi / hihyō no tanjō." In *Kitamura Tōkoku: "Hihyō" no tanjō*, edited by Shinpo Yūji, 242–52. Tokyo: Shibundō.

Hattori Motohiko. (1888) 1975. "Waka kairyōron o yomu." In *MTSS*, 91–96.

Hattori Yoshika. (1907) 1972. "Genbun itchi no shi." In *NKSK*, 327–30.

Hattori Yoshika. (1908) 1972. "Shiika no shukanteki ken'i." In *NKSK*, 359–67.

Hattori Yoshika. (1909) 1972. "Jikkan shiron." In *NKSK*, 381–86.

Hattori Yoshika. 1963. *Kōgoshi shōshi: Nihon jiyūshi zenshi*. Tokyo: Shōrinsha.

Heredia, José-Maria de. 1893 *Les trophées*. Paris: A. Lemerre.

Heredia, José-Maria de. 1897. *Sonnets of José-Maria de Heredia*. Translated by Edward Robeson Taylor. San Francisco: W. Doxey.

Higashinaka, Itsuyo. 1990. "Byron's *Manfred* and Kitamura Tōkoku's *Horaikyoku*." In *Literary Relations East and West*, edited by Jean Toyama and Nobuko Ochner, 207–14. Honolulu: University of Hawai'i Press.

Higashinaka, Itsuyo. 1995. "Politics or Cherry Blossoms? A Comparison of Byron's *Prisoner of Chillon* and Kitamura Tōkoku's *Soshu no shi*." In *Byron and the Mediterranean World: Proceedings of the Twentieth International Byron Conference in the University of Athens 20–21 September 1995*, edited by M. Byron Raizis, 131–39. Athens: Hellenic Byron Society.

Higuchi Megumi. 2000. "Uberusu to sutanzā no hassei: 'Shintaishi shō' to iu shomotsu." *Kokubungaku kenkyū* 132:20–30.

Hinatsu Kōnosuke. (1948) 1971. *Meiji Taishō shishi*. Vol. 2. Tokyo: Sōgensha.

Hiraoka Toshio. 1967. *Kitamura Tōkoku kenkyū*. Tokyo: Yūseidō.

Hitomi Enkichi. 1954. "Kōgoshi no shuppatsu (4)." *Gakuen* 16 (11): 6–65.

Hitomi Enkichi. 1975. *Kōgoshi no shiteki kenkyū*. Tokyo: Ōfūsha.

Hori Madoka. 2012. "*Nijū kokuseki" shijin Noguchi Yonejirō*. Nagoya: Nagoya Daigaku Shuppan Kai.

Hori Madoka. 2016. "Noguchi Yonejirō no shōchōshugi: Nihon bunka ni miidasareta shōchōshugi." In *Kindai nihon to furansu shōchōshugi*, edited by Sakamaki Kōji, 46–68. Tokyo: Suiseisha.

Horton, H. Mack. 2018. "Making It Old: Premodern Japanese Poetry in English Translation." *Asia Pacific Translation and Intercultural Studies* 5 (2): 110–204.

Howell, David L. 2005. "Civilization and Enlightenment: Markers of Identity in Nineteenth-Century Japan." In *The Teleology of the Modern Nation-State: Japan and China*, edited by Joshua Fogel, 117–37. Philadelphia: University of Pennsylvania Press.

Hugo, Victor. 1995. *Les contemplations*. Paris: Flammarion.

Hutcheon, Linda, with Siobhan O'Flynn. 2013. *A Theory of Adaptation*. 2nd ed. London: Routledge.

Ibi Takashi. 2002. "Kaigyōron: Kinsei chōka to meiji shintaishi no hazama." *Bungaku* 3 (2): 103–19.

Ikebukuro Kiyokaze. 1889. "Shintaishi hihyō 1." *Kokumin no tomo* 39 (January): 11–15.

Ikegawa Keishi. 1998. "Bungo teikeishi kara kōgo jiyūshi e." In *Kingendaishi o manabu hito no tame ni*, edited by Wada Hirofumi, 62–76. Tokyo: Sekai Shisōsha.

Inada, Hide Ikehara. 1971. *Bibliography of Translations from the Japanese into Western Languages*. Tokyo: Monumenta Nipponica (Sophia University).

Index Translationum FAQ. 2011. "What Does the Index Translationum Consist Of?" Last updated July 27, 2011. http://www.unesco.org/xtrans/.

Infante, Ignacio. 2013. *After Translation: The Transfer and Circulation of Modern Poetics across the Atlantic*. New York: Fordham University Press.

Inoue Tetsujirō. 1918. "Shintaishi no kigen oyobi shōrai no shikei." *Teikoku bungaku* 24 (5): 87–94.

Irokawa Daikichi. 1985. *The Culture of the Meiji Period*. Translated by Marius Jansen. Princeton, NJ: Princeton University Press.

Irokawa Daikichi. 2007. *Kitamura Tōkoku*. Tokyo: Tokyo Daigaku Shuppan.

Ishibashi Ningetsu. (1890a) 1995. "Inbun ron o azakeru." In *Ishibashi Ningetsu zenshū*, 3:196–99. Tokyo: Yagi Shoten.

Ishibashi Ningetsu. (1890b) 1995. "Shi (poejii)." In *Ishibashi Ningetsu zenshū*, 3:199–200. Tokyo: Yagi Shoten.

Ishikawa Takuboku. (1904) 1967. "Shidan issoku ('Tōkai yori' o yomite)." In *Takuboku zenshū*, 4:27–32. Tokyo: Chikuma Shobō.

Isogai Unpō. (1891) 1989. Review of *Hōraikyoku*. In *Shintaishi no senkusha Isogai Unpō sakuhinshū*, edited by Uchida Tadayuki, 252. Gunma Prefecture, Tsukiyonomachi: Uchida Tadayuki.

[Iwamoto Yoshiharu?] 1889. Review of *Soshū no shi*, by Kitamura Montarō [Tōkoku]. *Jogaku zasshi* 160 (May 4): 21.

Iwano Hōmei. (1907) 1972. "Shizen shugi teki hyōshōshi ron." In *NKSK*, 247–54.

Iwano Hōmei. (1908) 1972. "Sanbunshi mondai." In *NKSK*, 371–76.

Iwaya Sazanami, Iwano Hōmei, Sasagawa Rinpū, Kawai Suimei, Noguchi Yonejirō, Hayashida Shunchō, and Gotō Chūgai. (1907) 1972. "Genji no shintaishi no kachi (shō)." In *NKSK*, 193–204.

Jackson, Earl. 1991. "The Heresy of Meaning: Japanese Symbolist Poetry." *Harvard Journal of Asiatic Studies* 51 (2): 561–98.

Jacobowitz, Seth. 2015. *Writing Technology in Meiji Japan: A Media History of Modern Japanese Literature and Visual Culture*. Cambridge, MA: Harvard University Press.

Jacobs, Adriana X. 2018. *Strange Cocktail: Translation and the Making of Modern Hebrew Poetry*. Ann Arbor: University of Michigan Press.

Johnson, Jeffrey. 2011. *Haiku Poetics in Twentieth-Century Avant-Garde Poetry*. Lanham, MD: Lexington Books.

Kagawa Kageki. (1811) 1975. "Niimanabi iken," edited by Fujihira Haruo. In *Karonshū*, edited by Hashimoto Fumio, Ariyoshi Tamotsu, and Fujihira Haruo, 583–604. Vol. 50 of *Nihon koten bungaku zenshū*. Tokyo: Shōgakukan.

Kagawa Kageki. 2017. "Niimanabi iken." In *An Anthology of Kokugaku Scholars, 1690–1898*, translated by John R. Bentley, 265–77. Ithaca, NY: Cornell East Asia Program.

"Kaishaku 'Waga yuku umi.'" 1907. *Shijin* 6 (November): 4–6.

Kakuta Toshirō. 1966. "Ikebukuro Kiyokaze no 'Shintaishi hihyō': Yakushiron hikaku shiron toshite no igi." *Kokubungaku gengo to bungei* 45 (March): 23–32.

Kamei Hideo. 2014. *Nihonjin no "hon'yaku": Gengo shihon no keisei o megutte*. Tokyo: Iwanami Shoten.

Kamiyama, Tamie, William H. Matheson, Robert E. Morrell, J. Thomas Rimer, and Eugene Soviak. 1975. "Appendix C: *Kaicho-on* Related Materials: Extracts from the Preface." In "Toward a Modern Japanese Poetry," edited by Tamie Kamiyama, William H. Matheson, Robert E. Morrell, J. Thomas Rimer, and Eugene Soviak, special issue, *Literature East and West* 19 (1–4): 111–19.

Kanbara Ariake. 1901. "Ada naramashi." *Myōjō* 14 (August): 2–3.

Kanbara Ariake. (1903) 2009. *Dokugen aika*. Tokyo: Heibonsha.

Kanbara Ariake. 1905. *Shunchōshū*. Tokyo: Hongō Shoin.

Kanbara Ariake. 1907a. "Nihonshi no hattatsu sezaru gen'in." *Shinsei* 16 (1): 9–12.

Kanbara Ariake. 1907b. "Ware wa ika ni shite shijin to narishi ka." *Shinko bunrin* 3 (3): 227–32.

Kanbara Ariake. 1907c. "Hiru no omoi." *Shin shichō* 2 (November): 94–95.

Kanbara Ariake. 1908a. "Yo ga hansei no shijin keireki." *Bunshō sekai* 3 (5): 46–50.

Kanbara Ariake. (1908b) 1972. "Genbun itchi no shiika." In *NKSK*, 333–34.

Kanbara Ariake. (1914a) 1972. "'Hyōshōha no bungaku undō' ni tsuite." In *NKSK*, 282–91.

Kanbara Ariake. (1914b) 1980. "Shōchō shugi no inyū ni tsuite." In *Meiji bungaku kaikoroku shū*, edited by Usui Yoshimi, 2:272–78. Vol. 99 of *MBZ*.

Kanbara Ariake. 1922. "Ariake shishū jichū." In *Ariake shishū*, separately paginated at the end of the text, 27 pages. Tokyo: Arusu.

Kanbara Ariake. (1929) 1980. "'Ariake shū' zengo." In *Meiji bungaku kaikoroku shū*, edited by Usui Yoshimi, 2:280–82. Vol. 99 of *MBZ*.

Kanbara Ariake. 1947. *Shunchōshū: Kanbara Ariake shishū*. Tokyo: Tōkyō Shuppan.

Kanbara Ariake. 1957. *Teihon Kanbara Ariake zenshishū*. Tokyo: Kawade Shobō.

Kaneko Mitsuko. 2015. *Furansu 20-seiki shi to haiku: Japonisumu kara zen'ei e*. Tokyo: Heibonsha.

Karatani Kōjin. 1993. *Origins of Modern Japanese Literature*. Translation edited by Brett de Bary. Durham, NC: Duke University Press.

Karimi-Hakkak, Ahmad. 1995. *Recasting Persian Poetry: Scenarios of Poetic Modernity in Iran*. Salt Lake City: University of Utah Press.

Kasahara Kiyoshi. 2003. "Edo jidai no nihon de utawareta oranda kakyoku ni tsuite." *Hōsō daigaku kenkyū nenpō* 21:171–200.

Katayama Koson. (1905) 1974. "Zoku shinkeishitsu no bungaku." In *Kaneko Chikusui, Tanaka Ōdō, Katayama Koson, Nakazawa Rinsen, Uozumi Setsuro shū*, edited by Inagaki Tatsurō, 173–79. Vol. 50 of *MBZ*.

Katō Kaishun. 1934. "Waseda shisha to jiyūshisha." In *Nihon bungaku kōza*, 9:309–13. Tokyo: Kaizōsha.

Katō Shūichi. 1991. "Juriasu Shīzā." In *Hon'yaku no shisō*, edited by Katō Shūichi and Maruyama Masao, 442–52. Tokyo: Iwanami Shoten.

Kawai Suimei. 1908. *Shintaishi sahō*. Tokyo: Hakubunkan.

Kawaji Ryūkō. 1908. "Kankaku no shunji." *Bunko* 38 (2): 108–9.

Kawaji Ryūkō. 1909. "Jiyūshi kei: Kyōretsu naru inshō." *Shinchō* 10 (1): 23–30.

Kawaji Ryūkō. 1910. *Robō no hana*. Tokyo: Tōundō Shoten.

Kawaji Ryūkō. (1950) 1974. "Kaisō to kokuhaku." In *NGST geppō*, 2:4–5. Supplement to vol. 4 of *NGST*.

Kawaji Ryūkō. 1953. *Kurofuneki: Kaikoku shiwa*. Tokyo: Hōsei Daigaku Shuppankyoku.

Kawaji Ryūkō. 1955. "Jiden." In *Gendai nihon shijin zenshū*, 3:6. Tokyo: Sōgensha.

Kawaji Ryūkō. 2014. "A Moment of Sensation." Translated by Shō Sugita. *The Equalizer* 2 (1): 15–16.

Kawamoto Kōji. 1991. *Nihon shiika no dentō: Shichi to go no shigaku*. Tokyo: Iwanami Shoten.

Kawamoto Kōji. 2000. *The Poetics of Japanese Verse: Imagery, Structure, Meter*. Translated by Stephen Collington, Kevin Collins, and Gustav Heldt. With a Foreword by Haruo Shirane. Tokyo: University of Tokyo Press.

Kawamoto Kōji. 2015. "Modern Japanese Poetry to the 1910s." In *Cambridge History of Japanese Literature*, edited by Haruo Shirane, Tomi Suzuki, and David Lurie, 613–22. Cambridge: Cambridge University Press.

Keene, Donald. 1976. *World within Walls: Japanese Literature of the Pre-Modern Era, 1600–1867*. New York: Grove.

Keene, Donald. 1999. *Dawn to the West: Japanese Literature of the Modern Era. Poetry, Drama, Criticism*. New York: Columbia University Press.

Keene, Donald. 2013. *The Winter Sun Shines In: A Life of Masaoka Shiki*. New York: Columbia University Press.

Keene, Donald. 2016. *The First Modern Japanese: The Life of Ishikawa Takuboku*. New York: Columbia University Press.

Kenmochi Takehiko. 1973. "Gekishi to jojishi." In *Kōza nihon gendaishi shi*, vol. 1, edited by Murano Shirō, 161–92. Tokyo: Yubun Shoin.

Ki no Tsurayuki. 1957. *Tosa nikki*. Edited by Suzuki Tomotarō. In *NKBT*, vol. 20, edited by Suzuki Tomotarō, Kawaguchi Hisao, Endō Yoshimoto, and Nishishita Kyōichi, 27–80.

Kimata Osamu. 1965. *Kindai tanka no shiteki tenkai*. Tokyo: Meiji Shoin.

Kitagawa Tōru. 1974. *Kitamura Tōkoku shiron I: "Genkyō" e no tabi*. Tokyo: Tōjusha.

Kitamura Tōkoku. (1889) 1968. *Soshū no shi*. Tokyo: Kindai Bungakukan Meicho Fukkoku Zenshū.

Kitamura Tōkoku. (1891) 1977. *Hōraikyoku*. Tokyo: Kindai Bungakukan Meicho Fukkoku Zenshū.

Kitamura Tōkoku. 1950–55. *Tōkoku zenshū*. 3 vols. Edited by Katsumoto Seiichirō. Tokyo: Iwanami Shoten.

Kittler, Friedrich. 1990. *Discourse Networks, 1800/1900*. Translated by Michael Metteer, with Chris Cullens. Stanford, CA: Stanford University Press.

Klein, Lucas. 2014. "Translation, Nation, Metaphor." *The 2014–2015 Report on the State of the Discipline of Comparative Literature*. https://stateofthediscipline.acla.org/entry/institution-translation-nation-metaphor.

Klein, Lucas. 2017. "Reading and Speaking for Translation: De-institutionalizing the Institutions of Literary Study." In *Futures of Comparative Literature: ACLA State of the Discipline Report*, edited by Ursula K. Heise with Dudley Andrew, Alexander Beecroft, Jessica Berman, David Damrosch, Guillermina De Ferrari, César Domínguez, Barbara Harlow, and Eric Hayot, 215–19. London: Routledge.

Klein, Lucas. 2018. *The Organization of Distance: Poetry, Translation, Chineseness.* Leiden: Brill.

Kliger, Ilya, and Boris Maslov. 2016. "Introducing Historical Poetics: History, Experience, Form." In *Persistent Forms: Explorations in Historical Poetics*, edited by Ilya Kliger and Boris Maslov, 1–36. New York: Fordham University Press.

Klopfenstein, Eduard. 1981. "A Dialogue between Modern Poetry and *Haiku*: The Bashō Poems of Hoshino Tōru." In *Tradition and Modern Japan*, edited by P. G. O'Neill, 224–29. Tenterden, Kent: Paul Norbury Publications.

Kockum, Keiko. 2006. "The Role of Western Literature in the Formation of the Modern Japanese Novel." In *Literary Interactions in the Modern World 1*, edited by Margareta Petersson, vol. 3 of *Literary History: Towards a Global Perspective*, edited by Gunilla Lindberg-Wada, 97–140. Berlin: Walter de Gruyter.

Konakamura Gishō and Hagino Yoshiyuki. 1887. *Kokugaku waka kairyō ron.* Tokyo: Yoshikawa Hanshichi.

Kornicki, Peter F. 1999. Introduction to *Collected Works of Frederick Victor Dickins*, 1:ix–xxx. Bristol: Ganesha Publishing.

Kripke, Saul. 1980. *Naming and Necessity.* Cambridge, MA: Harvard University Press.

Krishnaswamy, Revathi. 2010. "Toward World Literary Knowledges: Theory in the Age of Globalization." *Comparative Literature* 62 (4): 399–419.

Kristal, Efraín. 2002. "'Considering Coldly . . .': A Response to Franco Moretti." *New Left Review*, 2nd ser., 15:61–74.

Kubo Tadao, Awazu Norio, and Hisamatsu Sen'ichi, eds. 1972. *Doi Bansui, Susukida Kyūkin, Kanbara Ariake shū.* Vol. 18 of *Nihon kindai bungaku taikei.* Tokyo: Kadokawa Shoten.

Kunikida Doppo. (1897) 1972. "Doppo gin: Jo." In *NKSK*, 119–21.

Kuroda Saburō. 1969. *Shi no tsukurikata.* Tokyo: Meiji Shoin.

Landresse, Ernest Augustin Xavier Clerc de. 1826. *Supplément à la Grammaire Japonaise, du P. Rodriguez.* Paris: Dondey-Dupré Père et Fils.

Lange, Rudolf. 1884. *Altjapanische Frühlingslieder aus der Sammlung Kokinwakashu.* Berlin: Weidmannsche Buchhandlung.

Lee, Yeounsuk. 2010. *The Ideology of "Kokugo": Nationalizing Language in Modern Japan.* Honolulu: University of Hawai'i Press.

Lento, Takako, ed. and trans. 2019. *Pioneers of Modern Japanese Poetry: Murō Saisei, Kaneko Mitsuharu, Miyoshi Tatsuji, Nagase Kiyoko.* Ithaca, NY: Cornell East Asia Program.

Lessing, Doris. 1997. *Walking in the Shade: Volume Two of My Autobiography, 1949 to 1962.* New York: Harper Collins.

Levy, Indra. 2006. *Sirens of the Western Shore: The Westernesque Femme Fatale, Translation, and Vernacular Style in Modern Japanese Literature.* New York: Columbia University Press.

Lindberg-Wada, Gunilla. 2006. "Japanese Literary History Writing: The Beginnings." In *Notions of Literature across Times and Cultures*, edited by Anders Pettersson, vol. 1 of *Literary History: Towards a Global Perspective*, edited by Gunilla Lindberg-Wada, 111–34. Berlin: Walter de Gruyter.

218 **REFERENCES**

Liu, Lydia H. 1995. *Translingual Practice: Literature, National Culture, and Translated Modernity—China 1900–1937*. Stanford, CA: Stanford University Press.

Long, Hoyt. 2021. *The Values in Numbers: Reading Japanese Literature in a Global Information Age*. New York: Columbia University Press.

Lotman, Yuri. 1977. "The Dynamic Model of a Semiotic System." Translated by Ann Shukman. *Semiotica* 21 (3/4): 193–210.

Lotman, Yuri. 2009. *Culture and Explosion*. Edited by Marina Grishakova. Translated by Wilma Clark. Berlin: Walter de Gruyter.

Lotman, Yuri. 2013. "On the Dynamics of Culture." Translated by Tyler B. Adkins. *Sign Systems Studies* 41 (2/3): 355–70.

Mack, Edward. 2010. *Manufacturing Modern Japanese Literature: Publishing, Prizes, and the Ascription of Literary Value*. Durham, NC: Duke University Press.

Maeda Ai. 1989. "Ondoku kara mokudoku e: Kindai dokusha no seiritsu." In *Maeda Ai chosakushū*, 2:122–50. Tokyo: Chikuma Shobō.

Maeda Ai. 2004. "From Communal Performance to Solitary Reading: The Rise of the Modern Japanese Reader." Translated by James Fujii. In Maeda Ai, *The Text and the City: Essays on Japanese Modernity*, edited by James Fujii, 223–54. Durham, NC: Duke University Press.

Maeda Ringai. (1890) 1973. "Kanshi waka shintaishi no aiirezaru jōkyō o joshite haikai ni oyobu." In *Kindai bungaku hyōron taikei*, 8:423–29. Tokyo: Kadokawa.

Maeshima Shiho. 2018. "Kakudai sareru haiku no shiteki kanōsei: Seiki tenkanki seiyō to nihon ni okeru aratana haiku kanshō no shutsugen." In *Nihon bungaku no hon'yaku to ryūtsū: Kindai sekai no nettowāku e*, edited by Kōno Shion and Murai Noriko, 67–100. Tokyo: Bensei Shuppan.

Manke, Michaela. 1997. "'Es ist Morgen' (Asa nari) von Kambara Ariake—in der Fassung der Veröffentlichung in 'Shunchō-shū' (Frühlings-Vögel-Sammlung) von 1905." *Seinan gakuin daigaku kokusai bunka ronshū* 12 (1): 149–61.

Marra, Michael. 2004. *Kuki Shūzō: A Philosopher's Poetry and Poetics*. Honolulu: University of Hawai'i Press.

Martin, Meredith. 2012. *The Rise and Fall of Meter: Poetry and English National Culture, 1860–1930*. Princeton, NJ: Princeton University Press.

Masaoka Shiki. (1895) 2001. *Haikai taiyō*. In *Masaoka Shiki*, edited by Tsubouchi Yūzō and Nakazawa Shin'ichi, 261–342. Vol. 20 of *Meiji no bungaku*. Tokyo: Chikuma Shobō.

Masaoka Shiki. 1975–78. *Shiki zenshū*. 25 vols. Tokyo: Kōdansha.

Maslov, Boris. 2016. "Metapragmatics, *Toposforschung*, Marxist Stylistics: Three Extensions of Veselovsky's Historical Poetics." In *Persistent Forms: Explorations in Historical Poetics*, edited by Ilya Kliger and Boris Maslov, 128–62. New York: Fordham University Press.

Masuda Michizō. 1954. "Kitamura Tōkoku to Rōdo Bairon." *Jinbun kenkyū: Ōsaka shiritsu daigaku daigakuin bungaku kenkyūka kiyō* 5 (11/12): 23–39.

Masuda Michizō. 1956. "Kitamura Tōkoku to Rōdo Bairon." In *Hikaku bungakuteki sanpo*, 132–56. Tokyo: Kenkyūsha.

Mathy, Francis. 1963. "Kitamura Tōkoku: The Early Years." *Monumenta Nipponica* 18 (1–4): 1–44.

Matsubara Shibun, Yabu Hakumei, Fukuda Yūsaku, Katō Kaishun, and Hitomi Tōmei. (1908) 1972. "'Ariake shū' gappyō." In *NKSK*, 260–68.

Matsubayashi Shōshi. 1996. *Nihon no inritsu: Goon to shichion no shigaku*. Tokyo: Kashinsha.

Matsumura Midori. 1965. *Kanbara Ariake ronkō*. Tokyo: Meiji Shoin.

Matsuo Bashō. 1979. *Oku no hosomichi*. Notes by Hagiwara Yasuo. Tokyo: Iwanami Shoten.

Matsuo Bashō. 2005. *Sendas de Oku: Versión castellana*. Translated by Octavio Paz and Eikichi Hayashiya. Illustrations by Yosa Buson. Mexico City: Fondo de Cultura Económica.

Matsuo, Kuni, and E. Steinilber-Oberlin. 1939. *Anthologie des poètes japonais contemporains*, 2nd ed. Preface by Kawaji Ryūkō. Paris: Mercure de France.

McCullough, Helen Craig, trans. 1985. *Kokin wakashū: The First Imperial Anthology of Japanese Poetry. With Tosa Nikki and Shinsen Waka*. Stanford, CA: Stanford University Press.

McVeigh, Brian J. 2017. *The History of Japanese Psychology: Global Perspectives, 1875–1950*. London: Bloomsbury Academic.

Mehl, Scott. 2015. "Early Twentieth-Century Terms for New Verse Forms ('Free Verse' and Others) in Japanese and Arabic." *Studia Metrica et Poetica* 2 (1): 81–106.

Mehl, Scott. 2021. "The *sanbunshi* (Prose Poem) in Japan." In *The Edinburgh Companion to the Prose Poem*, edited by Michel Delville and Mary Ann Caws, 262–80. Edinburgh: Edinburgh University Press.

Mellor, Anne K., and Richard E. Matlak, eds. 1996. *British Literature, 1780–1830*. Fort Worth: Harcourt Brace.

Mikami Sanji and Takatsu Kuwasaburō. (1890) 1982. *Nihon bungakushi ge*. Edited by Hiraoka Toshio. Nihon Bungakushi Shūsei 2. Tokyo: Nihon Tosho Sentā.

Miki Rofū. (1950) 1974. "Shi no kakushinki." In *NGST geppō*, 2:1–2. Supplement to vol. 4 of *NGST*.

Miki Shirahi. 1986. *Nihon kindaishi no rizumu*. Tokyo: Geijutsu Seikatsu Sha.

Miller, Christopher L. 2018. *Impostors: Literary Hoaxes and Cultural Authenticity*. Chicago: University of Chicago Press.

Miller, J. Scott. 2001. *Adaptations of Western Literature in Meiji Japan*. New York: Palgrave.

Miner, Earl, Hiroko Odagiri, and Robert E. Morrell. 1985. *The Princeton Companion to Classical Japanese Literature*. Princeton, NJ: Princeton University Press.

Miner, Earl. 1990. "Waka: Features of Its Constitution and Development." *Harvard Journal of Asiatic Studies* 50 (2): 669–706.

Moretti, Franco. 2000. "Conjectures on World Literature." *New Left Review*, 2nd ser., 1:54–68.

Moretti, Franco. 2003. "More Conjectures." *New Left Review*, 2nd ser., 20:73–81.

Mori Hajime. 1988. *Meiji shijin to eibungaku: Shizukana kanashiki shirabe*. Tokyo: Kokusho Kankōkai.

Mori Shingo. 2017. "Shiki to Mito." *Shiki kaishi* 152:1–12. https://open.bu.edu/handle/2144/36057.

Morita, James. 1970. "Shimazaki Toson's Four Collections of Poems." *Monumenta Nipponica* 25 (3/4): 325–69.

Morrell, Robert E. 1975. "A Selection of New-Style Verse." In "Toward a Modern Japanese Poetry," edited by Tamie Kamiyama, William H. Matheson, Robert

E. Morrell, J. Thomas Rimer, and Eugene Soviak, special issue, *Literature East and West* 19 (1–4): 9–33.

Morris, Mark. 1985. "Buson and Shiki: Part Two." *Harvard Journal of Asiatic Studies* 45 (1): 255–321.

Morris, Mark. 1986. "Waka and Form, Waka and History." *Harvard Journal of Asiatic Studies* 46 (2): 551–610.

Morton, Leith. 2004. *Modernism in Practice: An Introduction to Postwar Japanese Poetry.* Honolulu: University of Hawai'i Press.

Morton, Leith. 2009. *The Alien Within: Representations of the Exotic in Twentieth-Century Japanese Literature.* Honolulu: University of Hawai'i Press.

Morton, Leith. 2011. "Japanese Poetry and the Legacies of War." In *Legacies of the Asia-Pacific War: The Yakeato Generation,* edited by Roman Rosenbaum and Yasuko Claremont, 164–81. London: Routledge.

Mostow, Joshua. 2003. "The Revival of Poetry in Traditional Forms." In *The Columbia Companion to Modern East Asian Literature,* edited by Joshua S. Mostow, associate editors Kirk A. Denton, Bruce Fulton, and Sharalyn Orbaugh, 99–104. New York: Columbia University Press.

Motora Yūjirō. 1890a. "'Rizumu' no koto: Seishin butsurigaku 10." *Tetsugakkai zasshi* 42:330–43.

Motora Yūjirō. (1890b) 1975. "'Rizumu' no koto: Seishin butsurigaku." In *MTSS,* 439–58.

Murano Shirō. 1968. "Kawaji Ryūkō." In *Gendaishi kanshō kōza,* vol. 4, edited by Itō Shinkichi, 5–32. Tokyo: Kadokawa Shoten.

Murata Fumio. 1871. *Seiyō bunken roku kōhen,* vol. 4. Hiroshima: Izutsuya Shōjirō.

Mure Keiko. 1995. *Mure Keiko shishū.* Tokyo: Shichōsha.

"Musekinin naru hihyō." 1907. *Shijin* 6 (November): 66–67.

Nabokov, Vladimir. (1964) 1981. Foreword to Aleksandr Pushkin, *Eugene Onegin: A Novel in Verse,* translated with a commentary by Vladimir Nabokov, 1:vii–xii. Paperback edition in two volumes. Princeton, NJ: Princeton University Press.

Naff, William E. 2011. *The Kiso Road: The Life and Times of Shimazaki Tōson.* Honolulu: University of Hawai'i Press.

Nagashima, Yōichi. 1997. *Objective Description of the Self: A Study of Iwano Hōmei's Literary Theory.* Aarhus: Aarhus University Press.

Naipaul, V. S. 1994. *A Way in the World: A Novel.* New York: Vintage.

Nakajima Kotō. (1905) 1972. "Ankoku naru bundan." In *NKSK,* 235–39.

Nakamura Akika. 1898. *Shintai shiika jizai.* Tokyo: Hakubunkan.

Nakazawa Nobuhiro. 2008. "Kofū chōka no fukkō to sono chōraku." *Meiji Shōtoku kinen gakkai kiyō fukkan* 45:23–34.

Narita Takaaki. 1966. "Machine poetikku shishū (Nakamura Shin'ichirō, Katō Shūichi, Fukunaga Takehiko, Kubota Keisaku nado)." *Kokubungaku kaishaku to kanshō* 31 (1): 122–33.

Narita Tatsuo. 1988. "Shiki to Supensā: Meiji seinen no eigaku shūgyō." *Ōtani joshi daigaku kiyō* 22 (2): 45–74.

Natsume Sōseki. (1892) 1995. "Bundan ni okeru byōdōshugi no daihyōsha Woruto Hoittoman no shi ni tsuite." In *Sōseki zenshū,* 13:3–20. Tokyo: Iwanami Shoten.

Natsume Sōseki. 1995. *Sōseki zenshū,* vol. 13. Tokyo: Iwanami Shoten.

Nihon kokugo daijiten. 1972–76. 20 vols. Tokyo: Shōgakukan.

Nihon no shiika, vol. 2: *Doi Bansui, Susukida Kyūkin, Kanbara Ariake, Miki Rofū.* 1969. Tokyo: Chūō Kōron Sha.

"Nihon shiika no shinsō." 1895. *Teikoku bungaku* 1 (4): 91–92.

Nishi Amane. 1874. "Chisetsu 5." *Meiroku zasshi* 25 (December): 1r–3v.

Nishiwaki Junzaburō. 1971. *Nishiwaki Junzaburō zenshū,* vol. 2. Tokyo: Chikuma Shobō.

Noguchi Nobuya. 2007. *Shiteki kindai no seisei: Meiji no shi to shijintachi.* Tokyo: Tōseisha.

Noguchi, Yone. 1903. *From the Eastern Sea.* London: At the Unicorn.

Noguchi, Yone. 1907. "Twenty Four Paragraphs on Mr. Ariake Kanbara." *Shin shichō* 2 (November): 57–60.

Nomura Kiyoshi. 1954. "Ryūkōteki sekai no tenbyō." In *Kindaishi no shiteki tenbō,* edited by Sangū Makoto Kyōju Kakō Kinen Bunshū Hensan Iinkai, 102–9. Tokyo: Kawade Shobō.

Ogawa Kazuo. 1982. *Meiji bungaku to kindai jiga: Hikaku bungakuteki kōsatsu.* Tokyo: Nan'undō.

Ōi Sōgo. 1903. "Dokugen aika o yomu." *Myōjō* 9:83–84.

Okamura Chibiki. 1953. "Seishi hōyaku no ranshō." In *Kōmō bunka shiwa,* 114–38. Tokyo: Sōgensha.

Okkotsu Akio. 1972. "Kōgo jiyūshiron sono ta." In *NKSK,* 727–72.

Okkotsu Akio. 1991. *Gendai shijin gunzō: Minshūshiha to sono shūken.* Tokyo: Kasama Shoin.

Ōnishi Hajime. (1890) 2001. "Shiikaron ippan." In *Ōnishi Hajime zenshū shinsōban,* 7:435–49. Tokyo: Nihon Tosho Sentā. Reprint of vol. 7 of *Ōnishi hakase zenshū* (Tokyo: Keiseisha Shoten, 1904).

Ōoka Makoto. 1969. *Tōji no kakei: Nihon gendaishi no ayumi.* Tokyo: Shichōsha.

Oritake Ryōhō. (1908) 1972. "Genbun itchi shi." In *NKSK,* 350–52.

Oyanguren de Santa Inés, Melchor. (1738) 2009. *Arte de la lengua japona.* Edited by Otto Zwartjes. Madrid: Iberoamericana.

Ōwada Takeki. 1893. *Shintai shigaku.* Tokyo: Hakubunkan.

Paz, Octavio. (1970) 2005. "La tradición del haikú." In Matsuo Bashō, *Sendas de Oku: Versión castellana,* translated by Octavio Paz and Eikichi Hayashiya, 9–30. Illustrations by Yosa Buson. Mexico City: Fondo de Cultura Económica.

Paz, Octavio. 1971. *Traducción: Literatura y literalidad.* Barcelona: Tusquets.

Perloff, Marjorie. 1998. "After Free Verse: The New Nonlinear Poetries." In *Close Listening: Poetry and the Performed Word,* edited by Charles Bernstein, 86–110. Oxford: Oxford University Press.

Petrarca, Francesco. 1976. *Petrarch's Lyric Poems: The "Rime sparse" and Other Lyrics.* Translated and edited by Robert M. Durling. Cambridge, MA: Harvard University Press.

Pierson, John D. 1980. *Tokutomi Sohō, 1863–1957: A Journalist for Modern Japan.* Princeton, NJ: Princeton University Press.

Pondrom, Cyrena. 1974. *The Road from Paris: French Influence on English Poetry, 1900–1920.* Cambridge: Cambridge University Press.

Pound, Ezra. 1954. *Literary Essays of Ezra Pound.* Edited with an introduction by T. S. Eliot. London: Faber and Faber.

Rabinovitch, Judith N., and Timothy R. Bradstock. 2009. "Paulownia Leaves Falling: The Kanshi Poetry of Inaga Nanpo (1865–1901)." *Japan Review* 21:33–122.

Raffel, Burton. 1988. *The Art of Translating Poetry*. University Park: Pennsylvania State University Press.

Raud, Rein. 2016. *Meaning in Action: Outline of an Integral Theory of Culture*. Cambridge: Polity.

Ren Xing. 2007. "'Onsetsu/shiraburu/haku/mōra' no jutsugo kaishaku no hensen: Meijiki kara gendai made no kokugo jisho ni yoru kaishaku kara." *Meikai nihongo* 12:71–80.

Robinson, Peter. 2010. *Poetry and Translation: The Art of the Impossible*. Liverpool: Liverpool University Press.

Rodrigues, João. (1608) 1969. *Arte da lingoa de iapam*. Reprint of a photocopy of the original, with an afterword by Shima Masakazu. Tokyo: Bunka Shobō Hakubunsha.

Rosny, Léon de. 1871. *Anthologie japonaise: Poésies anciennes et modernes des insulaires du Nippon, traduites en français et publiées avec le texte original*. Paris: Maisonneuve.

Rosny, Léon de. 1878. *Les distiques populaires du Nippon: Extraits du Gi-retu Hyaku-nin Is-syu*. Paris: Maisonneuve.

Roth, Philip. 2013. *The Plot Against America*. In *Philip Roth: Novels 2001–2007: The Dying Animal, The Plot Against America, Exit Ghost*, 93–458. New York: Library of America.

Sadoya Shigenobu. 1969. *Kindai nihon to Hoittoman: Nihon ni okeru eikyō no zenbō*. Tokyo: Takemura Shuppan.

Saitō Mokichi. (1913) 2000. *Shakkō*. Tokyo: Shinchōsha.

Sakai, Naoki. 2009. "How Do We Count a Language? Translation and Discontinuity." *Translation Studies* 2 (1): 71–88.

Sakaki Yūichi. 2005. "Buntai jissen toshite no 'Shintaishi shō shohen.'" *Southern Taiwan University Department of Applied Japanese Bulletin* (*Nantai yingyong riyu xuebao*) 5:137–65.

Sakamaki Kōji, ed. 2016. *Kindai nihon to furansu shōchōshugi*. Tokyo: Suiseisha.

Sakurai Tendan. 1904. "Shijin Kanbara Ariake o ronzu." *Teikoku bungaku* 10 (3): 98–111.

Sakurai Tendan. (1905) 1972. "Shōchōshi o ronjite Ariake no Shunchōshū ni oyobu." In *NKSK*, 227–30.

Sasabuchi Tomoichi. 1959. *"Bungakukai" to sono jidai jō: "Bungakukai" o shōten to suru rōmanshugi bungaku no kenkyū*. Tokyo: Meiji Shoin.

Sasaki Hirotsuna. (1888) 1975. "Chōka kairyō ron." In *MTSS*, 159–62.

Sato, Hiroaki. 1987. "Lineation of Tanka in English Translation." *Monumenta Nipponica* 42 (3): 347–56.

Satō, Masako. 1995. *Karl Florenz in Japan: Auf den Spuren einer vergessenen Quelle der modernen japanischen Geistesgeschichte und Poetik*. Hamburg: Gesellschaft für Natur- und Völkerkunde Ostasiens.

Satō Nobuhiro. 2005. *Nihon kindai shōchōshi no kenkyū*. Tokyo: Kanrin Shobō.

Satō Nobuhiro. 2011. *Shi no arika: Kōgo jiyūshi o meguru toi*. Tokyo: Kasama Shoin.

Saussy, Haun. 2016. *The Ethnography of Rhythm: Orality and Its Technologies*. New York: Fordham University Press.

Saussy, Haun. 2019. "Contagious Rhythm: Verse as a Technique of the Body." In *Critical Rhythm: The Poetics of a Literary Life Form*, edited by Ben Glaser and Jonathan Culler, 106–27. New York: Fordham University Press.

Schamoni, Wolfgang. 1981. "Kitamura Tōkoku's Early Years and the Rise of the 'Poet' Concept." In *Tradition and Modern Japan*, edited by P. G. O'Neill, 196–205. Tenterden, Kent: Paul Norbury Publications.

Schamoni, Wolfgang. 1983. *Kitamura Tōkoku: Die frühen Jahre, von der "Politik" zur "Literatur."* Wiesbaden: Franz Steiner Verlag.

Scott, Clive. 1990. *Vers Libre: The Emergence of Free Verse in France 1886–1914*. Oxford: Clarendon Press.

Scott, Clive. 1998. *The Poetics of French Verse: Studies in Reading*. Oxford: Clarendon Press.

Scott, Clive. 2015. "The Rhythms of Free Verse and the Rhythms of Translation." *Style* 49 (1): 46–64.

Scott, Clive. 2018. *The Work of Literary Translation*. Cambridge: Cambridge University Press.

Screech, Timon. 2006. Introduction to Isaac Titsingh, *Secret Memoirs of the Shoguns: Isaac Titsingh and Japan, 1779–1822*, annotated by Timon Screech, 1–74. London: Routledge.

Seki Ryōichi. 1976. *Kindaishi no keitai to seiritsu*. Tokyo: Kyōiku Shuppan Sentā.

Shibusawa Takasuke. 1980. *Kanbara Ariake ron: Kindaishi no shukumei to isan*. Tokyo: Chūō Kōron Sha.

"Shikei no shinka." 1899. *Teikoku bungaku* 5 (2): 104–5.

Shimamura Hōgetsu. 1906. "Isseki bunwa." *Bunshō sekai* 1 (6): 67–74.

Shimamura Hōgetsu. (1907) 1972. "Gendai no shi." In *NKSK*, 331–33.

Shimamura Hōgetsu. (1908) 1972. "Kōgoshi mondai." In *NKSK*, 369–70.

Shimaoka Shin. 1998. *Shi to wa nani ka*. Tokyo: Shinchōsha.

Shimazaki Tōson. (1901) 1976. *Rakubaishū*. Tokyo: Kindai Bungakukan.

Shinada Yoshikazu. 2000. "*Man'yōshū*: The Invention of a National Poetry Anthology." In *Inventing the Classics: Modernity, National Identity, and Japanese Literature*, edited by Haruo Shirane and Tomi Suzuki, 31–50. Stanford, CA: Stanford University Press.

Shirane, Haruo. 2000. "Introduction: Issues in Canon Formation." In *Inventing the Classics: Modernity, National Identity, and Japanese Literature*, edited by Haruo Shirane and Tomi Suzuki, 1–27. Stanford, CA: Stanford University Press.

Shirane, Haruo. 2014. "Mediating the Literary Classics: Commentary and Translation in Premodern Japan." In *Rethinking East Asian Languages, Vernaculars, and Literacies, 1000–1919*, edited by Benjamin A. Elman, 129–46. Leiden: Brill.

[Shoberl, Frederic?] 1820. "Poetry of the Japanese." *New Monthly Magazine* 14 (79) (August 1): 121–25.

Sōma Gyofū. 1908. "Jisatsu ka tanshuku ka muimi ka." *Waseda bungaku* 29 (April): 37–45.

Somoff, Victoria. 2016. "Alexander Veselovsky's Historical Poetics vs. Cultural Poetics: Remembering the Future." In *Persistent Forms: Explorations in Historical Poetics*, edited by Ilya Kliger and Boris Maslov, 65–89. New York: Fordham University Press.

Spencer, Herbert. 1892. *Philosophy of Style: Together with an Essay on Style by T. H. Wright*. Introduction and notes by Fred N. Scott, 2nd ed. Boston: Allyn and Bacon.

Starrs, Roy, ed. 2011. *Rethinking Japanese Modernism*. Leiden: Brill.

Steele, Timothy. 1990. *Missing Measures: Modern Poetry and the Revolt against Meter*. Fayetteville: University of Arkansas Press.

Suematsu Kenchō. (1884–85) 1975. "Kagakuron." In *MTSS*, 11–47.

Suga Hidemi. 1995. *Nihon kindai bungaku no "tanjō": Genbun itchi undō to nashonarizumu*. Tokyo: Ōta Shuppan.

Susukida Kyūkin. 1906. "Waga yuku umi." *Myōjō* 1:10–11.

Suzuki Kazumasa. 2001. "Kitamura Tōkoku sankō bunken mokuroku: Meiji 22-nen-Shōwa 19-nen." *Kokubungaku kenkyū shiryōkan kiyō* 27:283–317.

Suzuki Sadami. 1998. *Nihon no "bungaku" gainen*. Tokyo: Sakuhinsha.

Suzuki Sadami. 2002. "What Is *Bungaku*? The Reformulation of the Concept of 'Literature' in Early Twentieth-Century Japan." In *Japanese Hermeneutics*, edited by Michael F. Marra, 176–88. Honolulu: University of Hawai'i Press.

Suzuki Sadami. 2006. *The Concept of "Literature" in Japan*. Translated by Royall Tyler. Kyoto: International Research Center for Japanese Studies.

Suzuki Sadami. 2009. "*Nihon bungaku*" *no seiritsu*. Tokyo: Sakuhinsha.

Suzuki, Tomi. 2000. "Gender and Genre: Modern Literary Histories and Women's Diary Literature." In *Inventing the Classics: Modernity, National Identity, and Japanese Literature*, edited by Haruo Shirane and Tomi Suzuki, 71–95. Stanford, CA: Stanford University Press.

Symons, Arthur. (1899) 2014. *The Symbolist Movement in Literature*. Edited by Matthew Creasy. Manchester: Carcanet Press.

Taketsu Yachio. (1888) 1975. "Kokugaku waka kairyō fuka ron." In *MTSS*, 123–37.

Takizawa Kyōji. 2011. *Kawaji Ryūkō*. Tokyo: Yumani Shobō.

Tani Masatoshi. 2014. "Waka kairyō undō to Keien-ha: Ikebukuro Kiyokaze o chūshin ni." *Kokugo to kokubungaku* 91 (7): 49–67.

Tatsumi-sei [pseud.]. 1903. "Dokugen aika o yomu." *Myōjō* 9:81–83.

Terhune, Alfred McKinley, and Annabelle Burdick Terhune, eds. 1980. *The Letters of Edward Fitzgerald*, vol. 2: *1851–1866*. Princeton, NJ: Princeton University Press.

Thomas, Roger K. 1994. "'High' Versus 'Low': The *Fude no saga* Controversy and Bakumatsu Poetics." *Monumenta Nipponica* 49 (4): 455–69.

Tillotson, Geoffrey, Paul Fussell Jr., and Marshall Waingrow (with the assistance of Brewster Rogerson), eds. 1969. *Eighteenth-Century English Literature*. Fort Worth: Harcourt Brace Jovanovich College Publishers.

Titsingh, Isaac. 1820. *Mémoires et anecdotes sur la dynastie régnante des Djogouns, souverains du Japon*. Edited by Abel Rémusat. Paris: A. Nepveu.

Titsingh, Isaac. 2006. *Secret Memoirs of the Shoguns: Isaac Titsingh and Japan, 1779–1822*. Annotated and introduced by Timon Screech. London: Routledge.

Todorov, Tzvetan. 1978. *Les genres du discours*. Paris: Éditions du Seuil.

Tomasi, Massimiliano. 2004. *Rhetoric in Modern Japan: Western Influences on the Development of Narrative and Oratorical Style*. Honolulu: University of Hawai'i Press.

Tomasi, Massimiliano. 2007. "The Rise of a New Poetic Form: The Role of Shimamura Hōgetsu in the Creation of Modern Japanese Poetry." *Japan Review* 19:107–32.

Toriyama Hiraku. 1873. *Seiyō zasshi shoshū*. Shikama-ken: Ogawa Kinsuke.

Toury, Gideon. 1995. *Descriptive Translation Studies and Beyond*. Amsterdam: John Benjamins.

Toyama Masakazu, Yatabe Ryōkichi, and Inoue Tetsujirō, trans. and comps. 1882. *Shintaishi shō*. Tokyo: Maruya Zenshichi.

Toyoda Minoru. 1939. *Nihon eigakushi no kenkyū*. Tokyo: Iwanami Shoten.

Tranströmer, Tomas. 2010. *The Sorrow Gondola = Sorgegondolen*. Translated by Michael McGriff and Mikaela Grassl. København: Green Integer.

Tsuboi Hideto. 2015. "Kanbara Ariake o omoidasu: Sono 4." *Gendaishi techō* 58 (8): 182–89.

Tsubouchi Shōyō. 1885. *Shōsetsu shinzui*. Tokyo: Shōgetsudō.

Tsubouchi Shōyō. 1981. *The Essence of the Novel*. Translated by Nanette Twine. University of Queensland Department of Japanese Occasional Papers, No. 11. [Brisbane]: Dept. of Japanese, University of Queensland.

Tsuji, Tomoki. 2012. "Japans 'Rezeption' der Germanistik und Deutschlands 'Aneignung' der Japanforschung: Lehr- und Forschungstätigkeit von Karl Florenz im Zeitalter des Kolonialismus." In *Transkulturalität: Identitäten in neuem Licht; Asiatische Germanistentagung in Kanazawa 2008*, edited by Maeda Ryozo, 713–19. Munich: Iudicium Verlag.

Tsunashima Ryōsen. (1903) 1922. "Dokugen aika o yomu." In *Ryōsen zenshū*, 7:298–305. Tokyo: Shunjūsha.

Tuck, Robert. 2018. *Idly Scribbling Rhymers: Poetry, Print, and Community in Nineteenth-Century Japan*. New York: Columbia University Press.

Twine, Nanette. 1991. *Language and the Modern State: The Reform of Written Japanese*. London: Routledge.

Uchida Roan. (1891a) 1984. "Shiben: Bimyōsai no inbunron o yomite." In *Uchida Roan zenshū*, 1:260–70. Tokyo: Yumani Shobō.

Uchida Roan. (1891b) 1984. "Bimyōsai ni ichigen su." In *Uchida Roan zenshū*, 1:281–82. Tokyo: Yumani Shobō.

Ueda Bin. (1890) 1985. "Ochiba no hakiyose." In *Teihon Ueda Bin zenshū*, 6:547–60. Tokyo: Kyōiku Shuppan Sentā.

Ueda Bin. 1896. "Pōru Verurēn yuku." *Teikoku bungaku* 2 (3): 100–101.

Ueda Bin. 1903. "Furansu kindai no shiika." *Myōjō* 1:1–14.

Ueda Bin, trans. 1905a. "Shussei." *Myōjō* 1:2.

Ueda Bin, trans. (1905b) 1972. *Kaichōon*. Tokyo: Kindai Bungakukan.

Ueda Kazutoshi. 1895. "Hihyō: Dichtergrüsse aus dem Osten, Dokutoru Furōrentsu yaku." *Teikoku bungaku* 1 (2): 98–99.

[Uemura Masahisa?] 1881. "Shiron ippan." *Rikugō zasshi* 12 (September 26): 292–94.

Unagami Tanehira. (1889) 1975. "Chōka kairyō ron benbaku." In *MTSS*, 171–88.

Venuti, Lawrence, ed. 2012. *The Translation Studies Reader*. 3rd ed. New York: Routledge.

Verlaine, Paul. 1986. *Oeuvres poétiques*. Edited by J. Robichez. Paris: Éditions Garnier.

Wachutka, Michael. 2001. *Historical Reality or Metaphoric Expression? Culturally Formed Contrasts in Karl Florenz' and Iida Takesato's Interpretations of Japanese Mythology*. Hamburg: LIT.

Wakabayashi, Judy. 1998. "Marginal Forms of Translation in Japan: Variations from the Norm." In *Unity in Diversity? Current Trends in Translation Studies*, edited by

Lynne Bowker, Michael Cronin, Dorothy Kenny, and Jennifer Pearson, 57–63. Manchester: St. Jerome Publishing.

Wakui, Takashi. 1994. "Prosody, Diction, and Lyricism in Modern Japanese Poetry (*shi*)." PhD diss., Columbia University.

Wakui, Takashi. 2017. "Maidens, Stars, and Dreams: Poems by Shimazaki Tōson and Kanbara Ariake." In *A Tokyo Anthology: Literature from Japan's Modern Metropolis, 1850–1920*, edited by Sumie Jones and Charles Shirō Inouye, 428–35. Honolulu: University of Hawai'i Press.

Weinberger, Eliot. 1992. "Translating." *Sulfur* 30 (spring): 226–27.

Wellek, René. 1970. "The Term and Concept of Symbolism in Literary History." *New Literary History* 1 (2): 249–70.

Wesling, Donald. 1980. *The Chances of Rhyme: Device and Modernity*. Berkeley: University of California Press.

Weston, Victoria. 2004. *Japanese Painting and National Identity: Okakura Tenshin and His Circle*. Ann Arbor: Center for Japanese Studies, University of Michigan.

Weston, Victoria. 2012. "What's in a Name? Rethinking Critical Terms Used to Discuss *Mōrōtai*." *Review of Japanese Culture and Society* 24:116–36.

Won, Ko. 1971. "The Symbolists' Influence on Japanese Poetry." *Comparative Literature Studies* 8 (3): 254–65.

Wordsworth, William. 1969. *The Letters of William and Dorothy Wordsworth: The Middle Years, Part I: 1806–1811*. Edited by Ernest de Selincourt. Revised by Mary Moorman. Oxford: Clarendon Press.

Wordsworth, William. 1984. *William Wordsworth*. Edited by Stephen Gill. The Oxford Authors. Oxford: Oxford University Press.

WReC (Warwick Research Collective). 2015. *Combined and Uneven Development: Towards a New Theory of World-Literature*. Liverpool: Liverpool University Press.

Yamada Bimyō. (1888) 1975. "Chōka kairyō ron o yonde." In *MTSS*, 165–68.

Yamada Bimyō. (1890–91) 2014. "Nihon inbun ron." In *Yamada Bimyō shū*, 9:82–137. Tokyo: Rinsen Shoten.

Yamamoto Kōji. 2012. *Meiji shi no seiritsu to tenkai: Gakkō kyōiku to no kakawari kara*. Tokyo: Hitsuji Shobō.

Yanagida Izumi. 1961. *Meiji bungaku kenkyū*, vol. 5, *Meiji shoki hon'yaku bungaku no kenkyū*. Tokyo: Shunjūsha.

Yano Hōjin. (1950) 1974. "Kaisetsu." In *NGST*, vol. 4, edited by Hinatsu Kōnosuke, 427–64.

Yoneyama Yasusaburō. (1892) 1975. "Kokushi ni tsukite." In *MTSS*, 511–17.

Yosano Hiroshi. 1901. "Shakoku." *Myōjō* 14 (August): 45–46.

Yosano Hiroshi, Baba Kochō, and Chino Shōshō. 1906. "Hakuyōkyū gappyō." *Myōjō* 7:1–37.

Zhuangzi. 1968. *The Complete Works of Chuang Tzu*. Translated by Burton Watson. New York: Columbia University Press.

INDEX

Printed in the USA
CPSIA information can be obtained
at www.ICGtesting.com
CBHW030805140224
4339CB00002B/4